More Praise for
INVESTMENT LEADERSHIP

"After 30 years as an active participant/observer of the investment management profession, I've seen every conceivable organizational structure, personality type, and management style. Or so I thought! *Investment Leadership* marshals a prodigious quantity of theoretical and empirical insights into the investment industry—how it works and who makes it work. Portraits of the characters who lead the firms made me envious, amused, and generally charged up to do a better job at my own firm. Ware, Michaels, and Primer observe people in top positions doing the *right* thing well."

—Theodore Aronson, Chair of the AIMR Board of Governors

"Investment managers tend to be a lot better at investing than at managing. This is unfortunate because investment success flows from quality leadership, culture, and creativity. *Investment Leadership* provides money managers with the necessary tools, diagnostics, and examples to improve their organizations—and their alphas."

—Michael J. Mauboussin, Chief U.S. Investment Strategist,
Credit Suisse First Boston

"Given that ours is a business of nurturing and managing human capital, this book provides a systematic framework with pragmatic exercises that will generate a meaningful impact on performance. A 'must read' for anyone seeking to create a culture that will survive market cycles and deliver value to clients."

—Keith F. Karlawish, CFA, President and CIO, BB&T,
Asset Management, Inc.

"According to the SEC there are 7,468 Registered Investment Advisors in the United States managing almost $1 trillion. How is it that when America's leading firms are cited not one of this very sizable group generally makes the list? *Investment Leadership* documents how and why the leadership vacuum that exists in the investment management industry has left the industry in a particularly precarious position. But, not content to simply document the leadership gap, Ware has identified the critical qualities and best practices of investment management leaders who have set the standard. This book should be required reading for all of us in the investment management industry."

—Margaret M. Eisen, CFA and Chair, The Institute for Financial Markets

"*Investment Leadership* is a nice, easy-to-read compendium of thoughts, ideas, and insights into the cultural aspects of investment organizations. The authors provide a broad landscape for the interested reader to traverse while seeking their own vantage point."

—Gary P. Brinson, CFA, GP Brinson Investments

Investment
Leadership

Founded in 1807, John Wiley & Sons is the oldest independent publishing company in the United States. With offices in North America, Europe, Australia, and Asia, Wiley is globally committed to developing and marketing print and electronic products and services for our customers' professional and personal knowledge and understanding.

The Wiley Finance series contains books written specifically for finance and investment professionals as well as sophisticated individual investors and their financial advisors. Book topics range from portfolio management to e-commerce, risk management, financial engineering, valuation, and financial instrument analysis, as well as much more.

For a list of available titles, visit our Web site at www.WileyFinance.com.

Investment Leadership

*Building a Winning Culture
for Long-Term Success*

JIM WARE
WITH BETH MICHAELS
AND DALE PRIMER

WILEY

John Wiley & Sons, Inc.

Preface

We missed the gravy, but we stayed out of the soup.
　　　　　　　　　—Edgar D. "Ned" Jannotta, Chairman,
　　　　　　　　　　　　William Blair & Company,
　　　　　　　　　　　　describing the company's
　　　　　　　　　　　　performance 1999–2001

Ned Jannotta's comment, from our interview in 2002, captures the essence of this book. William Blair & Company came under intense pressure during the tech bubble and bear markets at the turn of the century. They lost a few good people and asked some hard questions of themselves, but in the end, they survived and have prospered. Others, like Janus, did not fare as well. Bill McKenna, a 72-year-old retired commercial-laundry manager, removed all his money from Janus, explaining, "I've lost faith in the Janus culture. They've lost their direction."[1] Our research examines this issue: How do the best-run investment firms survive the highs and lows that inevitably come in the markets?

There are many good books on leadership and culture. If you do a search for "leadership" on Amazon.com, you'll find more than 12,000 titles. However, if you add the word "investment" to the search, it comes up empty. There simply are no books addressing leadership and culture specifically for investment professionals.

This book fills that gap. It is written for the busy and talented investment leader who knows that people are the firm's most important asset but isn't sure how to fully leverage that talent to get sustainable financial results. Throughout this book, we link the people factor with superior financial results.

It is also written for the investment leader who may never have intended to become a leader! While writing this introduction, I got a call from an investment professional who had just received a significant promotion.[2] During our conversation, he admitted that he wished he were still an analyst. He does not like or want the role of leader. Stephen Timbers, president of Global Investments, Northern Trust, stated it boldly: "Ninety-five percent of investment managers have no interest in managing people." (*Note:* All quotations, unless footnoted, are from interviews we conducted during the period January 2000 through April 2003.) In perhaps no other industry is the attitude "this is a great job except for the people" more prevalent. Most investment professionals are "idea" people, not "people" people.

So, what is the state of leadership in the investment industry? The truth is that there is a huge range of skill: from extraordinary (like Jack Brennan at Vanguard, who has written a book on the topic) to staggeringly poor (one CEO of a sizeable firm responded to our request for an interview on leadership by saying, "Leadership? What is there to talk about? People show up each day and do their work").

THE AUDIENCE FOR THIS BOOK

While writing this book, we had specific investment leaders in mind. Some of them were outstanding, like Brennan or Timbers. For these people, this book is an opportunity to fine-tune their already superior skills. We believe they will find useful ideas and tools for creating a winning culture and for measuring that culture. Ironically, almost every leader whom we consider excellent has expressed a strong interest in reading this book. They don't really need this information—they are already successful—but they are naturally drawn to the topic. Each one has a passion for the organization and its mission and are attracted to anything that will help.

"Bruce" is another person we're writing for. He has an MBA from Wharton and has earned the CFA designation. After serving as an analyst and portfolio manager, he has risen to the post of department head of a major investment operation. The chief investment officer (CIO) recently issued Bruce a tall order: double the amount of investments that the firm did last year. Bruce knows he needs the full talent and effort of the department's 13-person staff to pull this off, but he has no clue how to do it. To Bruce's credit, though, he has the good sense to call in help. He hires a firm to facilitate a series of meetings so that he can get his whole team on the same page. Bruce has expressed interest in this book and would probably read it. (He did read our first recommendation: John Kotter's *Leading Change.*)

Another person we had in mind as we wrote is the job candidate. Say you have just received your degree and are looking to work in investments. Which firm should you choose? Why, the one that pays the most money! We're joking, of course, but many people, especially in the investment field, would make that choice. (It's good to remember that Warren Buffett himself, arguably the world's greatest investor, chose his first investment job solely on the basis of the experience he would get, *not* for the money. He chose to work with his hero, Benjamin Graham [of Graham and Dodd fame], for nothing, just so he could learn from a master.) Along those lines, we believe that a person who is just starting in the investment field would benefit from joining a firm with excellent leadership and a strong culture. People blossom and do their best work in these environments. The key is knowing how to identify such a place. What questions would you ask in the interviews? What answers should you be looking for?

"Jane" is the plan sponsor head at a major organization. She hires a consulting firm to do searches on and monitoring of the investment managers that she retains. All major consulting firms recognize the qualitative side of evaluating investment managers, but the information in this book will help Jane ask the right questions when meeting with her consultants. She may even be persuaded to choose different consultants, based on their ability to analyze the qualitative aspects of a manager.

We also wrote this book for the stock picker. Though our focus is on how to run an investment firm, the lessons we've learned about the so-called qualitative side of the business also yield insights for stock selection. We provide a scorecard for identifying which nonfinancial firms will be outstanding performers. Want to avoid the next Enron, WorldCom, or Tyco? Read on.

The consultants themselves will benefit from reading this book. Many still rely on a gut-feeling approach to leadership and culture. The metrics and tools provided in this book should help them to formally assess investment managers and compare them to one another.

The book is intended for both U.S. and non-U.S. investment professionals. Originally we planned to have a chapter devoted to non-U.S. professionals so that we could address cultural differences and subtleties, making the material more relevant to Canadians, Europeans, and Asians. After speaking to non-U.S. audiences and asking colleagues from other countries to read drafts of the book, we decided the extra chapter was unnecessary. As our friend and colleague Fernand Schoppig—a Swiss-born consultant working in America—told us, "People are people. The material in the book is universal. The major difference is just the size of non-U.S. firms. European money management firms are huge. They have very few of the small entrepreneurial shops like the U.S." Several European audience members amplified this point by saying, "European audiences need it even more than U.S. audiences; we need to catch up on some of this material."[3] This gentleman's comment was reinforced by a woman working at a well-known European asset manager, who told me after the presentation, "Our firm could really use this." When I smiled in reaction to her candor, she gave me a look that said, "I'm not kidding." In the end, we decided not to include an additional chapter for non-U.S. investment professionals—but we invite comments and feedback from all readers: www.focusCgroup.com.

Finally, we believe that this book has valuable insights for any leader who is trying to build a sustainable organization, from a multinational company to a condo board or a Girl Scout troop. The principles are the same . . . though the Girl Scouts are probably a little easier to work with than most of the investment professionals we know.

LEADERSHIP AND CULTURE: TIMELESS FACTORS

In 2003, the world is dealing with the aftermath of Enron, WorldCom, Tyco, Andersen, Vivendi, and worldwide investment firm misbehavior. These events make it painfully clear how important and timely the discussion of leadership and culture is. Just half the respondents to a fall 2002 Gallup poll said that people in most companies are honest and ethical. And there may be worse to come. A majority of corporate businesses responding to a Conference Board ethics study predicted that at least a dozen more major scandals would be revealed during the next 12 months.[4] The premise of this book— that leadership and culture are the critical factors for sustainable success— couldn't be more relevant. Wall Street already knows this is true. In one study, Harvard professors Kotter and Heskett asked 75 analysts to divide the companies they follow into 2 groups: the best and the second tier. The analysts were then asked to identify the factors that separated the groups. All but one of the 75 analysts named "culture" as a differentiating factor. (*Culture* is defined as the values, beliefs, and behaviors that distinguish the members of one organization from another.) During our interviews with senior leaders in the investment world, time and again they acknowledged that culture is critical:

> "*Culture is the key to real future growth*" (*Bill Nutt, Chairman, Affiliated Managers Group*).[5]

> "*The key to attracting, motivating, and retaining employees lies with a firm's investment culture*" (*Thomas Dillman, while Director of U.S. Research, Scudder Investments*).[6]

> "*Culture and a set of shared values are absolutely critical and every bit as important as money management style to a firm's success*" (*Alison Winter, Executive Vice President, Northern Trust Company*).[7]

In this sense, many of the leaders we know see their primary role as being creators and caretakers of the corporate culture.

Because of current events, interest in the topic of investment leadership has never been higher. In 1999, during the dotcom explosion, I was asked by an industry trade group to make a conference presentation called "Leading the Investment Firm into the Future." In a beautiful ballroom that could easily have held 200 people, we gathered: 15 presenters and about 10 attendees. The room was so quiet you could hear the waiters pouring orange juice by the exit doors.

In contrast, that same conference presentation is fully subscribed in 2003. What's more, I've been asked to speak on the topic of "Leadership, Culture, and Investment Success" by more than 50 financial analyst societies, from Vancouver and Des Moines to Rome and Budapest. A survey on "hot investment topics" distributed to professionals by the Association for Investment Management and Research revealed that the overwhelming choice in 2003 is culture.

FOCUS CONSULTING GROUP

Since 1987, Focus Consulting Group (FCG) has been helping leaders build foundations for sustainable success using our expertise in leadership, culture, and change management. Our ideas and tools have been written up in *Consulting Magazine* and other trade publications. Beth, Dale, Jim Dethmer, Fran Skinner, and I work with organizations in many fields, although the focus of this book is on the investment industry. My background on the buy side, as a research analyst, portfolio manager, and director of planning and strategy, plus my experience as a Chartered Financial Analyst and an instructor of finance and investments at the graduate level, provided unique insights into the investment world. This book thus combines in-depth knowledge of the investment industry with our cutting-edge, solidly based ideas and tools in the areas of leadership and culture.

OVERVIEW OF THE BOOK

The book is divided into five parts. The first, called "Foundation Pieces," gives behavioral descriptions of leadership and culture and discusses our general mindset concerning them. It also describes the process of identifying, clarifying, and implementing your firm's values, vision, and culture.

The second part, "Assessment Tools," explains how you can quantify the people side of the business. By giving your firm a checkup, you can tell where to focus your improvement efforts.

The third part, "Getting Practical," uses the information garnered with the assessment tools to improve your firm's goal setting and implementation, innovation, compensation, and succession planning.

The fourth part, "Putting It All Together," provides a case study and complete analysis of an exemplary firm. Chapter 14 wraps up with concrete guidelines for continuous improvement.

The final part, "Other Audiences," addresses the special interests of consultants, those who perform manager searches, and analysts/portfolio managers who pick stocks for exceptional performance.

Throughout the book, we connect financial results with leadership and culture—the hard with the soft. We know that investment professionals in particular want quantitative evidence that time and attention to the "soft side" will pay off. It's here in spades.

THE RESEARCH PROJECT

In designing our approach to this project, we were heavily influenced by Jim Collins, coauthor (with Jerry Porras) of *Built to Last*[8] and author of *Good to Great*.[9] We knew that investment professionals would be a tough audience when it comes to the qualitative side of the business. Investment professionals have grown up in a culture that worships at the altar of formulas, statistics, and hard data. Jim Collins has done as much as anyone we know to quantify and legitimize the people side of business. Each of his books represents more than five years of research and endless hours of debate over cause and effect, and the validity of the findings. Rather than propose various hypotheses to be proven or disproven, Collins employed an empirical approach. Namely, he and his research team read about and studied the best organizations and their average counterparts to determine the differentiating factors. They looked for recurring themes and patterns that were present in the exemplary companies and absent in the mediocre ones. The result was a set of 21 factors that characterize the *Built to Last* companies.

In our research, we stood on the shoulders of Collins and asked, "Are these same 21 factors valid for investment companies? Or is there something unique about the investment industry (Collins did not examine any pure investment companies) that renders the Collins analysis irrelevant or inapplicable?" To discover answers to these questions, we researched and visited hundreds of investment firms. To our satisfaction, we found that the *Built to Last* principles were alive and well in the investment industry and went a long way toward explaining why certain firms had enjoyed remarkable long-term success.

The proof is always in the pudding. We eat our own cooking, which is to say that we practice these principles in our firm and with our clients. We know that they work. In taking on the challenge of this book project, our intention has been to clearly identify the elements of leadership that contribute significantly to a firm's sustainable success. We present them in a practical way so that you can use them in your firm as well.

JIM WARE
BETH MICHAELS
DALE PRIMER

Acknowledgments

We appreciate the support and encouragement of our colleagues: Jim Dethmer, Joe Mazzenga, Kary Miller, George Rounds, Jack Skeen, and Fran Skinner.

We would like to thank Jim Collins and the director of his research team, Stefanie Judd, for their help in understanding and integrating the *Built to Last* principles with our research. Same to Richard Barrett and Joan Shafer for their thoughtful input, and to Gay and Katy Hendricks, Kate Ludeman, and Eddie Erlandson. We also thank all the investment leaders who generously gave their time to share best practices and thoughts on leadership and culture. Their names are mentioned throughout the book.

We especially want to thank the "contact" people at the investment organizations who set up interviews, sent material, answered questions, filled in details, read and proofread draft versions, and so on. Most of these people are not named in the book and deserve to be named here: Jerry Bartlett, John Cole, Dennis Cook, Barry Gillman, Mark Gilstrap, Jane Hobson, Lisa Jones, Merrillyn Kosier, Isidora Lagos, Mark Toledo, Margaret Welch, John Woerth, and Jamie Ziegler.

We want to thank Lauren Topel for all the work that she did in arranging interviews, travel plans, speaking tours, and so forth. And speaking of speaking, thanks to the Financial Forum Speaking Bureau for their good efforts to help us get the word out to audiences around the world. In the same vein, thanks to Julie Hammond, Lisa Medders, Craig Ruff, and Katy Sherrerd at the Association for Investment Management and Research for their kind invitations to present this material at their conferences and to their member societies around the world. Truly, the feedback from these presentations has shaped and improved the material in this book. We have had running dialogues with people like Alida Carcano, Peggy Eisen, Jane Farris, Dave Fowler, Michael Frazin, Mike Gasior, K. C. Howell, Leandra Knes, Michael Mauboussin, Jeff Pantages, Jonathan Smith, Jay Taparia, Malcolm Trevillian, Steven Waite, and many other CFAs around the world.

We would be remiss in not mentioning our friend and colleague, Ted Aronson, who graciously consulted with us and provided insights and support throughout.

As always, special thanks go to our editor at John Wiley & Sons, Pamela van Giessen, who follows many of the *Built to Last* principles; most notably, she does not micromanage the process! She provides high-level input and lets us research and write as we see fit. The writers out there understand what a blessing this is.

On the production side, we work with a great team: Brooke Graves of Graves Editorial Service, who cleans up the editorial mess we've created; and Jamie Temple of Pageworks, who transforms it into a beautiful hardcover book.

Jim Ware

Jim wishes to thank his wife, Jane, who did more than her share of baby duties with Alexandra (two years) and Nicole (six months) while he sneaked off to read and write. Jim and Jane both want to thank family members Marilyn, Pat, Allene, Wendy, Marta, Mary, and Donna for their help in this regard. We don't know if it takes a village to raise a child, but it certainly takes more than just two sleep-deprived parents! He also wishes to thank his writing partners, Beth and Dale, for their invaluable assistance in collecting the data, designing the structure, writing the material, proofing it, debating and dialoguing, and finally proving that collaboration—while not necessarily the simplest path—is the most rewarding.

Beth Michaels

Helping people achieve their goals is my lifelong passion. This book represents many years of experience with people of all ages working diligently to create their preferred futures. I feel blessed and grateful to have been a part of your successes.

Teamwork and collaboration are at the heart of our work. In that spirit, I wish to thank the people who helped steer my professional growth: Shirley Lewis, Dan Stamp, and in fond memory of Pete Stursberg. To my partners, Dale Primer and Jim Ware, thank you for challenging me, for nurturing me, and for what we have built together.

I wish to thank my clients through the years, from whom I have learned so much and whose partnership I treasure. Learning and growing with you is a joy.

A big thank-you to all the investment firms who opened their doors to us, allowing us access to their inner operations and personal motivations. Your commitment to creating wonderful career experiences and results for clients is inspirational.

Lastly, to my husband and my children, thank you for your patience with me when I blurred the line between work and family time to complete this project. I love you dearly.

Dale Primer

My thanks to:

Jim Ware, for masterfully spearheading this entire book project.

Jim Ware and Beth Michaels, my coauthors, for your keen intellects and unwavering focus on both value to our clients and timely completion of this book.

Howard Primer, my brother, for your confidence, words of wisdom, continual mentoring, and ever-present support.

Dick Zalack, Andy Sherwood, and the late Pete Stursberg, for your many years of encouragement and ideas, which guide me every day.

Sgt. Sweeney (USAF), the late Tiny Mueller, Rich Tarsitano, and Truman Crawford, my coaches, for teaching me how to search and find excellence.

Betty and Seymour Primer, my parents, for inspiring me through your example of youthful vigor.

My wife and best friend, for being with me and behind me, all the time.

My children, Lisa and David, for bringing heartfelt love, pride, and loyalty continually into my life.

Contents

Foundation Pieces: Cornerstones of Long-Term Success

To make it crystal clear, Allstar's collapse was *not* caused by criminal acts. It was not an Enron or WorldCom or Andersen. No Allstar employees broke the law or created a scandal. So . . . what factors accounted for its success and then its collapse? How do you build a sustainable organization? What can be learned from Allstar's experience? That's the subject of this book. Our charge is to equip investment leaders, especially the "Bruces" and "Janes" discussed in the preface, with the mental models and tools that will help them create sustainable success.

UNIQUE ATTRIBUTES

Within the topic of strategies for building successful organizations, is there something unusual about the investment industry? In a word, yes. Investment professionals share a unique set of personality traits and personal values. To generalize, professional investors tend to be:

- Independent thinkers (nonconformists).
- Tough-minded (not sentimental).
- Naturally skeptical ("prove it" attitude).
- Anti-authoritarian (don't like to follow rules or sing company songs).
- Creative (question the status quo).
- Conceptual and task-oriented (rather than people-oriented).

When you add these characteristics up, you've got one hell of a management challenge! The television commercial that shows the ranchers herding cats isn't far from the truth.

Patrick O'Donnell, formerly a managing partner with Putnam, described the typical investment professional in similar terms, and noted that anyone charged with managing these folks "certainly needs a management structure that accommodates these individuals—a structure that develops and challenges analysts and one that provides for appropriate evaluation and compensation."[2] With this recognition and these characteristics in mind, we've written this book specifically for this audience. Later in the book we address the personality traits of investment professionals from a more objective, quasi-scientific perspective, using the Myers-Briggs Personality Type Indicator as a psychological measure. For now, let us just say that we know each investment firm will have its own set of challenges based on the people who are attracted to it.

ISTRY MYTHS

fore we discuss our findings from extensive research and experience, we begin with several myths—peculiar to the investment industry—that we discovered and shattered during our research of successful firms.

Myth 1: Money is everything

Reality   To be sure, investment professionals are fascinated by money, and the industry is clearly one of the most results-driven. Nevertheless, our research shows that the most successful firms do not focus on their own profit. Yes, they are fabulously profitable, but mostly because they focus on their clients and how to serve those clients (namely, through excellent service and performance). In this regard, the best firms reflected Warren Buffett's view: "I love the process more than the proceeds, though I've learned to live with them, too."[3]

When it comes to employee satisfaction and loyalty, again, money is not everything. Yes, compensation is important, but survey results from Capital Resource Advisors show that the two most important factors are leadership credibility and organizational culture and purpose. Other studies, by reputable firms such as Russell Reynolds and Associates, confirm these findings: Money is not the top motivator. Paul Schaeffer, formerly of CRA and now with SEI Investments, summed it up well: "The investment management business is about a lot more than just making money."[4] Compensation becomes a major issue when employees feel that they are not being treated fairly. In this sense, "fairness is everything" does generally hold true in the industry.

Myth 2: Brains are everything

Reality   As with Myth 1, many investment firms fail because they believe that sheer intelligence wins out over everything else. These firms recruit the top brains from business schools, pay them top salaries, and then turn them loose on the markets. In our Allstar example, this was the firm's strategy. It worked beautifully right up until the company fell apart.

The best firms realize that brains are enormously important, but also recognize that there is a second, equally important factor: cultural fit. Individuals need to share a sense of common purpose and guiding principles. The best firms hire for skills and fit. Gary Brinson, a legend in the investment business, addressed this myth head-on:

> *Given a choice between a highly talented but introverted, self-serving, and unenthusiastic person and another person who is not as smart but*

Our intention is not to create mutually exclusive descriptions. Rather, we will show that when the natural tension between investment professionals' traits and best "people" practices is actively managed, sustainable success follows.

Weathering the Tough Times: William Blair & Company

Because our emphasis is on long-term success, this book continually gives examples of companies that have weathered the tough times and emerged intact. William Blair & Company is one such firm. During the tech bubble in the late 1990s, Blair's performance came under intense pressure: Performance was strong, but it was not at "bubble" levels. Traditional approaches to money management fell way behind the hot dot-com funds. Some clients left. Blair also lost several young investment bankers who accepted jobs as CFOs at the hot new Internet companies. Understandably, senior leaders were concerned about the future of their firm.

Today, Blair has not only survived, but is flourishing. The details of how it weathered the ups and downs of the tech-bubble storm are related in various chapters, but the main point is summarized in comments made by vice chairman and CEO, E. David Coolidge III:

> On the business side, we tend to be financially conservative, so we weren't overextended during the rough period. Our operating model is to have relatively small salaries and high bonuses. Plus, as an independent firm, we avoid a lot of the outside pressure which can be very short-term oriented. So all that works in our favor through good times and bad. But the real strength here is our culture. We work very hard at recruiting and hiring and keeping talented people who love this field and who love our approach. We genuinely like working together.

Our extensive interviews at Blair support Coolidge's statements. David Ricci, an analyst hired from the retail industry by Blair, told us that the culture at Blair was "too good to be true. They actually practice a win-win philosophy here. My colleagues here want me to be successful. It sounds corny but it's true. I'd never go to Wall Street. Not after this." Ricci, who is now the Consumer Group head, also had worked at Procter & Gamble, a *Built to Last* company. Ricci prefers the Blair culture: "At Blair they are looking to make you a partner from day one. The retention rate is remarkable. At P&G nine out of ten employees were out after six years. The attrition rate was remarkable!" Ricci's belief in the power of culture extends to his company research, where he includes culture as an important analytical factor. Much of what we discuss in this book, albeit in relation to investment firms, he uses to analyze nonfinancial firms. The bottom line for Ricci: "I sleep better if I know a strong culture will carry the firm through hard times." Leaders of investment firms can sleep better by building a strong culture in their firm.

Another employee who echoed Ricci's endorsement was Isidora Lagos, a recent addition to the Blair team. With a background in consumer products, she told the Blair recruiters that she was not a financial services person. Their response? At Blair it's 90 percent fit and personality and 10 percent the smarts to figure it out. As a single mother, Lagos has found Blair to be an excellent blend of competition and compassion. She is challenged and excited by her work, but also told us many stories about the support she has received to help her balance work and family concerns. She made the same comment as Ricci: "It's too good to be true here."

I got a small taste of the genuine empathy these employees described when I had to cancel a scheduled interview with Blair's CIO because my infant daughter was having emergency surgery. Two Blair employees called and left lengthy phone messages that clearly indicated their level of concern. Their gist was, "Don't worry at all about the interviews, they can be rescheduled, just take care of your family."

This concern was also demonstrated in the way Blair handled layoffs during the rough times. Sources told us that president/COO John Ettelson, realizing what an enormous blow this was to people who had been part of the Blair "family," had trouble sleeping during that period. Blair employees stayed in touch with those who were laid off, providing leads for jobs, support, and references. As Lagos said, "No one told us to keep track of these people, we just naturally wanted to help."

Contrast our Blair experience with the one we had with a large, well-known West Coast firm. The day before we were to visit the firm, we received a call from the interviewee's assistant, saying that the person had been called out of town and would have to cancel. Of course, these things happen. But because we had already blocked out the day and paid for airline tickets, we asked if we could meet with another company representative. The assistant called back shortly, only to say curtly, "No, there is no one available." And that was that. We never got an apology from the interviewee, nor did we get an offer to reimburse us for expenses. We never had any further contact with that person, even after we sent a polite e-mail asking if we could reschedule. Our rule of thumb for culture research is to assume that leaders don't change their spots. If we got treated that way, the likelihood is that employees get similar treatment.

Strong cultures are built on respect. In the case of Blair, everyone at the company showed us respect—in spades. Firms that demonstrate a strong culture of respect and pride of membership can ride through the hard times without coming apart at the seams. As you will see, the Allstar Capitals of the world may flourish during bull markets, but they often implode when bad markets hit.

Leading versus Managing

Firm leaders often describe themselves as managers. In law firms, for example, the title "managing partner" is the designation for the person who makes decisions about the firm's internal operations. Though the leadership and managerial roles are not mutually exclusive, the successful development

TABLE 1.2 Differences Between Managing and Leading

Management	Leadership
Planning and budgeting: establishing the detailed steps and timetables needed to achieve results, then allocating the resources needed to make it happen	*Establishing direction:* developing a vision of the future and the strategies required to produce the changes to achieve that vision
Organizing and staffing: establishing structure to accomplish the plan, delegating authority, providing policies and procedures, establishing systems to monitor implementation	*Aligning people:* communicating direction, in words and deeds, to all whose cooperation is needed; creating teams and coalitions that understand the vision and strategies and accept their validity
Controlling and problem solving: monitoring results, identifying deviations from the plan, and solving problems accordingly	*Motivating and inspiring:* energizing people to overcome major political, bureaucratic, and resource barriers to change, by satisfying basic, but often unfilled, human needs
↓	↓
Produces a degree of predictability and order and has the potential to consistently produce results	Produces change, often to a dramatic degree, and has the potential to produce extremely useful change
Management Creates	**Leadership Creates**
Plans: The specific steps to implement the strategies	*Vision:* a sensible and appealing picture of the future
Budgets: The conversion of the plans into financial projections and goals	*Strategy:* A logic for how the vision can be achieved

of leadership and culture requires a clear and proactive distinction between them. What's the difference between leading and managing?

John Kotter, in *Leading Change*, charts the difference as shown in Table 1.2.[16]

We address vision and strategy in Chapters 2 and 9.

LEADERSHIP BEHAVIORS

If our economic organizations are going to live up to their potential, we must find, develop, and encourage more people to lead in the service of others. Without leadership, firms cannot adapt to a fast moving world. But if leaders do not have the hearts of servants, there is only the potential for tyranny.

—John P. Kotter, Harvard Business School[17]

I don't know what your destiny will be, but one thing I know; the only ones among you who will be really happy are those who have sought and found how to serve.

—Albert Schweitzer[18]

Service is at the heart of leadership, but what, specifically, does "acting like a leader" mean? Executive recruiters at Russell Reynolds Associates studied the critical success factors for chief investment officers. They intentionally targeted behaviors rather than vague generalities, and concluded that a top CIO:

1. Fosters a culture of intellectual curiosity and analytical rigor.
   —Creates an environment of respect and collaboration.
   —Shapes, articulates, and exemplifies the values of the group.
   —Promotes a meritocracy.
2. Interacts with respect.
   —Persuades rather than commands.
   —Sharpens focus.
   —Inspires with compelling thought leadership.
3. Develops investment capabilities.
   —Elevates judgment to an art form.
   —Stimulates insight.
   —Leads a thought process.
   —Coaches, mentors, and develops others.

4. Captains the investment process.
   —Establishes a philosophy and a framework for investing.
   —Clearly articulates core investment tenets.
   —Requires consistency in application of investment discipline.
   —Sets and holds high standards.
5. Seizes the moment.
   —Assesses the probabilities.
   —Makes timely decisions in the face of ambiguity.
   —Assumes personal accountability and holds others accountable.[19]

Leadership is not a matter of personality or charisma. It requires concentrated action in all these areas.

LEADING OTHERS

The preceding framework from Russell Reynolds provides a mental model for thinking about good leadership practices. You can use it as a checklist for leadership actions.

Remembering that our goal is to provide the reader with a number of useful mental models for leadership, let's look at another framework, developed by Paul Hersey and Kenneth Blanchard, called *situational leadership*. Their model is also based on findings from leadership research.[20] They discovered that leadership behavior toward others can be described as either task-driven or relationship-driven. When the leader is most interested in the task to be completed, task behavior is demonstrated. When the leader is emphasizing support of the person involved, relationship behavior is evident. Given that task and relationship behavior can be expressed strongly or weakly, there are four different combinations of them, called *styles*, as shown in Table 1.3. The appropriate style depends on the job maturity of the individual in regard to competence (Can the person do the job?) and job ownership (Can the person take responsibility for it?). Because the answers to these questions will change depending on the assignment, the appropriate leadership style is situational.[21]

RECOGNIZING CULTURE

If three of your top-notch people were asked to describe the culture of your firm, what would they say? What would they use as examples of your "culture"?

TABLE 1.3 Leadership Styles

Combination	Style Name	Appropriate for a Person Who
High task, low relationship	Directive, telling, hand-holding	Is unable and unwilling to perform the assigned task
High task, high relationship	Persuasion, influence, selling	Is unable but willing to do the job
Low task, high relationship	Participative	Is able but unwilling or a bit insecure
Low task, low relationship	Delegative	Is both able and willing to do the task

In all likelihood, you would hear descriptions of beliefs: beliefs about productivity, about client service, about coworker interaction, about attitude. Answers about culture address the questions "What's it like to work there?" or "What is our way of investing?" Another way to define culture is to ask employees, "What does it take to succeed in this organization?" Again, you will hear in their answers what they believe is true about the expectations of and within the firm.

High-performing cultures ask—and answer—four questions:

1. About clients: What do we believe about client service?
2. About excellence: What are our quality standards?
3. About groups: How do we treat each other?
4. About individuals: What do we do to create a truly satisfying work experience?[22]

The systems and processes you design to enact and integrate beliefs in real life create and solidify your firm's culture. In Chapters 5 through 8, we discuss these kinds of processes in detail and introduce metrics for measuring culture.

Culture and Financial Impact

Companies can have a long-standing culture and still fail if they cannot change with the needs of business or the marketplace. In their book *Corporate Culture and Performance*, John Kotter and Jim Heskett reported research on which types of culture were associated with the strongest financial performance.[23] They found that strong cultures were associated with the

TABLE 1.4 Adaptive versus Nonadaptive Cultures

Performance Measures	Firms with Strong Adaptive Cultures	Firms with Less Adaptive Cultures
Revenue growth	682%	166%
Employment growth	282%	36%
Stock price growth	901%	74%
Net income growth	756%	1%

best business results. These cultures got people aligned with the firm's goals, values, and strategy, and were able to change relatively quickly when business needs changed. Collins and Porras arrived at the same conclusions from their research: The strongest cultures also seem to be the most adaptive.[24] Like a flock of birds that stays in tight formation, companies with strong cultures "flock" around the same values, beliefs, and behaviors. The financial performance of firms with more adaptive and less adaptive cultures are compared in Table 1.4.[25]

Myths and models are examined in the rest of this book. We start our journey in the same place where Collins and Porras started theirs: the core values and vision of the firm. The best firms are clear about who they are and where they are going.

TEST YOURSELF

As a warm-up, see how you do with the following yes/no quiz.

	Yes	No

1. I can name three challenges of building and maintaining culture in an investment firm.
2. I can cite at least one study showing the link between the "people" side of the firm and the firm's profitability.
3. I can name actions that our leadership team is taking to build and maintain our culture.
4. We have clearly identified and defined our firm's values or guiding principles.
5. If I asked three different employees to name our core values, they would give the same answer.

Yes   No

6. Our values are central to our hiring and orientation procedures.
7. Our values are central to our performance evaluation system.
8. We can all clearly state our core purpose (vision/mission) in three minutes or less.
9. Our core purpose goes beyond making money.
10. This year's strategic goals/objectives are clear and well-known throughout the firm.
11. Our employees know when and how communication about progress on our goals will occur.
12. I know the essentials of leadership and motivating people for success.
13. I can quote a useful working definition of trust from memory.
14. I understand the basics of building and maintaining trust in my firm.
15. I understand the basics of managing continuous improvement or renewal.
16. We have a leadership development system, which addresses succession.

If you answered a resounding "Yes!" to each of these statements, then give this book to one of your less enlightened colleagues and get to work writing your own book! You obviously have much to offer in the way of leadership insights. For the rest of you, read on and test yourself again when you have finished.

People resources are critical; they dwarf technology or any other variable anyone might cite as being the key determinant of success.

—James Rothenberg, President,
Capital Research and Management[26]

People are the raw material in the investment management business.

—Thomas Luddy, Chief Investment Officer, J.P. Morgan[27]

CHAPTER 2

Core Values

I will devote a disproportionate percentage of my time to creating a corporate environment where the Company's Guiding Principles are clearly stated, and clearly heard, and where employees hold each other accountable to practice these statements.
—Bill Lyons, CEO, American Century[1]

You have to start with values—how you lead your life and what kind of an example you set.
—David Fisher, Chairman, Capital Group Companies[2]

Who are we as an organization? What do we care about deeply? Leadership's first imperative is to determine "who we are." That question is answered by the *values*, or guiding principles, that the firm adopts regarding what is most important. In this chapter, you will learn:

- The benefits and consequences of articulating company values.
- The financial impact on firms that have articulated their values.
- How firms walk their talk.
- How you can measure your firm's values and monitor progress.

By the time we were asked in to help with Allstar, much of the damage had already been done. They had lost one-third of the staff, assets were down more than 75 percent, and the company was operating in the red. Team members were battling one another at a time when they most needed to support each other.

For example, they scapegoated one analyst, saying that he was the primary source of their problems. They said he just didn't have the required skill level. Now, this analyst had graduated from Stanford's MBA program, earned the CFA designation, and been elected to the "Buy-side Allstar Team" by *Institutional Investor* magazine. According to his teammates, though, he had contracted a case of the "stupids" and had lost his analytical skills. When we heard this story, we doubted that the analyst had really lost his abilities. It sounded much more like a spell of bad luck, which every investor encounters, than a sudden onset of idiocy. His teammates' reaction did nothing, of course, to help his confidence and performance.

Another example of how bad things had gotten was the warning we received from Allstar's director of research. He told us that the tension was so high within this group that a fight might break out! With regard to this type of internal competition, David Fisher at Capital Group had an apt comment: "Beating external competitors is tough enough; we do not have the time and energy to worry about competing with each other. Everything in the organization has to be consistent with that philosophy of teamwork."[3]

When we met with the Allstar group, our first inquiry, as usual, was about the group's values. We got blank stares. We then asked about guiding principles. Nothing. Shared understanding of what was important here? Some grunts about basis points, benchmarks, better performance; nothing about clients, the staff, the working environment. Although we see many firms that haven't yet gone through the exercise of clearly articulating and defining their values, most of the time they can state their values in general terms. At Allstar, they couldn't. It was evident that they hadn't ever thought about it.

We'll return to the Allstar example shortly, but first let's cover some basics on leadership and values.

LEADERSHIP AND VALUES

Leadership starts with values. Whether they are referred to as *values, guiding principles, operating guidelines,* or *codes of conduct,* their purpose is the same: to indicate what is deeply valued. When something is important, we value it. Examples of common values are honesty, trust, integrity, client service, excellence, and teamwork. Good leaders identify what is important to them personally and to the organizations they serve. As shown at the beginning of this chapter, Bill Lyons at American Century has carefully written down both his personal vision and values, and those developed in his role of chief executive of the company. His personal statement begins:

> *I will find personal fulfillment in my life by consistently making deci-*
> *sions and taking actions that are strongly rooted in a set of core values*
> *and beliefs. These values and beliefs, which have been formed by a life-*
> *time of good—and bad—experiences, define the center of my being and*
> *serve as a compass against which I constantly check my direction.*[4]

Lyons's personal statement goes on to describe his commitment to various values, including honesty, integrity, family, learning, excellence, openness, and passion. Leaders at American Century encourage each employee to go through the exercise of writing out his or her own values statement. When Lyons's personal assistant introspected about her values, she realized that she really wanted to stay home with her kids—so she quit. There are some risks involved with this level of personal honesty!

Having stated what is important to him personally, Lyons builds on this set of values to describe a set of corporate values and his commitment to seeing that these values "live" in the organization. American Century's corporate values are:

- Providing value for our investors.
- Challenging and inspiring the best people.
- Building a financially sound company.
- Being adaptable and innovative.
- Working with integrity.

These values are well known to each of the 2,700 employees who work at the Kansas City–based investment firm. How do we know this? Because Bill Lyons (and, even more powerfully, Jim Stowers, the founder) meets with each new employee personally to describe these values and explain their importance to the success of this $80 billion organization. In addition to this initial meeting on values, employees find these five values reproduced on plaques all over the corridors of the building. Employees receive an average of 23 hours of training per year, some of it reinforcing these values and explaining how they are represented in the firm.

Each year American Century goes through an elaborate, employee-driven process of nominating and selecting five colleagues who best exemplify the company's five values. The winners are then honored in an Academy Award–type celebration called Recognition Day. The event is simulcast to all locations at a cost of nearly $250,000. In 2002, when the industry was struggling and American Century was laying off workers, the leadership decided it was still well worth the money to honor those who best lived out the company's values.

We know that this attention to values by American Century has raised employees' awareness. How? We practice what investment legend Phil Fisher called the "scuttlebutt" approach to research: We ask everyone we meet, from receptionist to chief financial officer, "What are the guiding principles of this firm?" And then we listen to what they say. Do their answers line up with the stated values? During the course of our interactions at the firm, employees at American Century demonstrated a clear understanding of their company's guiding principles.

The American Century CFO, Bob Jackson, went well beyond just identifying the values. He told us that senior management goes on at least two retreats each year where they talk about the values and how they are being manifested in the day-to-day life of the leaders and the employees. The result: "We're really a team here at AC. That wasn't true with prior employers." Importantly, the leaders at American Century realize that the only way a company can truly be values-driven is by the leaders "walking the talk." Gordon Snyder, marketing director at AC, said, "We screen everything we do through the guiding principles."

If there is the slightest suggestion or perception that the leaders are just paying lip service to the values, employees will sense it and move their values-imprinted paperweights to the bottom desk drawer. Outstanding leaders know this well, which is why David Fisher at Capital Group said, "Leadership is best accomplished by example rather than by telling others what to do."[5] Gary Brinson used his company's annual meeting to strengthen and reinforce the culture: "We try to take an active role in creating the corporate culture. When we get together each year at our annual meeting, we spend one hour discussing our beliefs and the culture of the firm. We solicit ideas about who we are and how we should think about ourselves."[6]

VALUES AND RESULTS

For leaders like Bill Lyons or David Fisher or Gary Brinson, it was probably evident very early on that values were important to corporate success. But for those of us who are naturally skeptical (read: investment professionals) and who are not terribly accepting of "touchy-feely" concepts, why should we pay attention to values? Where is the evidence that values-driven companies are superior to profit-driven ones?

Here is where we rely on Jim Collins and Jerry Porras and their findings in *Built to Last*. In their exhaustive study of 18 exemplary companies and 18 comparison companies, they found a marked difference between the great and the merely good companies in what they called "core ideology." In short, the great companies had a clear understanding of who they were and what they stood for. (They also had a clear sense of their corporate purpose and where they were going, which we'll discuss in Chapter 3.) This clear understanding of corporate identity serves as the glue that holds a company together, through good times and bad, up markets and down markets. Collins and Porras rated the studied companies using a three-point scale (High = +1, Medium = 0, and Low = −1), based on the evaluative statements about values and vision shown in Table 2.1.[7] The results for the 18 exemplary companies and their average counterparts are shown in Table 2.2.

TABLE 2.1 Study Results

A. Clarity of Values and Vision

+1 Significant evidence that the company has identified and articulated core values and purpose and uses them as a source of guidance. Key leaders speak of the values and vision and have communicated them to employees.

0 Some evidence of the above.

−1 No evidence that the company has made serious attempts to identify and articulate core values and purpose.

B. Historical Alignment around Values and Vision

+1 Evidence that the values and vision described in part A have undergone little change since inception and are continually reinforced by the leaders.

0 Evidence that the values and vision have changed over the years and that the company has been inconsistent in reinforcing them.

−1 Little evidence that there has been a consistent set of values or central purpose for the company.

C. Purpose Beyond Profits

+1 Evidence that the profitability or shareholder wealth is only part of the company's objectives, not the primary objective. Use of phrases such as "fair" return, rather than "maximal" or "highest possible" return.

0 Evidence that profits are highly important, equal to or more significant than any other goals or values.

−1 Evidence that profit is the main driving force, and all else comes second.

D. Alignment of Words and Actions: Walking the Talk

+1 Significant evidence that vision and values are "alive" in the company. Major strategic initiatives and/or company policies are guided by the vision and values.

0 Some evidence of the above, but less pronounced and inconsistent.

−1 Little evidence that vision and values tie into the actions and behaviors in the company.

TABLE 2.2 Results Comparison

Category	Average score: *Built to Last* Companies	Average score: Comparison Companies
A. Clarity of values and vision	.78	−.11
B. Historical alignment around values and vision	.67	−.89
C. Purpose beyond profits	.39	−.33
D. Alignment of words and actions	.72	−.22

The evidence from Collins and Porras's study clearly shows that the really top firms rigorously define their guiding principles (beliefs and values). Roger Siboni, CEO of E.piphany, would agree. As he put it:

> I think people underestimate the importance of values and vision. Having a clear, concise vision that everybody gets, alongside a set of values that become the fabric of the company and the rules to live by, creates consistency in your organization and makes it scalable. Companies that have a clear vision and values enjoy market caps that are consistently close to 20 times higher than those that don't have those qualities.[8]

Again, Collins and Porras made similar findings: The stock prices of their 18 exemplary companies consistently outperformed those of the comparison companies.[9]

BRINSON AND THE IMPORTANCE OF VALUES

My first boss in the investment business, Gary Brinson, understood this point well. When he left First Chicago to form Brinson Partners, he identified and wrote down the company values, which he called "Our Beliefs":

- Teamwork, collegial interaction, and collaborative activity form a common bond for achievement.
- Execution supersedes intention.
- Quality in everything we do preempts quantity.
- The pursuit of excellence must be pervasive and unrelenting.
- There are no higher ethical values than truth, honesty, and professionalism.
- Commitment, dedication, and hard work are our instruments of success.

- Enjoying ourselves and maintaining a pleasant working environment are important elements of our success.
- Individual rewards are tied to performance meritocracy.
- We will always benefit from critical review and a goal of constant improvement.

These beliefs were well known to each employee at Brinson. In fact, when the very successful Brinson Partners was finally acquired by UBS, this statement of beliefs lived on through many of the people who had worked at Brinson. In more than one instance, during a consulting assignment to identify and define values, we would meet a former Brinson employee (by then with a new organization) who would haul out this old, tattered set of beliefs and say, "We should use this as a model for our values." That is the sort of power these values had for the people who knew them and lived by them.

In our discussions, Brinson repeatedly came back to values as a key factor in his firm's success. At one point, using the broader term *culture* to define *values*, he summed it up thus:

> *In my mind, the worst thing that could happen is not that a firm chooses the "wrong" approach to culture but that a firm does not know what its culture is. If you know what your culture is, you can be successful. Firms that are not successful, not simply investment firms but any organization, do not know their culture.*[10]

VALUES GONE WRONG

Consider this example of corporate values. Imagine that a friend of yours, returning from a job interview, says that he has been offered a job by a firm with these values:

- Communication.
- Respect.
- Integrity.
- Excellence.

You consider them for a moment and then ask an excellent question: What do these words mean? After all, two people could differ widely on what "Respect" means.

Not to be put off, your friend triumphantly reveals a sheet of paper with definitions for each of the values:

■ **Communication**
We have an obligation to communicate. Here, we take the time to talk with one another . . . and to listen. We believe that information is meant to move and that information moves people.

■ **Respect**
We treat others as we would like to be treated ourselves. We do not tolerate abusive or disrespectful treatment.

■ **Integrity**
We work with customers and prospects openly, honestly, and sincerely. When we say we will do something, we will do it; when we say we cannot or will not do something, then we won't do it.

■ **Excellence**
We are satisfied with nothing less than the very best in everything we do. We will continue to raise the bar for everyone. The great fun here will be for all of us to discover just how good we can really be.

Defining values is important because many firms, having agreed on core values, don't go to the next important step of agreeing on what these values mean in a practical, day-to-day sense. But this firm has. You look at these values and can't help but be impressed. Having your friend's best interest at heart, you think, "Great, you should accept their offer. That will be a wonderful place to work." Right?

Wrong. These are the stated values of Enron before its collapse. What we all know now is that Enron's walk and talk were miles apart. The lack of congruence was shocking. A *New Yorker* cartoon made the point well: A boss who is standing at the head of a conference table says to his team, "Okay, honesty is the best policy, let's call that option A." For all that Enron's publicly stated values make it appear to be a wonderful workplace, an ex-employee told us that it was ruthless. (He said, "I wasn't worried about being stabbed in the back at Enron, I was worried about being stabbed in the front!") Jim Collins emphasized that healthy cultures are rigorous, *not* ruthless.

At this point, you may feel that we are preaching ethics or moralizing. Not so. The subject of ethics covers what is right and wrong; we are addressing the subject of congruence. Do actions and words align? There is no set of "right" values for an investment firm—or for any firm, for that matter.

To make this point clear, consider Nike, the sports apparel company. One of Nike's values is passion for competition. In fact, they talk about the thrill of crushing the opponent. Talk to any new employee (called an "ekin," which is *Nike* spelled backward) and he or she will tell you that

Nike is the best at firing up the competitive spirit. They parade the numbers from competitors in front of ekins and then show how Nike crushed them. Some may ask, "Is it ethical to enjoy beating the daylights out of someone?" Doesn't matter. Nike is expressing its own truth: Its employees are expressing what is real for and important to them. In this sense, the company's "walk" and "talk" are totally congruent. And, by the way, the company is very successful.

Glenn Carlson at Brandes, an $80 billion value manager of equities, expressed a similar delight when I asked him about his passion for investing: "I love kicking complete ass!" And Brandes does. It has the number one global equity value fund in the world over a 20-year period. Its record is so good it's almost laughable.

Another example from *Built to Last* is Philip Morris. They value personal freedom. If you want to smoke cigarettes, then, as an adult, you should have that freedom. Even though the Surgeon General has warned us that cigarettes are bad for our health, the leaders at Philip Morris don't care. They love their cigarettes and make no apologies for smoking. "I love cigarettes. It's one of the things that makes life really worth living. . . . Cigarettes supply some desire, some [aspect] of the fundamental human equation."[11] This declaration from Ross Millhiser, vice chairman of Philip Morris in 1979, sums up the company's position. Again, the issue is congruency, not ethics. In our examination of investment firms, we found ample evidence that the firms that had identified their true values and lived them passionately were the clear winners.

THE PARADOX OF PROFIT

Investment professionals, with their natural attraction to and fascination with money, may have more trouble understanding Collins and Porras's third differentiating factor:

> *Evidence that profitability or shareholder wealth is only part of the company's objectives, not the primary objective. Use of phrases like "fair" return rather than "maximal" return.*

This statement may seem like heresy to investors. Profit is everything to someone who watches stock prices bounce up and down because the company's results are a penny ahead of or behind the Street estimate. How can profits be anything less than paramount?

First, please understand that we are *not* suggesting that profits aren't important. Of course they are. We are merely saying that our findings in the investment industry mirrored those of Collins and Porras. Namely, we found that the top firms did not focus on financial results as a core value. To repeat what Paul Schaeffer of SEI said, "The investment management business is about a lot more than just making money."[12] Consistently, we found that values such as "client satisfaction" and "integrity" were the top values of the best-performing firms. Jeffrey Molitor at Vanguard says it this way:

> *The most important lesson we have learned from looking at the four P's is that performance is simply the residual factor. If we get everything else right in evaluating a manager—if the right people are in place and they have an enduring investment philosophy and a sound investment process—performance takes care of itself.*[13]

People + Philosophy + Process = Performance

Simply put, the firms that provide the best value to their clients also enjoy the highest profitability. To use a tennis analogy, the player who keeps his eyes on the ball does better than the player who keeps his eyes on the scoreboard.

WALKING THE TALK

Many firms may be able to meet the first three *Built to Last* factors: (1) identifying the vision and values; (2) maintaining the vision and values over time; and (3) placing vision and values ahead of profits. Still, there is a huge difference between meeting the first three and fulfilling the final one: making the vision and values live in the organization. Gary Brinson realized this and said, poignantly, "In our business, describing our principles is relatively easy; executing them, however, is not."[14]

A large investment firm that we consulted with is a good example. This $60 billion organization, with 300 employees, had gone to the effort of identifying a vision and four core values. These values were displayed prominently on plaques hanging on the walls and on paperweights on each employee's desk. Therefore, this organization met the first factor set out by Collins and Porras: identifying vision and values. They also met the second criterion of duration, because the vision and values statement was not new. It had been around for at least five years. This company even met the third factor, as none of the four core values had to do with profit or financial success.

Where this firm stumbled was on point four: making the vision and values "live" in the organization. Just as Brinson predicted, execution was the tough part. We discovered this as we worked with the employees over a three-month period and routinely performed our scuttlebutt research. In that period of time, we asked nearly every employee to name the four core values. We found only one who could do it—and she was, no surprise, the director of human resources.

Walking the talk is critical. Congruency between the stated values and the reality of what happens in the firm is where many firms fail.

TROUBLED TIMES AT ALLSTAR

Having established the importance of identifying and aligning with core values, we can better understand the reasons behind Allstar's collapse. In turbulent environments, a firm with clear guiding principles stands a better chance of survival. Allstar had never really formed as a team, that is, as a group with a shared purpose and common understanding of what was important at the firm. They were guilty of exactly what Brinson talked about earlier: not knowing their culture. When the going got tough—as it always does in the investment industry, sooner or later—they had nothing to fall back on. They couldn't appeal to a shared set of values because in truth, like Enron, they had never placed much importance on shared identity and had never truly developed any shared values. Instead, they spun out into emotions like anger, fear, and resentment. They turned on one another. All their fierce competitive instincts—needed to compete effectively in the market—were turned inward, on their coworkers and even on themselves. There was no mutual support, no pulling together, no trust. The assessment tool that we use to measure trust in an organization showed the lowest levels that we had ever seen in a group. The company's leadership had never recognized the importance of establishing a common identity, so when profits went south, there was no foundation to hang on to.

When we suggested that identifying values would be a good first step, the Allstar folks reacted with fear. What if they couldn't agree on core values? What if the discussion just spiraled down into more anger and dissent? We responded honestly that it could happen. (We decided not to make the obvious point that this is why firms should have this discussion first: so that they won't discover down the road that the group members are incompatible!) It took a bit of persuading to convince the leaders at Allstar that the "values question" must be addressed, but eventually they agreed. With relief, we can report that the values discussion did not erupt into fisticuffs—

just the opposite, in fact. We could feel the tension ease as they concentrated on common ground rather than on their intense personal feelings.

Some might ask, "Isn't what you've described here natural for any organization that is recording bad results?" No. Although it's natural to feel frustrated and dissatisfied, it is not natural—or necessary—for group members to turn on each other. It can happen, as it did in the Allstar case, but it doesn't have to. We have seen many instances in which performance was just as bad, and the employees felt just as frustrated, but they supported one another. Organizations that we interviewed and know well, such as First Quadrant, Aronson and Partners (now Aronson+Johnson+Ortiz), and Northern Trust, have all experienced difficult times, but their strong cultures allowed them to weather the storm. Their trust levels and culture assessments did not reveal cracks in the façade.

ESTABLISHING CORE VALUES: THE PROCESS

Now that you know it's crucially important, how do you create a sense of shared purpose in your organization? How do you collectively determine what you believe in, what you stand for? The process starts with identifying, defining, and measuring core values.

We'll use an extreme case from our consulting experience to show that even the most diverse group can succeed in this process. The group in question consisted of investment leaders from a large global company that had acquired firms from around the world and was endeavoring to integrate them into one, seamless operation. The 13 people in the room with us were from different companies (which had been acquired and merged together) and different countries and spoke at least four languages (English, German, French, and Japanese, and probably others we weren't even aware of). The only thing they appeared to have in common was their passion for investing and a healthy skepticism about the benefits of an offsite retreat. The leader expressed his urgent charge: to build a global team—in the true sense of the word—and begin delivering results within 10 months. We knew from experience that this group's best chance for success was to start at the beginning, by developing a foundation of shared values and a common purpose.

Uncommon Sense: Starting with the Soft Stuff

The leader's response to our suggestion to work on values was a huge, dramatic eye-roll. To him it seemed like the least productive of all possibilities.

"We're under tremendous pressure to produce significant results. We have to get to work! Don't you realize the challenges we're up against? Do we really have time to spend on 'values' and 'common purpose'?" In other words, are you nuts?

We experience this kind of resistance frequently. Investment professionals are focused and very hard-working. They have a distinct and hard-earned pride in their talents and skills, and enjoy applying those skills to the challenges of the day. To the uninitiated, values work seems terribly soft (as in *unfocused* and *unproductive*). "Please," we hear, "a few hours in the dentist's chair would be preferable to this touchy-feely stuff!" Additionally, because investors are traditionally so much more comfortable with numbers, investment models, and facts, the idea of a potentially personal discussion is pointedly discomforting. What happens if we don't agree? Won't we get into a bitch session? Won't this cause hard feelings?

The tendency we see, over and over again, is a rush to "do the work," without the understanding or appreciation that the articulation of "who are we" as a group is as much a part of the core work as the investment study and decisions themselves. The key point is the common understanding that investment results are everybody's business in the firm. Values work? That's the charge of leadership.

So, when is the best time to answer the question of "who are we" as a firm? If your organization already has long-standing values, we suggest that you revisit and refresh them periodically. See how your senior team defines them today and to what degree you share an understanding of what's really important at your firm. Remember Brinson's comment that his team reviewed the company values each year at the annual meeting. If you don't have your values stated and defined, we think the values work is most effective and influential if done at the startup of a new venture. *Venture* could be defined as the start of a new firm, the creation of a new division, or the restructuring of a department. When the senior leaders at Turner Investments decided to start the firm, this was their first action. They took time to decide what they stood for. Brinson did the same thing when he spun off from First Chicago's trust department.

Alternatively, a new venture could be the start of a new strategic plan or initiative, annual goal setting, or an important project the firm is about to undertake. Wrap the values work around an important business objective. Values work will not be as meaningful if it is seen as an end in itself. The point is to understand the connection between the "hard" business goal and the "soft" values work. You'll see how this played out in our case study of Global Investors, the multinational firm we described at the beginning of this section.

Global Investors: Finding Common Ground

At Global Investors, because of language differences, arguments arose over the nuances of certain words. For example, the European team members were eager to see the word *transparent* as a value. To them, this meant that the investment process was clear and easily understood. The Americans, however, were horrified at this proposal, because their association with the word was completely different; they understood it to mean someone who is phony and can easily be "seen through." When a team is selecting its values, all these distinctions are important. It's equally important to let people talk through the differences. After all, the team members are discussing what is deeply significant to them. If you shut down their conversation, you're bound to step on toes. Eventually, after intense discussions, the group reached a consensus, agreeing that *transparent* could be replaced by the word *accessible*.

In a relatively short time, this international team had identified its core values. Each team member could support these six they chose:

1. Unique insights.
2. Teamwork.
3. Integrity.
4. Results.
5. Accessibility.
6. Disciplined.

A team's successful agreement on core values may not seem like an extraordinary accomplishment, but consider the following. Barry, an actuary by training, approached us after his group had successfully agreed on five values. He showed us some figures on a notepad, and said, "This is incredible! Do you realize that the odds of a group of 18 people selecting the same 5 values from a list of 102 possible choices is 1 in 1.5 billion?!" (Leave it to an actuary to quantify this process! This really makes our point that financial people love to quantify things and may ignore aspects of business that don't lend themselves to measurement. We address this in Chapters 5 through 8.)

Sometimes groups fail to get the full benefit from values work because they stop after gaining agreement on the words. It's important to go the next step, which is to define what these values mean in practical, everyday behavioral terms.

Note that we are not getting specific about the process we use to facilitate these discussions. There are two reasons for this. First, we have found from experience that this sort of work requires outside facilitation. The best brain surgeon in the world doesn't operate on herself. Likewise, the smartest investment leader shouldn't try to both participate in and facilitate his own values session. It would be inappropriate for us to believe this and then suggest that you should undertake this process yourself, by carefully laying out all the steps. Second, and perhaps even more important, most self-respecting investment professionals would find that the description of the process goes well beyond boring and into "just be merciful and shoot me now" territory. (Interestingly, though, investment professionals don't mind doing the values work. In fact, most of them enjoy it—they just don't care *how* it gets done, anymore than they care about how their cars gets fixed.)

When the Global team pressed on and defined their six values, they came up with these bullet points:

Unique Insights:
We capture unique insights with processes, models, and analysis that are:
- Innovative.
- Non-consensus.
- Uncommon.
- High quality.
- Forward looking.

Teamwork:
- We acknowledge and leverage cultural differences and capabilities.
- We practice open, global communications and cooperation.
- We encourage constructive criticism, collegiality, and mutual respect.
- We have fun!
- We align our work with our values and vision.

Integrity:
We value integrity, by which we mean:
- Trust of colleagues and clients.
- Professionalism and honesty.
- Knowing our limitations.
- Acknowledging accountability and taking responsibility.

Results:
We value and reward results. These results include positive impact on:

- Investment process.
- Reputation.
- Client satisfaction.
- Investment performance.

Accessibility:

- We accomplish this by effective communication and strong internal and external relationships.
- We provide transparency and usability for process, analysis, models, and strategy.

Disciplined and Consistent Processes:
These globally integrated processes are:

- Investment research.
- Risk analysis.
- Portfolio construction.

Defining your values helps you bring them to life. When people understand what the values mean, it's more likely that they'll use them in day-to-day activities.

We encourage simple, everyday language. The values of Harley Davidson, the motorcycle manufacturer, are a good example:

- Tell the truth.
- Be fair.
- Keep your promises.
- Respect the individual.
- Encourage intellectual curiosity.

We showed Harley Davidson's values to a team that was working on this exercise, and they were so moved by the language that they almost simultaneously yelled, "Yes, let's make those OUR values!" This was after three hours spent selecting a significantly different set of values. We had to remind this team that values, no matter how good they might sound, have to emerge from the group's own discussion of identity. Never underestimate the power of language. We encourage people to find compelling language to express their important values.

Another challenging aspect of values work is social expectations. People are tempted to describe what they feel could—or should—be the ideal work environment. That's why words like *teamwork*, *collaboration*, *quality*, *service*, and *innovation* instantly come up when a group starts values work. The trick is to discern what is actually true for the group. Nordstrom's, for example, is well known for high-quality merchandise—but *quality* is not one of its defined values. The Nordstrom folks don't believe that quality has to be explicitly stated as a value. Customer service? You bet. Quality? Not core.

Additionally, you do not have to excel at a value to call it your own. Your firm may highly value teamwork or communication, yet know there are serious issues with these at present. When you have identified the firm's true values, though, people will have an easier time prioritizing the changes that will have to be made to embed those values and integrate them into effective, values-driven, day-to-day business.

In light of Enron, WorldCom, Andersen, and other corporate debacles, we have also moved toward having teams rank their values. The fall of Andersen, for example, can be attributed to a shift in the priority of its values: "In the 1990's, the firm embarked on a path that valued hefty fees ahead of bluntly honest bookkeeping, eroding Andersen's good name."[15]

Which is it for your team: hefty fees or honesty? This may seem like an easy decision, but Andersen, whose core business was financial integrity, got it wrong and thus destroyed itself. Consider the values of your team. Which one comes first? Do any of the values conflict? Have you chosen two that are natural opposites, such as "risk-averse" and "entrepreneurial"? Which gets top priority? Ranking values makes for interesting dialogue and serves as important guidance for team members. In the Global Investors case, the team decided that Integrity, Teamwork, Unique Insights, and Results were their most important values. When pressed, they decided that Integrity and Teamwork would contribute to the success of the other two and therefore were most important.

For clarity, have your team rate the values they've chosen. Ask them how well they are living each individual value as a team. For example, the Global team picked "Unique Insights" as a value. They believe that to be a high-performing, successful team, they have to be innovative. Fine. On a scale of 1 (lousy) to 10 (excellent), how well are they doing in this regard?

That's why it's important to spend time defining your values; thereafter, you can evaluate yourselves more accurately. We had each Global team member write down the six values on a sheet of paper and give each a number from 1 to 10. The rating was to reflect how the team was doing currently, not an aspiration for the future.

Figure 2.1 shows, at left, the six values of the Global Investors financial firm; the bars quantify how the value ratings have improved over time. The rating for each of the six values has improved since they started measuring in May 2001. Aligning around these six values has helped this organiza-

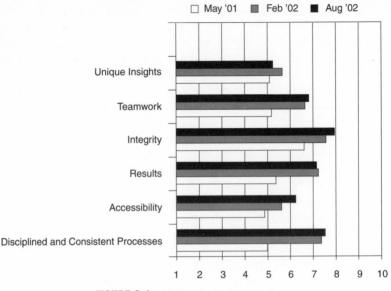

FIGURE 2.1   Value Rating Improvements

tion's performance significantly. It met and exceeded the 10-month goals mentioned earlier and are continuing to perform ahead of expectations. The measurement process involves an investment of time and effort for sure, but as Peter Drucker, the renowned management guru, says, "What gets measured, gets done."[16]

The Value of Values: Getting the Right People on Board

The process of establishing core values and company identity is critical to getting the right people on board. Those "right people" will have great skills and be a great fit with one another (that is, they will have shared values). There are three powerful benefits of values work:

1. Hiring and promoting decisions become easier.
2. Termination decisions become clearer.
3. Morale is improved as individuals de-select themselves from a team.

A clear corporate identity certainly makes hiring and promotion decisions easier. Consider the case of Mike Miller, director of planning and development at Vanguard, who had worked at a law firm before moving to

Vanguard. His switch to Vanguard is a strong statement about culture. Jack Brennan learned from a friend that a fellow named Miller, who was then working in the D.C. area, would be a perfect fit for Vanguard. Pursuing this tip, Brennan contacted Miller and talked to him about the possibility of joining the Vanguard team. The friend was exactly right: Miller found it a perfect fit and raves about the culture at Vanguard. "This is one firm, one vision. And with my values, I'm a perfect fit," he says. In particular, Miller enjoys the friendship with his senior colleagues. "At other jobs, I had good relationships with my colleagues, but here we've become good friends. I like socializing with these guys."

The second effect of values work pertains to whether people stay or go, once the culture is more clearly defined. The deeper discussions of corporate identity sometimes cause conflicting values to surface. Troublesome as it may sound, the issue of conflicting values must be addressed head-on. There is no way to fake alignment. In fact, this phrase was the rallying cry at Fannie Mae, when David Maxwell took over as CEO: "You can't fake it at Fannie Mae."[17] After Maxwell carefully described the core values that he wanted his team to live by, 14 of the top 26 executives left the company.

We had a similar experience working with the Global team: 3 of the 13 members left the team within 3 months of establishing the core values. They saw clearly that they didn't fit. We call this *deselection*, and it is a very healthy, logical consequence of setting the company's foundation. Most often, no one in the group is surprised by who chooses to leave. Often everyone is relieved.

Top leaders must act when the fit is bad. These tough decisions become easier when those involved realize that it is not personal. It is no longer a subjective decision about liking or disliking someone, but rather an objective decision about fit with the company's values. Investment professionals are unusually smart, and they often see the handwriting on the wall clearly after the values have been identified. Fortunately, many people who leave are thankful down the road because they find a much better environment for themselves.

The third consequence is a surge in morale. After an individual has deselected himself or been released, there is usually a collective sigh of, "Phew, it's about time." When action is taken, the word gets out: "We mean business. Our values have teeth. Leadership is willing to protect and defend them. This is our group and I'm proud to be here." The drive to identify with a group is powerful. What makes your group different from others? Its values, for starters. Furthermore, the willingness of a firm's leadership to walk its talk is one of the key elements of trust, which we discuss fully in Chapter 8. But first we turn our attention to the question that logically follows "Who are we?": namely, "Where are we going?" Vision is the subject of Chapter 3.

SUMMARY

Core values establish a group's identity. They define what is important and how group members will treat others. They act as the glue that holds people together through tough times. Something that occurred while we were writing this chapter illustrates the point. An investment manager whom we admire very much was shocked when five brokers left to form their own company, taking 10 percent of the firm's assets with them. I called to discuss the incident with the chief investment officer, an excellent leader. She and the other members of the senior management team were sorry to see this group leave, but she noted that they did not leave to join a competitor. Nor did they leave with guns blazing. Rather, they simply wanted a more entrepreneurial environment. They wanted to do their own thing. The CIO maintained an open-door policy for several days after the incident, and constantly reassured her remaining staff that this was not an indication that the firm was being sold or that any other dire event was imminent. As things returned to normal, the CIO made a comment to me that summed up much of what this chapter is about: "Sure, it made a lot of us angry at first, but you know this stuff rolls off our back because we know who we are as an institution." That, in a nutshell, is what core values are all about: identity. When you know who you are, you don't sweat the small stuff. And you survive the big, hard stuff.

TEST YOURSELF

Ask yourself the following yes/no questions.

Yes   No

1. Are your firm's values clearly defined?

If you answered no, skip to the exercise.

2. If your firm has articulated its values or guiding principles, are there fewer than seven?
3. At your workplace, if you stopped three people at random and asked them to name the firm's values, could they do it?

Yes   No

4. Do you use your values in the context of hiring and orientation?

5. Do you use your values in the context of separation or termination?

6. Do you use your values in the context of performance evaluations?

7. Do you use your values in the context of awards and recognition?

8. What are your next steps to reinforce the firm's values throughout the firm?

EXERCISES

Do each of these with your senior team.

1. Examine your firm's written materials (brochures, web site copy, etc.). Do they contain value words that pop out?
2. If one of your highly regarded, senior people were to give an "elevator pitch" about your firm, what would you hear?
3. If one of your most committed clients were to give an "elevator endorsement" about your firm, what would you hear?
4. If you were seeking to fill a senior position and had a number of candidates of equal ability (experience, IQ, skill levels), what personal characteristics would generate enthusiasm about a particular candidate?
5. Given your responses to these four questions, what values are surfacing? (Remember, we're not talking about ideal states; we're answering the question, "What do we most care about?")

CHAPTER 3

Vision: Where Are We Going?

An effective leader has a clear vision of where the firm is going and what is necessary to get there and has the ability to effectively communicate that vision across the entire organization.

—Alison Winter, Executive Vice President,
The Northern Trust Company[1]

"Why are we here?" addresses the firm's core purpose and its image of a preferred future. In this chapter, you will learn:

- The benefits of articulating the core purpose of the firm for employees, clients, and shareholders.
- A process for discerning your core purpose.
- The elements of a good vision and vision story.
- The quantifiable difference in business results between firms that define and use their values and vision and those that do not.

When the Allstar team successfully agreed on five core values, the tension in the room lessened considerably. They had found common ground, some overlaps in the Venn diagrams to which they could point and say, "We'd all like to work together in this way." The group was ready to move to the next question, "Where are we going?" Other ways to phrase this question include:

- What's our purpose?
- Why do we exist?

- What is our mission?
- What are we here to do?

Values answer the question "How we are going to work together?" but not "What are we working on?"

We turned to the Allstar leader and said, "So, what is your vision? What are you and your team here to do?" He furrowed his brow and after a few seconds said, "To achieve an investment return of 50 basis points over our benchmark." This was his compelling vision. This numeric goal was the reason why his teammates should jump out of bed on a cold morning, fight the blizzard and traffic, and show up for work. (Can you say, "I think I'll sleep in?") As Collins and Porras noted in *Built to Last*, the exemplary companies always had a motive beyond profit, something that inspired people to rise above themselves, to achieve the impossible—something that connected them to a purpose greater than themselves.[2] People who have never had this experience cannot fully understand the concept of vision. They may make fun of it, perceiving it as adolescent, fatuous, or cultish.

As the hard evidence shows, they should not be so quick to dismiss it. When people feel connected to something important and larger than themselves, they often produce their best results. Connection is powerful and has even been linked to physical health. Dr. Edward Hallowell, of the Harvard Medical School, has researched this topic and found that people who feel connected to their work and colleagues actually are healthier and live longer.[3] When we met with Jack Brennan and his senior team, we mentioned this fact, and Jack polled the group for the number of sick days. The 7 people present, who had 70 years of combined experience, had taken only 3 sick days in all those years of work.

The Allstar vision didn't work this way. It did not connect the staff to anything larger than themselves. Rather, it reduced them to a number (50 basis points, to be exact). Given the survival mode that Allstar was operating in, we decided not to push for a richer, deeper statement of purpose. The group had come together to be allstars, to produce the numbers, and performance defined their culture. Despite our numerous discussions, we did not hear much about clients, except for the obvious concern that Allstar was losing them weekly.

Several times since the Allstar experience, each of us has expressed sadness about it. Much of our professional joy comes from helping leaders create a working environment that brings out the best and highest in their people. The Allstar experience was nearly the opposite. The environment brought out the lowest and worst in these otherwise decent and talented people. The absence of a strong culture, in which values and vision are clearly identified, had the very effect that Brinson predicted in his earlier statement: disaster. It is no wonder that David Fisher, one of the most highly respected leaders in the industry, reiterates, "We talk a great deal about values and vision."[4]

VALUES, THEN VISION

First comes identity, then comes direction. Collins makes this point forcefully in his second book, *Good to Great*. He goes so far as to say, "Great vision without great people is irrelevant."[5] We agree, which is why we start a client's work with the question: "Who are we?" Your charge as leader is to answer this question, which will get the right people on the bus. Once the right people are assembled, you can then ask,

- Why are we here? (purpose)
- Where are we going? (vision)

Combining these questions—Who are we? Where are we going?—yields what Collins calls "core ideology." In Chapter 2, we showed the evidence, from *Built to Last,* that the truly excellent companies are passionately driven by core ideology. It is their clarity of identity and their passion for their purpose that propels them to greatness.

Is this true for investment firms? Emphatically, yes.

Imagine two investment firms that are remarkably similar in many ways. They both have so many billions of dollars under management, they both employ about the same number of people, they both focus on the same market niche, and so on. From the outside, you might say it would be impossible to predict which firm would prosper and which would falter. Now imagine, though, that you were privy to the deep motivation of the leadership of each firm. Let's call this deep motivation the *core purpose*. Why does the firm exist? What is its reason for being? For one of the two imaginary firms, the answer is "to provide the highest and best service to our clients." For the other, the answer is "to get fabulously wealthy for ourselves."

Based on just this information—the core purpose of each firm—we could predict confidently that the former will flourish and the latter will falter. This was Collins's finding in *Built to Last* and ours in our study of the investment industry.

TURNER INVESTMENTS: A VISION OF SERVICE

Consider the case of Turner Investments. Turner was founded in 1990 in Berwyn, Pennsylvania, near Philadelphia. It is 100 percent employee-owned, and currently manages more than $8 billion for institutions and individuals. The firm invests in growth and value stocks of all capitalizations and in bonds of various maturity averages. The first thing you see when you go to the Turner Investments web site, in bold letters, is: "Putting Our Clients First." One click takes you to Turner's mission statement:

> *It's been said that the more one gives, the more one receives. Thus the mission of Turner Investment Partners, Inc. is to give of ourselves:*
> - To our clients: *consistently superior investment returns combined with the highest level of client service.*
> - To our prospects: *a straightforward presentation of our logical and common-sense investment philosophy, approach, and process.*
> - To those who serve us: *courtesy, respect, and a timely response to any questions or comments.*
> - To our employees: *the opportunity for career growth in a positive and enjoyable work environment and, to the extent it is financially possible, compensation and benefits which are at the upper-end of industry levels.*
> - To our employees' families: *recognition of the importance of family to each employee and respect for each individual's family needs.*
> - To each other: *recognition of the personal dignity of each individual and, although we may have different talents, that we all contribute in a unique way to the firm's goals as a team.*
> - To our profession: *strict adherence to the AIMR Code of Ethics and the Standards of Practice and a commitment to the advancement of the AIMR.*
> - To our community and society: *a commitment to activism to see the communities and society in which we live prosper.*
> - To ourselves: *recognition that success is not necessarily defined by money or position, but by happiness in our daily lives and growth in human potential.*

How did we first learn of Turner? Paul Schaeffer, formerly of Capital Resource Advisors and now with SEI Investments, nearly trampled a few innocent bystanders in his effort to reach me after a talk I delivered. He said with conviction, "The things you just talked about, Jim, that's exactly how

Turner operates." Beth and I packed our bags soon thereafter and left for Berwyn to see for ourselves.

The first thing that we noticed about Turner's mission statement was that the opening lines sounded more like something from the Salvation Army, Red Cross, or United Way. It didn't sound like the hard-boiled stuff you would find on Wall Street. Could an investment firm with this mission statement be taken seriously?

We also noticed a few other things. The first group of people to be served was clients. Right on top. This was a good sign. We also noticed that the tone of the mission was disarmingly—and refreshingly—honest. We liked the feel of it, but were skeptical: Was this another Enron-type statement? Sounds great, but has no substance behind it?

We arrived in Berwyn and began with our scuttlebutt research technique. Before we could even ask the receptionist, Bev, to describe the company's mission, she said, "I want this to be your best visit of the day." Good opener. When asked about the mission of the company, she effortlessly recited the key points in the previously quoted statement. Further, we noticed that she had her business cards prominently displayed next to her name plaque, and later we learned that she was an owner and partner in the firm. These are all good signs! As we were making these mental notes, Bev proudly announced that she was the "chief executive officer in charge of first impressions."

She escorted us to a conference room where Stephen Kneeley, CEO, John H. Grady, COO, and Thomas R. Trala Jr., CFO, met with us to discuss how the mission relates to Turner's daily functions. What we learned from them over the next few hours reassured us that the "walk" and the "talk" were beautifully aligned.

First, these three officers understood clearly the distinction between running the business and running the money. Imagine for a second working in an investment environment where you can focus on investment ideas all day long, without interruptions, silly meetings, bureaucratic red tape, and the like. You are surrounded by other bright investment professionals whose incentive compensation is structured to motivate them to help you perform.

Okay, you're drooling, so grab a hankie and mop up. Sound too good to be true? The environment I just described—investment nirvana to many—is the mission of Steve and his senior team. Their approach to service is to eliminate any obstacles that might keep their investment professionals from doing their absolute best work. They rigorously protect and defend this vision. Kneeley said, "Don't attack our commitment to client service; you might as well insult my mother!"

The Turner structure reminded me of the days when I followed the advertising industry as a securities analyst. Ad firms structured themselves in the same way: Separate the creative talent from the "suits" so that the former could spend all their time thinking up new, innovative campaigns. Likewise, Turner has created an ideal environment for investment pros to do their best thinking.

Another aspect of Turner that impressed us was a generally positive attitude, despite the difficult markets they were experiencing. There were no defections by key personnel and morale was good. To simplify, leaders can motivate with the carrot or the stick; through recognition and inspiration or punishment and fear. One story in particular revealed that Turner has largely driven fear out of the workplace. Kneeley told us that each morning he looks in the mirror and asks, "Am I the right guy to lead Turner Investments?" He said if he ever thought the answer was no, then he would step aside and do something else. Well, of course, this sounds good, but would it really happen? Kneeley said that the woman in charge of human resources at Turner had done just that. She felt safe enough at Turner to go to Kneeley and tell him that she thought she might not be the right person for a new initiative. They subsequently reassigned her, with no negative consequences, and moved someone new into her old role. The message here is that the company's mission, *to be of service*, helps employees focus on the positive aspect of serving clients, rather than on the fearful activities needed to protect the holy triumvirate of me, myself, and I.

Another story from Turner also supported the idea that Kneeley and his team have created a real community. Kneeley was describing a new initiative that involved sending two employees to start up a new facility. As he described the events, he referred to the two people in question as "remaining behind" at the new facility. Then Kneeley stopped and said, "But you know, it's not like they were really leaving us, because we'll be with them in spirit and we'll be talking to them every day." As we packed up to leave Turner, Beth commented that this story reinforced something Bev had said in our first few minutes there: "Welcome to the Turner family." There was very much a family feeling at Turner, and that family feeling was entwined with the core purpose of service.

All this is very well and good . . . but does it translate into results? After all, most investment professionals would not be happy joining a warm, fuzzy family that had stinko investment performance. Not to mention the reaction of clients! Table 3.1 shows the numbers in the three critical areas that we measure.

Contrast the experience at Turner with that at Enron and Andersen,

TABLE 3.1 Critical Areas

	Record
AUM growth (5 years)	31.4%
Performance (R1000 growth, 5 years)	10.03% vs. 7.58%
Staff turnover (12 years)	1 senior portfolio manager

where profit had surfaced as the core purpose. You can see why we claim that we would confidently bet on the client-driven firm over the profit-driven firm.

Another client-driven firm that operates like Turner is Perigee in Toronto. Like Steve Kneeley at Turner, Perigee's CEO, Alex Wilson, considers himself a businessperson, not an investment professional. His vision is for the firm to become one of the top five institutional money managers in Canada. Through his efforts to define and build a strong culture, Wilson and his team have grown Perigee from an 18-person organization, managing about $1 billion, to an 80-person firm with $20 billion in assets. Perigee's core values are "Integrity, Client service, Collaboration, Fun, and Innovation." Greenwich Associates ranked Perigee number 1 for client service in Canada. Employee turnover at the firm is virtually nonexistent, largely because Wilson, like Kneeley, has created an environment in which investment professionals can thrive and do their best work.

VISION, MISSION, PURPOSE: WHAT'S THE DIFFERENCE?

You may already have noticed that although this chapter is entitled "Vision," we used the word *mission* to describe Turner's purpose. Companies frequently use *vision* and *mission* interchangeably. Our experience is that the terms used are not nearly as important as the core concept: the importance of defining and using a statement of your firm's reason for being. For clarity's sake, let's look at how the purists describe vision and mission and then you can decide what would be useful for your purposes.

- *Vision.* A statement describing our preferred future. In his book, *Liberating the Corporate Soul*, Richard Barrett describes vision in this way: "It declares the company's intention with regard to the future it desires to create. The vision represents a deeper level of motivation than a mission. The mission describes the 'means,' the vision describes the 'end.' It makes a compelling statement about what the company is striving to achieve."[6] A vision statement doesn't necessarily reveal what kind of enterprise has embraced it. For example, Motorola's "Tap the creative power within us" could be for an advertising firm or an art school. The beginning of Turner's statement, "to give of ourselves," does not necessarily describe an investment firm (to say the least).

- *Mission.* A statement describing what the firm does. As Barrett put it, this is the "means to the end" and tells us what kind of business the firm is in. Turner's statement goes on to describe that giving, in the context of their clients and business, means delivering "consistently superior investment returns combined with the highest level of client service." So now we know what Turner does.

- *Core purpose.* Collins and Porras, in their *Build to Last* research, avoided the whole terminology conundrum by using "core purpose" to integrate vision and mission. Many companies, like Turner, combine the two anyway.

COMPONENTS OF VISION

Because so many companies combine their vision statements with their missions, we will use the broad term *vision/mission* to capture the spirit of both the end goal and the means. A good vision/mission serves three important purposes:

1. It signifies where the firm is striving to go, thereby simplifying many detailed decisions.
2. It motivates people to move in that direction, even when it's painful to do so.
3. It helps coordinate the actions of many in an efficient way.[7]

John Kotter specified the characteristics of an effective vision as follows:

- *Imaginable.* Conveys a picture of what the future will look like.
- *Desirable.* Appeals to the long-term interests of employees, clients, stockholders, and others who have a stake in the business.
- *Focused.* Is clear enough to provide guidance in decision-making.
- *Flexible.* Is general enough to allow individual initiative and alternative responses in light of changing conditions.

■ *Communicable.* Is easy to communicate; can be successfully explained within five minutes.[8]

Another take on the components of an inspiring vision comes from Interaction Associates, a global consulting and training firm, based on its vision work with many companies:[9]

■ *High standards.* Almost by definition, vision suggests a stretch goal, something that will require us to go above and beyond the call. Collins and Porras, in their book *Built to Last,* call them BHAGs: Big Hairy Audacious Goals.[10] Examples range from Sony's vision of becoming the premier name in quality electronics, and thereby transforming Japan's image as a maker of shoddy products, to Motorola's goal of winning the Baldrige Award for excellence (which it did). The purpose of setting high standards is to energize and encourage employees to reach beyond what they believe is possible. As Walt Disney said, "It's fun to do the impossible."[11]

■ *Unique attribute.* Visions inspire us because they highlight what is unique about our capabilities. They ask the question, "What are we truly best at?" Wells Fargo achieved excellent results in the banking industry because CEO Reichardt concentrated on streamlining its operations and remaining geographically focused in the western United States. One of his colleagues remarked on Reichardt's ability to focus on the unique attribute: "If Carl were an Olympic diver, he would not do a five-flip twisting thing. He would do the best swan dive in the world, and do it perfectly over and over again."[12] Visions highlight our brilliance.

■ *Future focus.* Visions are about the future. They may indirectly extol the past, but they must direct our attention to unrealized possibilities. They excite our imagination about what has not happened but could. Often they include a time line or date of completion, as in Kennedy's vision of a man on the moon by the end of the 1960s.

■ *Vivid imagery.* Visions paint a picture. Many visions fall flat because the leader does not infuse them with life and energy. As any writer will tell you, the way to do that is with details and stories. A leader at one of the major airlines was preparing to tell a group of employees about the importance of customer service. He felt deeply about this topic. In creating his vision statement, though, all he could come up with was stock phrases, such as "the customer is always right" or "treat the customer as you would a friend." These phrases had no juice. Finally, we asked him to tell a story about customer service at his airline. Without hesitation, he told a story about a pilot who stepped out of the cockpit of the 747, went to the gate area, picked up a microphone, and personally apologized for the long delay. Bingo! Here was a real-life situation that people could feel and understand. (How many times have you been there? Wanting *somebody* to apologize for the delay!) Similarly, consider the vivid description below from Sony in the 1950s:

We will create products that become pervasive around the world. . . . We will be the first Japanese company to go into the U.S. market and distribute directly. . . . We will succeed at innovations that U.S. companies have failed at—such as the transistor radio. . . . Fifty years from now, our brand name will be as well known as any in the world . . . and will signify innovation and quality that rival the most innovative companies anywhere. . . . "Made in Japan" will mean something fine, not something shoddy.[13]

- *Unifying theme.* Great visions bring people together. Great leaders understand this. Jim Stowers, founder of American Century, tells all the new employees personally that the company's unifying theme is to help people achieve their dreams. This is the common purpose that joins all the employees. For Robert Bagby, CEO at A.G. Edwards, the unifying theme is: "We are dedicated to building a one-on-one relationship between an investor and a professional financial consultant." Effective CEOs and politicians understand the importance of finding and focusing on common ground.
- *Shared values.* As discussed in Chapter 2, shared values are powerful. For this reason, vision statements often appeal to them. Sony's statement, in vivid imagery, emphasizes the Japanese people's shared value of elevating their culture and national status, which were devastated after World War II.

SIMPLE FORMULA FOR VISION/MISSION

In the investment industry, we've found a remarkable absence of compelling vision statements. Go to the web sites of the leading investment firms, and you'll find that only a handful even have a stated vision/mission. When we ask investment CEOs to share their company vision, most launch into a careful description of the investment process, complete with asset class descriptions, benchmarks, and investment philosophies. Though this is important to a company's success, it doesn't answer the fundamental questions posed by the vision inquiry. Imagine asking Bill Ford to describe the vision of his company and getting a lengthy explanation of anti-lock brakes and dual exhaust systems. Dale put it well after we interviewed the leader of a top 20 mutual fund: "He sounded like a Chief Operating Officer." The discussion was all about the mechanics of getting the job done, not the "why" behind it.

To reiterate, the formula is fairly simple: Our company exists to create _____, by doing _____. Examples of these two components are given in Table 3.2.

Of all the major investment firms, Lehman Brothers follows this formula most closely. Here is its statement of mission:

Our mission is to build unrivaled partnerships with and value for our clients through the knowledge, creativity, and dedication of our people leading to superior returns for our shareholders.

Notice that Lehman snuck in the additional piece about shareholders. As a publicly traded company, that's understandable, but it's not necessary. Execute the mission and the shareholders will benefit. They have in Lehman's case: The stock is the second-best performer (up 86 percent over 5 years) of the 13 that we monitor.

In the case of Turner, the company exists to be of service, and serves by providing the best investment returns possible to its clients. A variation on this theme is American Century's vision statement, which declares that the company exists to help people achieve their dreams by providing financial prosperity to its clients.

Each of these companies uses the vision as its polestar in tough times. The folks at American Century thought for a long time about using the word *dream* in the vision statement of a financial company. Ultimately they went

TABLE 3.2 Component Samples

Company	Purpose: Why We Exist	Mission: How We Do It
Ford	We are about cars	Democratize the automobile
Motorola	Tap the creative power within us	Invent a way to sell 100,000 television sets at $179.95
Disney	Make people happy	Build Disneyland
Merck	Preserve and improve human life	Become the preeminent drug maker worldwide

with it because they believe that vision statements should inspire employees, and nothing is more inspirational to people than their dreams. Now American Century is considering rewording this vision statement, because it has become so popular for financial firms to use *dream* that it has lost any impact. Nevertheless, imitation is the sincerest form of flattery: American Century was there first.

The motivation concept seems trickier for most investment firms. Professional investors love their work, which involves money. They watch screens all day long that show prices and trading volumes. They read quarterly reports of earnings per share and dividends. In a sense, to tell them that their careers must be motivated by something beyond profit doesn't jibe with their reality. Their day-to-day work is filled with money and profit. Furthermore, many investment professionals will tell you flat out that they are in it only for the money. They are going to pursue their dreams at some other time in life, presumably after they get rich.

This attitude poses a problem for investment leaders. But Warren Buffett, perhaps the greatest investor, made a most important point when he said, "I enjoy the process more than the proceeds, though I've learned to live with them, too."[14] Sharath Sury, chairman and CEO of Chicago Analytic Capital Management, agreed that at his firm "the focus is on the process, not on the fruits." Sury and his team emphasized that they enjoyed being part of something bigger than themselves. It wasn't just about the money. In our view, investment leaders must walk this fine line between proceeds and process; they must hire professionals who are motivated, like Buffett, by something beyond just the money. In fact, there were several people like this on the Allstar Capital team, and it was sad to listen to them describe their experiences at Allstar. One of them, an ex-military officer, told us several times how much he missed the camaraderie of the military, as well as his former investment job. This man said of his old boss (whom we've written about in this book) that he would "have run through a wall for him."

DEVELOPING A VISION

In Chapter 2, on values, we said, "Don't try this at home." The values process is best done with some outside help, specifically experts who have worked with lots of firms and who understand group facilitation. Vision, however, is different. Vision development is a top-down process. The leadership team, having gone through a values process and assembled a great team, is then charged with discovering and expressing a vision. We say *discovering* because great visions are not flights of fantasy, imagined with an eye toward what might be nice. Rather, they result from the deep introspection and soul-searching inquiry needed to answer the questions: "What are we here to do? What is our purpose?" Crafting a vision is a bit like Michelangelo sculpting a statue: chip away the unnecessary marble until all that is left is the masterpiece. The truth of our purpose lies within, and our job is to chip away all the excess material that keeps us from seeing it clearly.

The main tool required is a colleague who can ask "Why?" repeatedly. (Three-year-olds are ideally suited for the job.)

Colleague: "Why do you come to work each day?"

As noted earlier, your first response might be, "To make money." Fine. But beyond that, why do you choose to earn money this way? Why not any of the myriad other ways?

Perhaps you respond that you come to work each day to provide customers with the right investment plan for their needs. This leads to the next "Why?"

Colleague: "Why do you want to do that?"

In other words, what is your underlying motivation to help them with their investments? To this, you may answer: because it will give them financial security. Again, the "Why?" question.

Colleague: "Why do you want to do that?"

You might answer this question so: because having a sound financial future gives them peace of mind.

At this point you may feel that you've found the final underlying reason for your work: to provide peace of mind for people. When you have found the deep purpose of your work, you will know it, because you will feel it. It is no longer an intellectual exercise; you should feel it in your gut or heart. The old line about "the longest journey that a leader makes is the 18 inches from his head to his heart" is becoming accepted wisdom in leadership circles. Ask yourself this: If you were working for a leader who stated his vision and then said, "But I don't have any passion for it," how motivated would you feel? Leaders must love their calling and show it. When Bill Lyons became CEO at American Century, he committed himself to being more open and revealing of his passion for the business.

In addition to the "why" exercise, here are some other good vision questions that open up the mind and heart:

- How would you describe the ultimate objective for your organization?
- If you overhear a conversation about your team five or ten years down the road, what do you want people to be saying about you?
- What would it be like around here if you were really excited about coming to work every day?
- If you could create the ultimate work environment, how would you describe it?
- What would we be doing that would have you excited about being a part of it?[15]

We are not suggesting that you make the necessary vision work into some sort of frantic Richard-Simmons-meets-Tony-Robbins break-dancing exercise. But it is important for vision to have an emotional component, and investment professionals can be just as passionate as anyone else. Typically they just don't like to show their emotion. Therefore, the trick to working with investment leaders is to create the right environment—often by using the right language—in which they can talk with passion about their love of investing and winning and creating something exceptional. The common theme of all great investors is their love of investing. The masters—Buffett, Lynch, Soros, and the like—all use passionate language. They *love* it. *Note:* they don't just like it; they *love* it. (When Lynch got up one morning and realized that he had lost his passion, he quit managing the Magellan fund.) Good vision taps into these deep feelings and ties them to the organizing principles of the firm. That's why good leaders use the vision again and again to motivate their teams.

As an example, one of the most successful companies ever is Southwest Airlines. Its market capitalization is larger than those of the next seven U.S. airlines combined. The company has never experienced a loss—and we're talking about the *airline* industry! It comes as no surprise to us that Southwest's logo is a heart and its ticker symbol is "LUV." Good leaders know how to harness the emotions of the troops, and vision is a primary tool for drawing out that commitment and excitement. Warren Bennis wrote that the leader "[a]rticulates the vision and gives it legitimacy, expresses the vision in captivating rhetoric that fires the imagination and emotions of followers, and empowers others to make decisions that get things done."[16]

The leader of Allstar Capital did not understand this aspect of leadership. His idea of a great vision for the team was to "outperform the benchmark by 50 basis points." Despite this dull and uninspiring vision, a few of his team members did finally get fired up about turning the operation around. This often occurs when people get away from the daily pressures and refocus on what is really important to them. In the face of this new-found enthusiasm, the leader commented, "Yes, we can turn it around but it's going to be a long, dry march between here and there." With lines like that, he could star on the de-motivational speaking circuit. When his team needed to hear a "finest hour" speech (à la Churchill), they got the "dry march" talk.

DELIVERING THE VISION

We've given some examples of what not to do. Now, how does a leader deliver the vision? How does she make it compelling and motivating? What effect does she have on the listener? Does she come across as intellectual? Emotional? Holier-than-thou? Effective leaders are aware of how they deliver a vision statement. Typically, a good leader recognizes what Freud realized decades ago: that each listener has a child, adult, and parent in his or her psyche. Children are emotional and animated. Parents are full of advice ("shoulds") and beliefs about right and wrong. Adults are objective and mature in their approach. To be effective, leaders must deliver their visions in a way that speaks to each of these parts of the psyche.

The 1996 presidential campaign with Clinton, Dole, and Perot provided a good example of this model. Clinton appealed to the child in us: He was clearly the most emotional of the three candidates, talking about poverty and racism and remarking to voters that he could "feel their pain." Dole came across as the parent, talking about ethics and what was right for the country. Perot, with his charts and graphs, came across as the objective, adult personality, presenting the facts and providing logical solutions to the country's ills.

Leaders understand the need to cover all the bases as they deliver vision statements—and those statements have to come from both their hearts and their heads. Leaders have to go beyond well-scripted speeches and *actually* care about their followers. When Rob Arnott at First Quadrant came to the decision that they would have to lay off 30 employees, he personally went and gave each one the news. Bill Lyons at American Century told us that he knew he needed to be more vulnerable as a leader, and he wrote it into his personal vision statement: "I will invite people to see the man behind the curtain—I will not be afraid to openly show and express the entire range of human emotions, regardless of what their expectation of me, or my position, may be."[17]

Time and again during our research and interviews, we saw that the most effective vision statements were delivered by leaders who were perceived by their employees as real, human people. In his statement, Lyons acknowledged that this takes courage. We would amend his statement slightly to say that it is not about leaders being fearless, but rather about walking through their fear. (Alexander the Great was so frightened before one battle that his knees started shaking uncontrollably. He looked down at them and said, "Shake on, knees! You'd shake even harder if you knew where I was taking you!")

Some leaders are not especially emotional or imaginative by nature. How can they deliver a compelling vision? A case in point was an engineer at the Woodward Governor Company, which makes parts for jet engines. A classic task-oriented person, precise and careful, Stan was much like many of the investment professionals who question the "vision thing." When asked about it, Stan said, "I don't get it. My father taught me to work hard and take pride in my work. I have never missed a day of work in 23 years. I show up early each morning and work hard until closing time. My employees do the same. I don't have some grand vision of work." When Sam reflected on his vision statement, he found that several of the components mentioned earlier were indeed part of it: high-quality products; the values of precision, hard work, and discipline; and the unifying theme of loyalty. He took these elements and constructed a vision statement that accurately conveyed his deep conviction about what it means to do an excellent job and how important that is. He liked the content of the vision and agreed that it conveyed the deep truth about how he felt.

The problem of delivery remained. Stan was a mild and soft-spoken man. He could not imagine himself jumping on a table, Zig Zigler style, and delivering his vision in a soul-rocking fashion. From this perspective, he believed his efforts would always be second-rate. But the truth about vision statements is that their power comes from the speaker's authenticity. Once Stan understood this simple point, he was able to deliver his short vision statement with amazing power, because of his level of personal conviction.

PERSONAL CONVICTION AND POWERFUL VISIONS

The story of Stan reveals an important aspect of vision statements: They are only as powerful as they are true for the leader. When executives cannot touch their own personal passion, they cannot hope to express a vision with fire and conviction.

When executives go on retreat, away from the culture of corporate America, it seems to be easier for them to tap into their truth and passion and deliver inspiring personal visions. Once they have had the experience of touching on some deep inner truth, they often find that their professional interests stem from the same core belief. John, an executive with a medical products company, found that his early childhood experience of losing his mother to cancer related directly to his personal and professional calling of health care. He had originally gone on a weekend experience because he was feeling burned out in his career. When he touched upon the personal mission and then the professional mission of healing, he returned to his work with new passion and a vision about health care for his employees.

But is this ability to create and deliver an inspiring vision really so important? Two experts on leadership, Kouzes and Posner, believe it is: Leaders must have "a vision for the future. This capacity to paint an uplifting and ennobling picture of the future is, in fact, what differentiates leaders from other credible sources."[18]

SUMMARY

Vision work is tough for five reasons:

1. It requires effective leadership skills rather than effective management skills. Investment firm leaders tend to think of themselves as the senior managers of the company. The managerial equivalent of vision creation is planning. Many times, when we ask investment leaders for vision statements, we get elaborate technical answers, but no vision. Technical plans can never direct, align, and inspire others to act, the way a vision can.

2. It requires a great deal of time and thought, and usually some soul-searching, to develop a vision. We've had senior leaders say to us after the vision exercise, "I had no idea that this process was going to be so gut-wrenching."

3. Both head and heart are required for this work. As we indicated earlier, investors tend to pride themselves on their by-the-numbers focus. A vision process requires more than assessing market opportunities and lagging indicators. The "who we are" question from Chapter 2 is a critical part of this discussion, and can cause acute anxiety in those who are not given to introspection.

4. Teamwork is required, or people will end up just trying to protect their interests. Input from across the firm will help the discussion center on the whole firm, not on specific departments or areas of interest.

5. Urgency is necessary. Without it, people will find excuses to avoid the work. This is particularly dangerous in the investment field, where most people are naturally skeptical or even cynical. If vision work is not completed once it has been started, the leadership team will pay, one

way or another. Articulating your values and vision is an investment in your successful and sustainable future—well worth the time it takes.[19]

Values and vision are the foundation of a firm's culture. Culture is the competitive edge in winning over the long term, which is why strong culture is the subject of the next chapter.

TEST YOURSELF

Ask yourself the following yes/no questions.

	Yes	No

1. Do you have a clearly articulated vision/mission statement?

If you answered no, skip to the exercise.

2. If you randomly stopped three people at work and asked them to state the firm's vision/mission, would you get one clear, immediate answer?
3. Does your vision/mission elicit any kind of positive emotional or personal response?
4. Does your vision/mission statement answer the big question about what you at this firm are ultimately here for?
5. Is your firm's vision/mission statement used as a basis for goal setting or annual planning?
6. Is your firm's vision/mission revisited periodically to see if it continues to accurately reflect the preferred future of the firm as it might be described today?

7. What are your next steps for reinforcing or exemplifying the importance of the firm's vision/mission?

EXERCISES

With your senior team,

1. Go through the "why" exercise described in this chapter.
2. Complete the grid that answers the "why" and "how" questions concerning vision and mission.
3. Plan your strategy for communicating the vision to all stakeholders.

CHAPTER 4

Strong Cultures

The Goldman Sachs culture is what sets our company apart from other firms and helps to make us a magnet for talent.
—Pat Ward, Co-Chief Executive Officer,
Goldman Sachs International[1]

Values and vision create the foundation for building your firm's culture. In this chapter you will see:

- Methods for evaluating the strength of your firm's culture.
- Examples and characteristics of strong cultures.
- The four types of investment cultures.
- The impact of culture on organizational success.
- Ways to solidify your culture.
- The benefits of a solid performance evaluation process.

During a break at the Allstar retreat, Phil commented on his social interactions at the firm. "It's mostly just work. We don't go out for drinks or a bite to eat. It's not at all like the last firm where I worked. At that firm, we did lots of outside activities together. Here work and play are separate," he said regretfully.

"Do you still see some of those ex-colleagues?" Dale asked.

"Yeah, in fact, we still socialize a lot. I'm really more connected to them than this group."

Connection is important to strong cultures, and not necessarily in a touchy-feely way. It doesn't always involve coffee houses or cocktail lounges or long dinners or golf outings. Employees may feel tremendously connected to the firm's mission and the importance of the work it does. The connection may stem from a deep respect for the abilities of those around them. It may be an intellectual connection, involving the thrill of exchanging ideas with really smart people. I once worked with a man who absolutely loved investing and talking about investment ideas. He was one of the kindest and brightest people you could ever meet. He was definitely connected to the mission of the department and to those around him. He was the biggest kidder of the bunch, yet he made it an unbendable policy never to socialize outside the office. He just didn't do it. Period. And that was fine with the rest of us. We still had a strong connection.

In contrast to Allstar, The Burridge Group LLC (TBG), founded in Chicago in 1986, values personal connection within the firm. When interviewing a candidate, Nancy Prial, CIO, and her senior staff use the "rubber band" test to see if there is a good potential fit. The interviewers ask themselves, "How would this person react if we playfully shot a rubber band at him?" Would he explode into fireworks or looked shocked? Or would he react playfully and with a sense of humor?" Given the value that TBG places on good fit and the right chemistry, the latter response is important. Mind you, TBG is serious about its investment performance and reputation as a winner. Its employees work long and hard, but they're equally committed to enjoying the company of their colleagues. They will tell you that both are important to success.

CHARACTERISTICS OF STRONG CULTURES

The key to attracting, motivating, and retaining employees lies with a firm's investment culture.
            —Thomas Dillman, Director of Research, Scudder Kemper[2]

The importance of corporate culture cannot be overstated.
                —Stuart Robbins, as Managing Director,
                Donaldson, Lufkin & Jenrette[3]

The preceding quotations go to the heart of our message. The top investment firms have moved beyond simply hiring smart people who embrace continuous learning. They hire both for talent and for fit. Fit with what? With the firm's defined and cohesive culture. Combining the concepts from the last two chapters—values and vision—helps us understand the idea of culture. Firms that have consciously addressed their values and vision have taken important steps toward shaping their culture.

Earlier we defined *culture* as the values, behaviors, and beliefs that distinguish the people of one organization from those in another. Perhaps a more hands-on way to get a feel for culture is to ask yourself, "How would I coach a new recruit to succeed in my organization?" We often ask this question when interviewing senior leaders, because their answers go to the heart of culture. What we consider important and the rules of how we work together define culture.

In *Built to Last*, Collins and Porras identify strong cultures as having the characteristics shown in Table 4.1.[4]

Table 4.2 shows the average scores of the *Built to Last* companies versus the comparison companies on the preceding criteria.

To summarize Collins and Porras's findings, strong cultures have:

- A fervently held ideology (who we are and what we're about).
- A precise indoctrination process.
- Tightness of fit.
- Elitism.

VANGUARD: A STRONG CULTURE

If you want to experience a strong culture, visit Vanguard. Named by Jack Bogle for a famous naval vessel, the HMS *Vanguard* (which, under the direction of Lord Nelson, defeated Napoleon's forces), Vanguard's culture starts with physical appearance. The buildings are named after famous naval vessels and paintings of these ships adorn many of the walls in the corridors. Employees are referred to as "crew members." The cafeteria is the "galley" and the bathroom is the "head." (One wonders if absent employees set off cries of "Man overboard!")

During meetings with Jack Brennan and several members of the senior staff (Jim Gately, Gus Sauter, and Mike Miller), we got a firsthand look at a close-knit culture. The values and guiding principles are clearly stated and fully lived out. The client comes first in everything that Vanguard does. When telephone activity is heavy, a Swiss Army flag goes up, and senior officers, like the ones around the table with us, drop their duties and man the phones. Brennan is no exception.

Brennan's willingness to jump in and answer telephones reflects Vanguard's fanatical attachment to teamwork, as opposed to the star system. Anyone looking for ego strokes should steer clear of Vanguard. Brennan and

TABLE 4.1   Characteristics of Culture

Cultural Indoctrination: "Molding the new hires"

+1   Significant evidence of a formal indoctrination process, which may include:
     Orientation program that teaches values, traditions, guidelines.
     Ongoing training that reinforces the values, traditions, and guidelines.
     Internal publications that emphasize company values and traditions.
     Leaders who discuss and promote the values and traditions.
     Use of unique language or terminology that reinforces a frame of reference.
     Hiring young, promoting from within, shaping the employee's thinking from
     the start.

 0   Some evidence of the above, but to a lesser degree.

−1   Little or no evidence that the company has a formal indoctrination process.

Strong, Active Culture: "Our way or the highway"

+1   Strong evidence that the culture is well defined and binary (that is, some
     people love it and others hate it). Indications of strong culture are:
     Rewards and recognition for those who fit in with the culture, and negative
     reinforcement for those who do not.
     Severe penalties for those who violate core values.
     Hiring for fit and careful monitoring of employees based on vision and values.
     Heavy emphasis on loyalty.
     Expectations of joining fully into the company and espousing its virtues.

 0   Some evidence of a strong culture, but not to the extent indicated above.

−1   Little or no evidence of a strong culture.

Elitist Attitude: "We're special"

+1   Significant evidence that the company reinforces a sense of belonging to
     something superior or special. Some indications of this are:
     Verbal and written reiteration that employees belong to something special.
     Secrecy as to internal information or processes.
     Celebration to reinforce successes, belonging, and elitism.
     Nicknames or special terminology, such as "crew members" at Vanguard,
     "cast members" at Disney.
     Emphasis on feeling of family.
     Physical isolation: The company has its own campus and minimizes the need
     for employees to deal with outsiders.

 0   Less evidence that the company has reinforced a sense of belonging to
     something special.

−1   Little or no evidence that the company creates or emphasizes a sense of
     belonging to something special.

TABLE 4.2 Cultural Characteristics: Comparison of Scores

Strong Culture Factors	*Built to Last* Companies' Average Score	Comparison Companies' Average Score
Cultural Indoctrination	.61	–.39
Strong, Active Culture	.44	–.33
Elitist Attitude	.83	.06

his team go after ego like Mark McGwire after a piñata. First and foremost is allegiance to Vanguard's unique, strategic position: lowest cost to clients. Examples of this dedication abound:

- There are no executive automobiles.
- There are no executive parking spaces.
- There is no executive washroom.
- There is no executive dining room.
- Everyone is on a first-name basis.

Compensation is based mostly on company performance, not individual performance.

- Officers have inside offices, not corner ones.
- There are no private jets for officers.
- Officers fly coach.

This egalitarian approach even extends to employees' private cars. We surveyed the officers around the table and found that they drove a Jeep, a Pontiac, a Dodge, and an eight-year-old Audi. Comments from the officers about their relationships in this tight-knit organization were revealing. Gus Sauter, CIO, had worked for five other companies before arriving at Vanguard. He immediately recognized and liked the fact that at Vanguard the client came first. (The client to Vanguard is what winning was to Vince Lombardi: the only thing.) Interestingly, Sauter said that none of the other five places at which he'd worked had had a distinct culture. Not so with Vanguard; there, in Sauter's words, employees "bleed the company colors."

The story of Mike Miller, director of planning and development was described earlier. His switch to Vanguard is a strong statement about culture.

Jack Brennan recruited Miller after learning from a friend that Miller would be a good fit with Vanguard. The friend was right: Miller raves about the culture at Vanguard. "This is one firm, one vision. And with my values, I'm a perfect fit," he says. In particular, Miller enjoys the friendship with his senior colleagues. "At other jobs, I had good relationships with my colleagues, but here we've become good friends. There is a deep respect and friendship between us."

BINARY: LOVE IT OR HATE IT

John Woerth, associate director of public relations, picked up on this theme and said that at a recent holiday party, one of the attendees learned that John worked for Vanguard and said, "Oh, you mean that cult company!" Woerth was not offended, nor did he deny it. "We are a close-knit family here," he said.

A common misconception about culture is that there is a universal good culture and a universal evil or bad culture. The good culture is kind and decent and moral and practices good hygiene. The bad culture is epitomized by Nazi Germany. The stereotype is that all cultures fit on this continuum somewhere, and your goal should be to get as close to the "good" end as possible. But culture doesn't work that way. As Collins and Porras point out, strong culture has nothing to do with right or wrong.[5] In this sense, their view of culture is amoral (for example, both the Catholic priesthood and criminal street gangs have very strong cultures). Importantly, strong cultures are also binary. This means that people either love them or hate them.

Vanguard is a good example of the elitism described by Collins and Porras as a key element of a defined culture. Elitism is fostered by:

- Extremely difficult requirements or criteria for entry into the group.
- Acceptance into the group that is followed by intensive training.
- Challenging and high-risk team assignments that are given early in the individual's career.
- Tests to ensure that individuals measure up to the elite standards of the group.
- Autonomy to take risks, which is not normally permitted at other organizations.
- Training that is continuous and related to assignments.
- Individual rewards that are tied to collective rewards.
- Managers who are seen as experts and mentors, rather than administrators.[6]

Leaders must define, defend, and maintain the organization's culture. If they don't, culture will take on a life of its own, independent of leadership desires and intentions. In other words, culture exists and spreads with or without direction from the leaders. Without direction, the heaviest influencers of culture will be the most negative people. Whose voice do you want heard at your firm?

Returning to the Vanguard example, I was asked by an investment professional at a cocktail party what company represented an excellent culture. For some of the reasons just mentioned, I said Vanguard.

The woman looked at me as though my hair had suddenly burst into flames. "What?! Vanguard? Oh, I hated working at that company," she declared.

Somewhat taken aback, and thinking, *Tell me how you really feel about it*, I asked, "Why?"

"It was so militaristic," she said, putting one hand to her head. "Ugh, I felt like I was suffocating."

"Where do you work now?" I asked.

"Brown, Brothers Harriman in Philadelphia."

"Do you like it?"

"Yes, it's wonderful," she said.

A cartoon from the *New Yorker* captures how this woman felt while working at Vanguard. A dog is standing in front of the boss's desk. The boss is a cat, and both are surrounded by hundreds of cats hard at work at their own desks. The cat boss says, "Well, it's true that you never really fit in around here." Simply put, the dog was totally out of place. I had a similar feeling about one investment firm where I worked when I saw that my Myers-Briggs personality profile was completely different from all the other staff members'. More importantly, their profiles were largely identical! I was the dog in a cat's world. To use an old expression, one man's meat is another man's poison.

The conversation with the Brown Brothers woman caused me to reflect on my visit to Vanguard. As I thought back on it, I recalled that Beth had left the interview feeling elated and saying things like, "Wow, they love working here! This is exactly what we've been talking about as far as strong cultures." My personal reaction was completely different. I had actually felt progressively more nauseated during our time at Vanguard. (No reflection on their hospitality, which was very gracious.) It might have been all the naval references, as I get seasick at the mere sight of a boat. More likely, though, is that I was reacting like the Brown Brothers woman. I don't like formal or regimented environments, preferring instead casual and free-wheeling ones.

Like Vanguard, Northwater in Toronto has a strong culture and insists that employees subordinate their ego needs to the needs of the group. North-water has its own Swiss flag story: they call it "filling the fountain." On the 33rd floor of their offices, there is a fountain that has become legendary be-cause it requires the whole team to periodically fill it with water. From the rookie employee to David Patterson, the CEO, team members roll up their sleeves and pitch in when the water level is low. These sorts of symbolic ex-ercises have a powerful effect on the team, making the point that "we're all in this together."

Patterson has structured compensation and ownership to make the same statement. Northwater differs from Vanguard, though, in that the culture is much more casual and unstructured. Their physical structure—open of-fices—testifies to this, as did a comment by Dennis Cook, human resource director: "We're in a low-grade meeting all the time." He added that there are no formal performance reviews; rather, employees get running updates throughout the year. This culture is entirely appropriate for a firm that con-siders itself cutting-edge in innovation. Does it work for Northwater? The firm has grown to more than $5 billion in assets under this management, which is a 100 percent increase over 5 years. It is one of the world's leading fund-of-funds in the market-neutral segment. A large European company chose Northwater from a search of 75 Canadian fund-of-funds firms. In the past 5 years, Northwater has lost only 2 key employees from its team of 51. Its culture is very different from Vanguard's, but clearly very successful.

The binary concept was reinforced by Thomas Dillman, who said when he was at State Street Research:

> I have met many bright and talented people who should work at Fidelity Investments, whose culture is different from ours at State Street Re-search, and I have met other people who would hate to be at Fidelity, and would probably like our firm because it is collegial and sedately en-trepreneurial, not aggressively entrepreneurial.[7]

As important as this notion of fit is to the hiring process, Richard Lanna-mann at Stern Stewart told us that, in his experience, "Fit is still not a big part of the way that some firms do executive search."

DOES STRONG CULTURE MATTER TO FINANCIAL RETURNS?

We continually return to the link between the so-called soft stuff and the bottom line. It is tempting to ignore culture because it is ambiguous, varies even among successful firms, and is difficult to measure. The old joke about Joe, who is looking for his keys at night under the street lamp, is a good analogy. A curious stranger sees him searching and says, "Where exactly did you lose them?"

Joe points to the dark alley and says, "Over there."

"Then why are you looking here?" says the stranger.

"Because the light is better here!" says Joe.

(Trust me, at one point in the history of the human race, this joke was hilarious . . .)

Old as it is, this joke perfectly makes the point. Culture is much harder to analyze and evaluate than sales, earnings, dividends, and the other solid, hard data available online from any computer. Therefore, unless investment leaders are convinced that there is a strong case for the importance of culture, they're going to continue to look where the light is better.

Is there a link between culture and financial results? Should leaders take the time to look in the dark alley where the keys to leadership and culture are hidden? Mark Huselid, a researcher at Rutgers, says yes. He conducted one of the most comprehensive studies of this kind. Using a sample base of 700 companies, he looked at management practices that dealt with employee motivation, such as evaluation and pay, as well as those pertaining to recruitment, training, and participation. These are the leadership practices that we argue contribute to building a strong culture. The data show a positive association between increasing and strengthening these practices and increasing financial results. He also found a decrease in employee turnover relative to the average. Table 4.3 summarizes Huselid's results.[8]

TABLE 4.3 Employee Motivation Practices and Financial Returns

	Number of Motivation Practices			
	Bottom 25%	Second 25%	Third 25%	Top 25%
Annual shareholder return	6.5%	6.8%	8.2%	9.4%
Gross return on capital	3.7%	1.5%	4.1%	11.3%

FOUR BASIC INVESTMENT CULTURES

Having stated earlier that there is no right or correct culture for investment firms, we nevertheless find it useful to think of investment firms as falling into one of four broad categories. Defining your culture is critically important, but culture is also invisible, so this approach provides a structure for the conversation. These categories were formulated by the ancient Greeks 2,500 years ago, and were revised more recently by David Kiersey, in his work on temperaments. In the course of our research, we've surveyed more than 100 global firms, and find that they can be characterized in these four general ways:

1. Guardians.
2. Rationalists.
3. Communalists.
4. Adventurists.

In Chapter 5, we'll explain more fully how you can measure the prevalence of these four categories in your firm and the implications for performance.

Guardians

As the name implies, Guardians are keepers of tradition, and cautious by nature. Their attitude toward money is to preserve it. Their value statements would include words such as *efficiency*, *accountability*, and *quality*. They are the banks, insurance companies, and large mutual funds. Their core competency is processing. Vanguard, Bank One, and State Street are examples. Thirty years ago, the Guardian spirit dominated nearly every investment firm. Now, many of the top active managers are Rationalists.

Rationalists

Rationalists are great strategists. They excel at big-picture thinking. Their attitude toward money is acquisitive; they like to take it from others. Typically, when a Rationalist group determines its values, the members agree on words such as *excellence*, *knowledge*, and *winning*. Their core competency is strategic thinking—basically, smarts. Rationalists abound in the ranks of active managers: Wellington, Wanger Asset Management, and Brandes are good examples. This type has become so prevalent among the top-performing asset managers that we are surprised when we see the few exceptions.

Communalists

Communalists are team-oriented and typically are found in firms that focus on individual clients. Their attitude toward money is holistic; they see money as part of the person's entire physical, emotional, and mental well-being. Unlike the Guardian and Rationalist, who probably have earned the CFA designation, the Communalist goes for the CFP (Certified Financial Planner), because he or she wants to work closely with individuals and families. Values for this group include loyalty, team, and open communication. Edward Jones and Ferguson Wellman are examples of Communalist cultures. This role in the financial world has become much more prevalent as consumers seek financial advisors whom they can trust and enjoy working with. Guardians and especially Rationalists can be a bit blunt and brusque for the average person.

Adventurists

Only recently, with the advent of day trading and the increased popularity of hedge funds, has the Adventurist type moved into the investment world. Having run personality profiles on a number of investment organizations, we can state confidently that this personality is rare in the mainstream world of active investment managers. Therefore, you would not expect to see an investment firm take on the values of these types: risk-taking, fun-loving, thrill-seeking. Outside of day trading and hedge fund management, the other place you might see a culture of Adventurism is the institutional sales force. In fact, this was the case with a major New York firm that we surveyed.

MFS: CULTURE AS COMPETITIVE ADVANTAGE

Regardless of which of the four basic cultures you manage, it's very clear that you can take steps to strengthen the culture. Hiring is a good place to start. Leaders who are savvy about culture understand that their competitive edge lies in creating a cohesive culture, because that culture enables them to attract and retain the best talent. The old model was to hire for brains. As knowledge workers, our smarts were the most important talent we had. Competition has pushed us to the next level. Hiring for talent isn't enough anymore; now the top firms hire both for talent and for fit.

A good example of this phenomenon is MFS in Boston. America's oldest mutual fund, started in 1924, MFS (originally Massachusetts Financial Services) now employs more than 2,500 people and manages nearly $112 billion. When we met with CEO John Ballen and his senior team, we were surprised—no, flabbergasted—at their answer to one of our standard interview questions: How many people at MFS will a candidate meet with? We had heard from some top firms on this issue, and thought that 8 or 10 was an average number. Ballen responded, "30 to 35 people at the firm before the person will get an offer." Lisa Jones, executive vice president at MFS, told us that employees jokingly say that MFS stands for "My Final Stop." That's the sort of culture they have created. People go to work there and don't leave.

A week later, as we reviewed our notes, we wondered if we had really heard Ballen correctly. Then later that day, while talking to Dave Coolidge at William Blair, we heard the same statistic: When you interview at Blair you'll talk to as many as 30 people, or more. Still wondering if this was possible, I called my friend Dave Chalupnik, who had just become CIO at US Bank in Minneapolis. I asked him how many people he had met with at the bank before he was hired. Same answer: 30 people. Patrick O'Donnell, when he was managing director at Putnam, said:

> *Our interview process is extremely extensive. We do not try to make hiring a fast process. We do try to make it a process that involves the largest number of people who want to be involved; all analysts in the department are allowed to interview every single candidate if they want to. One of the things I believe about this business is that, to some degree, we all come to work each day to make each other smarter or to acknowledge that we need each other's skills. This sentiment is especially true for recruiting.[9]*

What happens when firms aren't this rigorous in their hiring? Ray Nixon, president of Barrow Hanley in Dallas, Texas, knows the consequences firsthand. His firm, with 47 employees, manages about $30 billion for 125 clients, including Vanguard in a subadvisor role. Barrow Hanley is a Graham and Dodd value shop. Normally, they are very conscious of people and culture. Nixon told me, "You can be the smartest guy in the world, but if you're a jerk with a big ego, you won't work at Barrow Hanley. We believe in teamwork and work hard to create an open, honest culture where people can yell, 'Bullshit!' when appropriate." When asked if they had ever made a hiring mistake, Nixon confessed to one. In 1999, they interviewed a bright, 35-year-old candidate for an analyst job. The candidate came highly recommended, had experience, and was very smart. After just a few conversations, the senior team at Barrow Hanley agreed to bring him on board. Within months of being hired at this value shop, the young man ordered six subscriptions to high-tech magazines. Soon after that, he began bringing in recommendations for companies that paid no dividends because they had no earnings . . . because they had no sales! Despite the clear value philosophy at Barrow Hanley, this analyst could not kick his habit. Like an alcoholic who knows that drinking will do him in, this fellow nevertheless kept diving into the high-tech end of the pool. Eventually, they had to part ways.

Given the standard formula that headhunters in the investment business use for calculating the cost of turnover, this example represents a $300,000 mistake. For Ray Nixon (who, true to his value investing philosophy, allowed me to pick up the $16 lunch tab), this must have been a bitter pill. Michelle Seitz, who heads up the investment management division at William Blair & Company, echoed this conclusion, saying, "Missteps in hiring can kill you."

Has paying close attention to people and culture paid off for Barrow Hanley? In 2001, Barrow Hanley was ranked number 1 in the Greenwich Quality Index. From a group of 109 equity managers, the clients of Barrow Hanley gave it the highest ranking of the entire group.

In addition to multiple interviews with many people, the hiring process should specifically address cultural issues. Each interviewer should discuss the firm's vision and values. In turn, the interviewer should inquire of the candidate, in the context of past work experience, which values were important. Did the candidate feel that any of his or her personal values were not respected or welcomed in the last job?

This sort of testing for fit actually helps both participants. For example, if the candidate is looking for a job at Vanguard and wants to work 40-hour weeks with lots of time at home with the family, forget it. Jack Brennan's idea of goofing off is to take one Friday afternoon in the summer and play hooky with his senior staff at the golf course. He told us that this was okay and that he didn't feel guilty about it. *One* afternoon! Brennan is fond of saying to his colleagues, "Today had better be your worst day," meaning that you had better continually improve from this day forward. Brennan also has no use for managers who rest on seniority. His test for any manager is, "Would I hire you again today?" So, if you're a job candidate and you don't value the work ethic and long hours, don't apply at Vanguard. Neither of you will be happy.

CULTURE ORIENTATION

Strong cultures involve clear orientation processes. Once hired, the new employee can expect a rigorous indoctrination into the firm's way of doing things. Consider how orientation works at Disney. Before he is allowed even to answer the telephone at Disneyworld to take a dinner reservation, the new recruit spends four weeks learning about the Disney culture: its history, Walt Disney's life, and the special language of the Disney culture. Employees are called "cast members." Customers are "guests." Jobs are "performances." In the investment world, Ariel Capital in Chicago has a 100-day Ambassador Program. No, new employees are not in training for 100 straight days! (Assuming the worst, someone actually shrieked when I told them about this program.) The new employees do, however, get continual training during their first 100 days. At the end of this program, which was named after the traditional time reference to a United States president's first 100 days in office, a new employee has a thorough understanding of Ariel and can be an effective ambassador for the company.

Contrast these approaches with that of a restaurant in Toledo where I was making a presentation. Having arrived early to set up and prepare, I overheard a server say to the boss, "I understand there's some kind of meeting at 2:00 P.M. today." The boss responded, "Oh yeah, that's the orientation meeting. It only takes about 15 minutes, you should probably attend." Can you say, "Weak culture?"

CHANGING A CULTURE

What if your organization needs a transformational change? Can you change a culture? What would have to happen? Don't despair. Cultural transformation takes time, but many success stories exist. We can share one of them concerning a large, well-established bank. One of the executives explained:

> I've worked at this company all my life and had begun to lose hope. But once we became clear in our own minds about what we really stand for and began to change the organization to fit with that, well, the release of human energy has been amazing. People all the way down to the individual branch level feel that their work has more meaning than it used to.[10]

John Kotter considers the following to be key points to remember, once you've started down the path of major change:

- Culture change comes last, not first (baby steps, concrete actions first).
- Culture change depends on results: new approaches will sink in only after it's very clear that they work and are superior to old methods.

- Culture change requires a lot of talk: without verbal instruction and support, people are often reluctant to admit the validity of new practices.
- Culture change may involve employee turnover: Sometimes the only way to change a culture is to change key people.

Culture change makes decisions about succession critical: If promotion practices are not changed to be consistent with new practices, the old culture will reassert itself.[11]

WEAVING CULTURE INTO DAY-TO-DAY OPERATIONS

Beyond hiring and orientation, culture must be integrated into the fabric of everyday organizational life. It must be part of performance reviews, compensation, and promotion. This is especially true in the investment world. Investment professionals watch the money as carefully as any group in business. If there is no link between values and money, they will almost reflexively flout (or ignore) the guiding principles. Remember, this is a group that worships at the altar of market principles, and cherishes the idea that the invisible hand is always at work. To suggest that people should altruistically follow new guiding principles smacks of heresy, and to some degree raises the suspicion that people will think you're stupid if you follow the rules for no incentive. Nothing speaks more loudly and clearly about what the firm values than the criteria in a performance review. If you're serious about your firm's values, they must be tied to this process. Danielle McDonald, from Hewitt Associates, believes strongly that performance management is the fundamental management practice by which a business aligns its employees to achieve its desired outcomes. Her team, consisting of colleagues Sally Shield, Katherine Donohue, and Professor Abbie Smith of the Graduate School of Business at the University of Chicago, studied the performance management processes and financial results of 437 publicly traded firms. They found that 232 companies used only year-end reviews or had nothing at all; only 205 used a formal process. Table 4.4 compares the differences between the two groups.[12]

SUMMARY

If you do nothing else as a result of reading this book, we encourage you to take a good look at your performance management process and format to see if you're evaluating people against the key drivers of your firm's success. We believe so strongly in this statement that we brought in an expert in this

TABLE 4.4   Comparison of Companies With and Without Formal Performance Management Processes

Companies with Performance Management	Companies without Performance Management
Higher profits	Lower profits
Better cash flows	Weaker cash flows
Stronger market performance	Weaker market performance
Greater stock values	Lower stock values
Between 1990 and 1992	
Return on equity: 10.2%	4.4%
Return on assets: 8.0%	4.5%
Total shareholder return: 7.9%	0.0%

area, Fran Skinner, just to make sure that we were doing it right in our consulting work.

Aside from performance reviews, here are other ways to reinforce your firm's culture:[13]

- Include values, norms, history, and tradition in your orientation and ongoing training programs.
- Create internal universities and training programs.
- Make on-the-job socializing opportunities.
- Promote from within, with rigorous "up through the ranks" policies that include criteria tied to firm values and norms.
- Recognize and reward those who display great consistency with the firm's values and vision.
- Penalize those who cross the ideological boundaries; don't punish for making mistakes.
- Share stories about firm exemplars.
- Reinforce a sense of belonging through unique language, mottoes, or logos.
- Screen for fit and take action when it's apparent that the fit is wrong.

- Create buy-in mechanisms for shared ownership and investing.
- Communicate consistently as to what's special about belonging to this organization.

If you're an investment professional and you've read this far, you may well be thinking, "Yes, this makes some sense, but I want to see measurements!" Are there tools for quantifying your firm's leadership and culture? For example, how do you assess the decision-making and communication styles of your leaders? How do you know which of the four common cultures (Guardian, Rationalist, Communalist, Adventurist) best describes your environment? How do you determine if you have a strong culture? How do you go about improving it? How do you measure trust levels in the organization? Most importantly, how do you use all this information to be more successful? In the next part of this book, we present measurement tools for assessing and benchmarking the qualitative aspects of the firm.

TEST YOURSELF

Ask yourself the following yes/no questions:

                                                                   Yes No

1. Quick: Can you identify the three keys to being successful at your firm?
2. Would your five best clients all respond the same way if asked to describe what is distinctive about the way you do business?
3. Would these five clients agree on your value proposition? That is, what value do you provide for them? Where is your competitive edge?
4. Does your performance evaluation process align with what you care about the most?
5. If not, do you have a plan for improving it?

Assessment Tools: Putting Numbers to the Soft Stuff

CHAPTER 5

Leader Types

Self-evaluation is not a strength for anyone in this business.
—Ned Jannotta, Chairman, William Blair & Company

The Myers-Briggs Personality Type Indicator is useful for identifying and understanding:

- The way you prefer to take in information.
- The way you process information.
- The way you make decisions.
- The way you communicate those decisions.
- Ways in which you can build on and leverage your strengths and minimize or shore up your weaknesses.
- Ways to address and resolve conflict.
- Your leadership style.

Alpha Investment's research director originally asked us to help him resolve a conflict with his team of 10 analysts. Though the members are smart and motivated, the team is beginning to fray around the edges as the market drops and bad relative performance numbers pile up. The research director (we'll call him RD here) believes that the way of the future for investment shops is collaboration, not individual analysts working behind closed doors. He is convinced that his research team would perform better if its members interacted more. According to RD, they spend too much time alone in their offices and not enough time with company management and their teammates. However, the more he pressures them to interact, the more resistance he gets. The last staff meeting ended with a shouting match and a mass walkout by the analysts.

Another investment firm is on a two-day retreat. The first day is spent brainstorming some approaches to quantitative research that are considered to be thought leadership. These ideas are truly cutting-edge. Of the 12 participants, the chief investment officer appears most excited about these attempts to gain unique insights. Three analysts are having an animated discussion about research findings and possible areas for pioneering a whole new approach to asset allocation. As a way to help this team get even further out of their box, we use an imagery-and-metaphor technique from the Center for Creative Leadership. That evening, after dinner, the directors of fixed-income and equity investments meet with me privately to say that they both are truly worried about what is happening at this offsite retreat and are considering quitting the firm.

These are just two examples, from our firsthand experience, of situations in which psychological type can be useful in addressing conflict and helping teams to be more effective. In the Alpha case, the problem involved a clash between an introverted style and an extroverted one. The research director of Alpha was a strong Extrovert, as measured by the Myers-Briggs Personality Type Indicator (MBTI or Myers-Briggs). His focus was mainly outside of himself, on people, places, and things. He processed his thinking out loud and preferred spoken communication to written. His preference for extroversion indicated that his deeply held belief about success in the investment business was: I will succeed if I can collect enough information out there in the world. To this boss, it was investment suicide to sit quietly in one's office when all the important information was being gobbled up by the competitors, who all appeared to be attending conferences, meeting with company leaders, or talking to analysts about breaking news.

Here's the rub: Every member of this boss's team was an Introvert. They preferred to be with their inner worlds of thoughts and ideas. They preferred to go deeply into one idea, rather than bouncing along the surface, hopping from one thought to another. They viewed conferences and large meetings as just barely necessary evils of the job. In fact, many of them would retire to their rooms after a full day of conference meetings, putting the "Privacy Please" sign on the door and ordering room service. Quite the opposite of their boss, these Introverts held a deep-seated belief that victory in the investment game depends heavily on getting enough private time to study and think deeply about an investment thesis. In their view, their boss was literally—and apparently intentionally—sabotaging any chance they might have of winning.

The MBTI is one of the most useful tools we've ever found for resolving these sorts of conflicts. For example, at Alpha Investments we used Myers-Briggs to uncover and explain the hard-wiring of the people involved. Because of their new comprehension, the tension among the team members eased enough to allow them to work toward a solution. A compromise was struck between the two extreme positions: on the one hand, frantically racing about to every imaginable meeting, and on the other hanging a "gone fishing" sign on the door. The analysts committed to more interaction with one another and the investment world, and the research director committed to more respect for private work time and individual styles. In the end, both sides admitted that the balanced approach was more powerful than either extreme. (This decision supported the premise of my earlier book, *The Psychology of Money*, in which I argued that the great money masters—Buffett, Lynch, Soros, and others—achieved their outstanding performance by striking just this sort of balance.)

WHAT IS MYERS-BRIGGS? BASIC PREFERENCE SCALE

Before we address the second of the preceding examples, let's briefly explain the Myers-Briggs method of identifying personality types. Originally conceived of by the Swiss psychologist Carl Jung, and named for the mother-daughter research team that converted it into a practical assessment tool, the Myers-Briggs Personality Type Indicator measures the ways in which we prefer to use our brains.

A simple analogy is handwriting. If asked to write your name, you could undoubtedly grab a pen and do so with ease. The hand you use is your preferred hand. You don't even think about it, you just do it, skillfully and effortlessly. Now try writing your name with the opposite hand. Arrgh . . . awkward, slow, and unskillful. The same is true of our brain preferences: some modes of thinking come naturally and easily, but others are difficult and underdeveloped. Table 5.1 shows the four pairs of brain preferences measured by Myers-Briggs. For each person, one of each pairs will come fairly easily, the other with greater difficulty.

The conflict with the Alpha research staff involved the first pairing, Extrovert (E) versus Introvert (I).

SECOND PREFERENCE SCALE: BIG DREAMERS VERSUS "JUST THE FACTS, MA'AM"

The second case described at the beginning of this chapter is even more interesting, because it touches on a major paradigm shift in the investment

TABLE 5.1   Myers-Briggs Preferences

Extroversion (E):
- Focus is outside the self, on other people, places, things
- Tends to "do-think-do"
- Prefers verbal to written communication

Introversion (I):
- Focus is inside the self, on ideas and feelings
- Tends to "think-do-think"
- Prefers written to verbal communication

Sensing (S):
- Linear thinking
- Practical; likes details
- Step-by-step approach

Intuiting (N):
- Creative thinking
- Theoretical; likes big picture
- Jumps from idea to idea

Thinking (T):
- Objective decision making
- Tough-minded
- Competitive
- Prizes truth and clarity

Feeling (F):
- Subjective decision making (based on personal values)
- Tender-hearted
- Cooperative
- Prizes warmth and kindness

Judging (J):
- Organized
- Decisive
- Deliberate (plans carefully)

Perceiving (P):
- Flexible
- Open to new options
- Goes with the flow

industry—a shift that can also be explained by personality types. As part of our preparation for the retreat with the second exemplar firm, we had all the participants take the Myers-Briggs assessment (it's free online and only takes 10 minutes: www.humanmetrics.com/cgi-win/JTypes2.asp). What we found in this case was that the CIO and his three animated analysts had a preference for big-picture, new-paradigm thinking. Their brains were literally hard-wired to naturally and comfortably think this way: creatively, intuitively, jumping from thought to thought. The heads of fixed income and equity were just the opposite. Their brains were wired to focus on details and undertake step-by-step thinking. Jung called such people *Sensors* because they rely on and trust their five senses. They tend to be very practical sorts with a healthy skepticism about anything new.

There's a little story that highlights the basic difference between these preferences. Two men are on their knees laying bricks. You ask the first one what he is making and he responds, "I'm building a huge cathedral in which to worship God and give thanks for this wondrous universe." Wow, there's a big thought!

You approach the second man, who is doing exactly the same thing, and ask the same question: "What are you making?" This fellow, a practical, down-to-earth Sensor, interprets the question totally differently and responds, "$10 an hour."

Same question, same job, but utterly different answers, based on their mental preferences.

Similarly, the investment group on retreat was snared by this difference between a practical, detailed approach and an imaginative, big-picture approach. Much has been written about these different approaches, including an excellent book by Clayton Christensen called *The Innovator's Dilemma*.[1] Christensen explains in great detail the difference between continuous improvement, where slight adjustments are made to a product or process; and what he calls "disruptive technologies," where the whole existing approach is tossed out in favor of a new one. An example of a disruptive technology is the inkjet printer displacing laser printers.

Given their orientation, it's easy to understand why the heads of fixed income and equity were horrified with the CIO's attention to and fascination with disruptive technologies. In their opinion, the firm was operating fine, with good results, and they were very comfortable with the "if it ain't broke, don't fix it" principle of management. By contrast, the CIO saw the offsite retreat as a perfect opportunity to get away from the day-to-day grind and come up with unique insights that would give their firm a competitive edge for years to come. In fact, the CIO told us the following story, which confirmed our suspicions about his view of the industry.

Three executives from Acme Investments (a top, innovative firm) are in Grand Central Station in New York, boarding a train to Philadelphia for a conference. Next to them are three executives from Benchmark Capital (a large, mediocre firm). The Benchmark people each buy one ticket and head for the train. The Acme group buys only one ticket. This strikes the Benchmark guys as odd, so they make a point of sitting next to the Acme team.

Once on the train, the Acme team members wait until the conductor is just about to enter their train car, and then they scurry to the bathroom and close the door. The conductor collects the three tickets from Benchmark's staff and then knocks on the bathroom door, saying, "Tickets, please!" The door opens, and one hand holding a ticket emerges. The conductor takes it and moves to the next car.

"Very clever," say the Benchmark people.

The two groups attend the conference in Philly and return to the train station in the evening. The same scene is replayed, but this time the

Benchmark people only buy one ticket. The Acme folks don't buy tickets. Again, the Benchmark people are surprised and puzzled by this action.

When the conductor is about to enter their car, both groups split for opposite bathrooms: three in one, three in the other. Just before the conductor comes into their car, one Acme fellow opens the bathroom door, runs down to the other bathroom, knocks on the door and says, "Tickets, please!"

The CIO told us this joke with absolute conviction that it was a metaphor for the industry. If you don't completely reinvent yourself—come up with a disruptive technology—you'll be left behind and taken advantage of like the poor, slow-witted fellows from Benchmark.

With this offsite team, we had a nearly even split between the continuous-improvement faction and the disruptive-technology faction. Again, the Myers-Briggs assessment aligned exactly with the rift. Those in the continuous-improvement group were all identified as Sensors; that is, practical and linear thinkers. The disruptive-group members were all Intuitives: big-picture, creative, smash-the-mold types.

Knowing this about the team members doesn't, of course, automatically solve the conflict. There is still genuine disagreement about which path to take. Still (getting back to our notion of mental models), understanding the differences between the ways in which these groups think helps frame the conflict and point the way toward mutual respect and constructive discussion. When people realize that their apparent adversary is not simply trying to annoy them or make life difficult, it goes a long way toward removing the resentment. It's a bit like learning why your new friend refuses to come to dinner. Before you discover the reason, you may be angry that he keeps blowing you off—but when you find out that he's allergic to cats and that's why he's been refusing your kind dinner invitations, then you see the whole problem differently. Your friend can't help the fact that he is allergic. He has no choice in the matter, so now you don't feel resentment toward him.

This was what happened with the Alpha offsite investment team. They were able to address the interests of both parties once they had identified the underlying problem. A portion of the remaining retreat was set aside for improving existing operations and another time block for covering unique insights and breakthrough ideas.

The dilemma faced in the second example by the CIO and his team is a demonstration in microcosm of a larger shift that's occurring in the industry. In our work with investment firms, we are seeing a decided shift from the Sensor personality, which is most interested in improving the status quo, to the Intuitive personality, which is interested in dumping the status quo and inventing or instituting the new next thing. In a *Fortune* article entitled "Does Your Fund Manager Play Piano?" psychologist Ted Bililies stated that "[i]f you had to brand fund managers with psycho jargon, they'd be **STJ** [Sensing-Thinking-Judging, per Table 5.1] on the widely used Myers-Briggs personality test."[2] Though he wrote the article more than a decade ago, Bililies argued (probably correctly) that most investment professionals have the practical, detail-oriented mindset.

From the Myers-Briggs results that we've seen recently, the top active managers are now led by Intuitives, not Sensors. Interestingly, the president at Alpha was a Sensor, whereas leaders at many of the top firms are Intuitives. What's more, we have found that birds of a feather do flock together: In almost every firm where we've done Myers-Briggs assessments, the preferences of the leader are reflected in the team. The only notable exception has been Alpha's Extroverted research director and his Introverted team, and this may be explained by the fact that he inherited the team when he got the RD job.

Why are more investment teams being led by Intuitives? Simply because the investment world is changing from the times when the folks at bank trust departments and insurance investment divisions could buy blue-chip stocks and make 60/40 asset allocation decisions and then sleep contentedly at night, knowing that they had made good, well-founded decisions. In a two-year study by PricewaterhouseCoopers, which ended in 1999, the authors wrote: "Tomorrow's leading companies need senior managers who have vision, creativity, flexibility, and a broad perspective."[3]

These are not the characteristics of the Sensor. Rather, this is a perfect job description for the Intuitive. In a similar vein, Katrina Sherrerd summarized the AIMR speeches given by 10 senior people: "A unifying theme is the need for innovative strategies to meet the challenges of the 21st century."[4]

Investment professionals often ask us, "What is the best type for being an investment leader?" Although we strongly believe that there is no one best type, many great investors have a preference for Intuition. Nevertheless, Sensors can take heart: Gary Brinson is a Sensor, and he founded one of the most successful active management shops ever. Note, though, that this success was due in part to the fact that Brinson's right-hand man was Jeff Diermeier, a very intuitive thinker.

Sensors can also take comfort in the fact that there are niches in the investment market that are perfect for them. It's likely that both Jack Brennan and Jack Bogle are Sensors (though we haven't seen their MBTI results), and they are perfect for the job of running an indexed mutual fund. Imagination is the enemy of the big index fund. Also, many analysts have achieved success and fame by leveraging their Sensing abilities. A famous one is James

Chanos, who is credited with blowing the whistle on Baldwin United in the 1980s and then again on Enron at the turn of the century. Reporters used the same words in their articles to describe his detail orientation:

> *"Mr. Chanos started poring over piles of Baldwin's financial statements . . ."*
>
> *"The key to spotting that pattern lay in obscure reports that Baldwin was required to file with the state insurance regulators, and Mr. Chanos obtained the reports . . ."*[5]
>
> *"In poring over Enron documents, Chanos took note of an odd and opaque mention of transactions that Enron and other 'Entities' had done . . ."*[6]

Our point here is certainly not to discount the value of Sensing abilities. They are enormously important—and the master investors all rely on them. Rather, the point is that we've seen a shift in leadership from the Sensing types to the Intuitive types.

THIRD PREFERENCE SCALE: TOUGH-MINDED VERSUS TENDER-HEARTED

If the first important point to be made about investment leaders involves the shift from practical, detail-oriented types to creative, big-picture types, then the second major point involves the feeling/thinking preference. Traditionally, investment professionals, especially leaders, have shown a preference for Thinking (T). The definition is important here. Thinking and Feeling (F) in the Myers-Briggs framework do not signify cold, analytical, Alan-Greenspan types versus wildly hysterical Robin-Williams types. Rather, these preferences address the question of how a particular person makes decisions. Thinkers tend to detach from a problem and view it objectively, as if from a distance. They look for independent facts and criteria that will help them make a logical decision. Feelers tend to operate just the opposite. They project themselves into the problem and ask, "What would I do if this were my personal problem?" In this way, they call on their personal values to help them decide.

Again, an old story illustrates this difference quite well:

> *A Feeling brother goes on vacation and leaves his dog, Lucky, with his Thinking brother. In two days, the Feeling brother calls to ask after the dog.*

> *Thinking brother responds, "Oh, Lucky is dead."*
> *Feeling brother, stunned, says, "What do you mean, dead?"*
> *"Well, he got hit by a truck and died."*
> *Feeling brother, "Well, that's the last straw. You are just so incon-siderate, so unfeeling."*
> *Thinking brother, "What should I have done?"*
> *"You should have said, 'Lucky has had an accident. He's not doing well.' Then when I called back the next time you could say, 'I'm sorry, he's not improving.' Finally, on the third call, you could say, 'Lucky didn't make it, I'm so sorry.'" Then Feeling brother, sighing heavily, says, "Well, I'm sorry I blew up at you. Anyway, how is Mom?"*
> *Thinking brother: "She's had an accident."*

This story emphasizes that Thinkers aren't trying to be rude. They're interested in telling the truth, so they do just that—sometimes too harshly, in the opinion of Feelers. Often Feelers have a very hard time breaking bad news; for example, they dread giving bad performance reviews or layoff notices to employees. Instead of giving it to people straight, they bob and weave, dance around the subject, and often deliver only a half-truth. Once, when I mentioned this during a speech, a woman sitting near the front shot up out of her chair and screamed, "That's the cruelest thing you can do!" My first thought was, *Well, thanks for revealing your preference for Thinking!* It was true: As a Thinker, this woman believed that the kindest thing to do was give it to people straight, even if it meant hurting their feelings.

Those whom we've surveyed in the investment world (more than a thousand professionals, in what is a reasonably random sampling) prefer Thinking by nearly 80 percent. The industry, with its competitive nature and emphasis on objective analysis, has not historically attracted many Feelers. (Peter Lynch said, "The stocks don't know you own them, so don't take it personally."[7]) This is currently changing in at least one respect. The private-wealth area is attracting financial advisors, many with CFP designations, who are interested in personal consulting roles. Feelers are well suited for these jobs.

In this book on leadership and culture, we want to emphasize the importance of the Thinking/Feeling distinction. The best leaders we've seen are able to weigh decisions from both perspectives. They can look at a problem from a tough-minded, objective perspective, asking, "How will this affect profits and stock performance?" Then they can shift to the tender-hearted question, "How will this affect people?" The ability to wrestle with the legitimate tradeoffs that occur in these thinking-versus-feeling debates is at the core of great leadership. For instance, time will tell if the Compaq/Hewlett-

Packard merger will pay off. Our guess is that Carly Fiorina didn't give enough consideration to the "heart" side of the deal. Like most mergers in the past, the "head" side got nearly all the attention, so the main question was: Is it a good strategic fit? Questions of cultural fit are considered secondary, and dealt with like an unwanted stepchild—as a necessary evil.

This behavior persists in spite of the evidence (from Jeffrey Krug and others) showing that in the first two years after a merger, nearly 25 percent of the executives leave each year (50 percent total) and that 15 to 20 percent leave each year thereafter over the next 7 years. This latter exodus rate is about twice that of companies that have not undertaken a merger. There is a reason why companies like Goldman Sachs and Vanguard don't make major acquisitions, and why companies like Brandes and William Blair don't allow anyone to acquire them. Thinkers typically ignore Krug's advice, "Companies contemplating an acquisition should focus on retaining key incumbent executives for the long haul."[8] If they ignore the people side of the equation, Krug says, "[t]he exodus of incumbent executives decreases leadership stability, disrupts lines of communication, and fractures the organizational culture."[9] Findings from studies of mergers indicate that nearly 80 percent are declared failures, and mostly for the reason given by Krug: culture clashes. This is why Michael Goldstein, of Sanford Bernstein, said, "Success in the money management business has mostly been built, not bought."[10]

Another benefit of acknowledging the "feeling" aspect of decision making appears in company research. Twenty years ago, analysts were trained to direct questions mostly to the CFO (the "numbers" guy), about margins, growth rates, unit pricing, costs of raw materials, number of new facilities, sales results by region, and the like. Nowhere in their training were they encouraged to ask the kinds of questions that we've discussed in this book, about leadership and culture: What is your corporate identity? How strong is your culture? Do you develop and train leaders? What is the turnover rate of key executives? Leaders who are in touch with the people side of the equation include it in their approach to company analysis, and encourage their staff to do so as well. Jeff Diermeier, CIO at UBS Global, told us that after one of their analysts visits a manufacturing facility, she is encouraged to go to the tavern where the workers hang out, to determine their morale level. Do they seem happy about the work and their company, or is there a general atmosphere of bitching and moaning about those "jerks who run the place"? This "soft" assessment has become part of UBS's formal research process.

It should be no surprise that one of the books on Diermeier's office shelf is Dan Goleman's *Emotional Intelligence*. A key premise of that book is that the best leaders have a heightened sense of self-awareness.[11] They are attuned to how their actions affect other people. Example: One leader we know, who has a strong preference for Thinking, has oil paintings of black people working in fields and two Aunt Jemima–style dolls on his desk. When asked about these artifacts, this white male said, "I like Haitian art." No doubt, but we wondered how his black secretary and other employees reacted to it. We know for a fact that this leader is not a racist, but doesn't it seem like bad judgment to display this artwork?

Another investment professional who uses the people factor in his analyses is David Ricci of William Blair & Company. He watches for signs that a company has a strong, positive culture. He cites companies like Wal-Mart, Bed, Bath & Beyond, and eBay as examples of companies that benefit from the synergy of "being on the same page." The best company analyses come from analysts who can deliver the one-two punch: They can crunch the numbers *and* judge the soft side.

Appreciation of their own personality styles helps leaders increase their emotional intelligence and avoid the kinds of problems just discussed. Two Myers-Briggs pairs in particular—Sensing/Intuiting and Feeling/Thinking—hold enormous importance now for investment leaders. The best leaders are able to shift from strategies of continuous improvement to breakthrough ideas. They are also able to evaluate decisions from both the Thinking and the Feeling perspectives.

FOURTH PREFERENCE SCALE: FELIX AND OSCAR

The final preference in the Myers-Briggs matrix underlies the natural tension between those who like to plan and organize their lives and those who are comfortable just going with the flow. We call these the Felix approach and the Oscar approach, respectively, after the characters in Neil Simon's play, *The Odd Couple*. Much humor, in books, movies, and television shows, is based on the juxtaposition of these two types. In the Myers-Briggs lingo, organized, decisive, plan-driven people are called Judgers and flexible, accepting, roll-with-the-punches types are called Perceivers. Our experience in the investment world uncovered an overwhelming majority of Judgers. In fact, many senior investment teams have either none or at most one Perceiver on them.

Notable Perceivers include Jeff Diermeier and Rob Arnott. Often Perceivers fit well in the role of strategist or big-picture thinker. They like to keep their options open and enjoy discussing lots of scenarios. Leadership teams that are heavy on Judgers must be careful not to close down conversations too quickly. Their unofficial motto often seems to be "All action and no talk!," meaning that they hate long brainstorming sessions and feel much better when a decision has been reached and they can move on it. An old poster captures this spirit well: Two buzzards are sitting on a tree limb, and one is saying to the other, "Patience, my ass, I'm gonna kill something!" Judgers must guard against their tendency to close up and move on before all the good options have been considered.

Occasionally, when presented with this information, a leader will say, "Do we try to change the Judgers we have, or do we bring in some Perceivers?" First, remember that it is possible for any type to succeed in any job. It is really a matter of desire, effort, and awareness. There have been successful basketball players who were less than six feet tall. There haven't been many, though, and the ones that made it had tremendous drive and heart.

Typically, it's better for us average folks to do what we were designed to do: namely, work in line with our natural talents. Rather than try to change a zebra's stripes to spots, it's better to get a leopard in the first place. Hiring for investment firms should be like recruiting in professional sports. In fact, Jonathan Niednagel has created a hugely successful business by recruiting professional athletes using Myers-Briggs. He wrote:

> *Once I learned about the characteristics Jung had identified in people, I set out to disprove him. In doing so, I not only found out that he was correct, but I made a connection between personality types and motor skills. The single greatest determinant about what people do, on or off the field, is inborn, genetic brain type. We are generally hard-wired to act and think and even play a certain way.*[12]

It comes down to this: If you need a center on your basketball team, you look for someone with certain attributes. The same is true when you need a creative strategist for your quant group.

BRANDES

Consider the Myers-Briggs makeup of the Brandes leadership team. Table 5.2 shows the preferences breakouts for the five leaders (2 Extroverts, 3 Introverts, etc.).

The Brandes leaders represent the typical active manager type: INTJ. Given the nature of investment analysis, this is no surprise.

TABLE 5.2 Brandes Leaders' MBTI Preferences

Extroversion (E):	2	*Introversion (I):*	3
• Focus is outside the self, on other people, places, things		• Focus is inside the self, on ideas and feelings	
• Tends to "do-think-do"		• Tends to "think-do-think"	
• Prefers verbal to written communication		• Prefers written to verbal communication	
Sensing (S):	1	*Intuiting (N):*	4
• Linear thinking		• Creative thinking	
• Practical; likes details		• Theoretical; likes big picture	
• Step-by-step approach		• Jumps from idea to idea	
Thinking (T):	5	*Feeling (F):*	0
• Objective decision making		• Subjective decision making (based on personal values)	
• Tough-minded			
• Competitive		• Tender-hearted	
• Prizes truth and clarity		• Cooperative	
		• Prizes warmth and kindness	
Judging (J):	5	*Perceiving (P):*	0
• Organized		• Flexible	
• Decisive		• Open to new options	
• Deliberate (plans carefully)		• Goes with the flow	

Introversion: Analysts and portfolio managers tend to be good at concentrating for long periods of time. They like to think and work with ideas.

Intuition: They tend to like complex problems and playing with theories and investment themes. They are naturally curious and often ask "what if?"

Thinking: They tend to be competitive and like a good challenge. (Remember Glenn Carlson's declaration, quoted earlier: "We love to kick complete ass!")

Judgment: They are decisive and organized.

All these traits contribute to excellent analysis and performance. Our view, however, which is based on extensive experience and research, is that the best analysts and portfolio managers draw from both sides of the preference chart. This means that a typical INTJ team must be careful to consciously acknowledge and use the strengths of the other preferences as well. Here are some tips in this regard:

> *Extroversion:* Get out and kick the tires. Talk to company officers, suppliers, customers, and competitors. Make sure your ideas are tied to experience.
>
> *Sensing:* Ground all your theories in facts. Dig, dig, dig. Think "James Chanos."
>
> *Feeling:* Consider the culture of the companies you invest in. What is happening with their people and their leadership practices? Use the scoresheet from Chapter 16 of this book.
>
> *Perceiving:* Take time to consider different options. Be willing to take extra time with key decisions, even if it makes you a bit uncomfortable. Your tendency is to move quickly to closure, possibly too soon.

From a leadership perspective, INTJ investment firms are very strong at strategic thinking and discipline. Brandes, for example, has established a premier record because of its employees' adherence to value investing principles and their discipline in sticking with the company's philosophy in tough times. Theirs is very much a Rationalist leadership team, according to our earlier description of the four basic investment cultures. It is to that discussion that we turn in Chapter 6.

TEST YOURSELF

1. What is your Myers-Briggs type?
2. Based on this information, what are your strengths and weaknesses?
3. How do preferences affect the way your team members work together?
4. How do preferences affect your stock research? Stock selection?
5. Has your team explored how diversity in thinking styles can add value to decision making?
6. Can you think of a team conflict that might be explainable by the members' varying preferences?

CHAPTER 6

Measuring Culture

What gets measured, gets done.
—Peter Drucker[1]

The four culture quadrants discussed in this chapter help you to:

- Identify the dominant culture in your own organization.
- Assess how a firm's dominant culture fits with its core business.
- Determine if there is alignment and congruence in the employees' view of the company.
- Achieve balance between the four dominant culture types for best performance.

Based on the earlier description of the four common investment cultures, what would you guess was the dominant culture at Allstar?

> *Guardian:* Were they primarily interested in smooth processes and efficiency?
> *Rationalist:* Were they mainly interested in winning and competence?
> *Communalist:* Were they deeply involved in creating a great work experience and excellent client relations?
> *Adventurist:* Were they constantly looking for new product ideas and markets?

Pretty clear, right? They were mainly interested in winning. Their vision was stated in terms of a numerical goal and included the idea of beating the benchmark. Performance was measured and discussed daily. Each team member had been recruited based on past success and impressive credentials. Pay and expectations were both high.

The tool we discuss in this chapter allows us to measure this aspect of culture with an eye to improving it for your firm.

FROM 16 TYPES TO 4 QUADRANTS

The Myers-Briggs Personality Type Indicator ties directly into the four cultures described here and in Chapter 4. David Keirsey, in his work on temperaments, asserted that the 16 Myers-Briggs personality styles (e.g., ISTJ, ENFP, etc.) translated into the 4 temperaments: Rationalist, Guardian, Communalist, Adventurist, as shown in Table 6.1.

Based on this correlation between Myers-Briggs and the four basic cultures, we can usually tell just from the Myers-Briggs assessment data what the dominant culture is. Typically, the leader's personality type is mirrored in the team; that type, when translated into the language of the four cultures, will be the dominant one.

IMPORTANCE OF MEASUREMENT

Drucker has it exactly right, especially for the investment industry, in the quote that opens this chapter. We know of one economist who, when asked about the role of culture in developing a firm's talent, said, "It can't play any role. As an economist, I can't quantify culture, so I don't believe in it."[2]

This view is changing. Most investment professionals recognize the importance of culture, both for the success of their own firms and in the selec-

TABLE 6.1 Myers-Briggs Temperament Correlations

Myers-Briggs Type	Keirsey Temperament
ESTJ, ISTJ, ESFJ, ISFJ (all have "SJ" in common)	Guardians
ENTJ, INTJ, ENTP, INTP (all have "NT" in common)	Rationalists
ENFP, INFP, ENFJ, INFJ (all have "NF" in common)	Communalists
ESTP, ISTP, ESFP, ISFP (all have "SP" in common)	Adventurists

tion of companies to invest in. After a presentation on culture to a group of financial analysts, David McLellan, a senior manager with ATB Financial in Calgary, approached me and said, "Besides being a senior manager here, I'm an officer in the army reserves. I like things pretty cut and dried and don't have much patience for the soft side of business. I figure if this stuff really got my attention, there must be material here we would benefit from." At some point in most of our interviews with senior management, we ask flatout about the importance of culture. Without even pausing to think, we can name a dozen CEOs—Jim Tyree at Mesirow; Dave Coolidge at William Blair & Company; Jack Brennan at Vanguard; and Gary Brinson, founder of Brinson Partners, among many others—who would echo Charles Ellis's comment that "over the very long term, culture dominates."[3] Earlier we cited a study of 75 Wall Street analysts, 74 of whom said that culture was a characteristic that distinguished outstanding from average companies.[4] The issue, then, is not that we are still battling for recognition of the importance of culture; rather, we have to establish good measurement tools for culture. Culture is a bit like the Abominable Snowman: Many people have seen the footprints, but no one has seen the thing itself. We know that culture exists and that it is critical to success, but how do we quantify it?

FOUR BASIC INVESTMENT CULTURES

Consider the four basic investment cultures:

1. Guardian.
2. Rationalist.
3. Communalist.
4. Adventurist.

The tool that we created for measuring this phenomenon is the Culture Assessment Tool (CAT). This assessment is designed to force the respondent to choose between conflicting values. For each of 6 questions, you are asked to allocate 10 points among 4 choices (see the end of this chapter for the full assessment tool). This makes it hard simply to say, "We care about all of these things." (You would have to divide your 10 points into 4 equal portions of 2.5 each, which most people don't do.) Instead, through their allocations people reveal their sense of what is most important at the organization.

The CAT Scan is useful for first steps into culture work. It is nonthreatening (because all the answers are positive) and fast (10 minutes), and it can be scored in-house. Its usefulness lies primarily in its ability to start a dialogue among team members about key elements of culture. For example, if two divisions of your company complete the CAT Scan and score very differently, this difference is worth talking about. Why do your employees see your company's culture so differently? How does this disparity (and their views) affect their work? Should steps be taken to gain agreement on core values, vision, guiding principles, and the like?

Another useful question to ask, when viewing results, is whether your culture matches your core business. An intensely competitive, strategic group may not be the best suited for work with retail clients. A communal group probably would not excel in a hedge fund environment. These questions help identify and clarify culture and provide excellent insights into improving the hiring, orientation, and training of new hires.

Once you are familiar with the four basic types (Guardian, Rationalist, Adventurist, and Communalist), you will recognize them in many different settings. For example, in the wildly popular Harry Potter stories, these four temperaments show up as characteristics of the four different Houses at the Hogwarts School. With regard to investors, portfolio managers might exhibit the four temperaments shown in Table 6.2.

The CAT Scan is useful in identifying which of these four temperaments is strong and which is weak in a culture. From a leadership perspective (as opposed to an investment perspective), Table 6.3 shows what each temperament tends to emphasize in running a firm.

Notice how the final category, "Main focus," connects this framework to the industry standard, the Four Ps of Processes, People, Performance, and Philosophy (with one minor exception: here Philosophy is replaced by Pioneering). Depending on the nature of your business, your firm will tend to excel at certain Ps and be weaker in others. For example, Vanguard, with its emphasis on index funds, is very much a Process shop. We argue, as intermediaries usually do, that all the Ps are important, but also point out that it's natural to see stronger and weaker Ps depending on the firm's strategy.

Returning to the Allstar example, we worry when a culture is out of balance. Yes, all firms will have strengths and weaknesses, but in the case of Allstar, the CAT Scan needle was virtually stuck on Performance. The amount of attention given to People, Processes, and Pioneering (innovation) was little to none. Borrowing from the wisdom of the balanced scorecard (developed by Robert S. Kaplan and David P. Norton[5]), we look at how much emphasis a firm puts on each of the Ps. Beyond the clear need for some balance, we also like to see a logical alignment between the firm's core competency (active management, index funds, client relations, etc.) and the firm's culture.

TABLE 6.2 Temperament and Portfolio Management

	Four Temperaments			
	Guardian	**Rationalist**	**Communalist**	**Adventurist**
Animal	*Beaver*	*Owl*	*Dolphin*	*Fox*
Market view	"It's a battle to be won by patience, precision, and discipline."	"It's a challenging puzzle to be solved."	"It's a garden to be weeded and cultivated for growth."	"It's a fun game to be played with flair."
Investment strength	Discipline and execution	Creative analysis	Collaboration and intuition	Fact-finding, risk seeking
Investment style	Technical, rules-oriented	Value, quantification, contrarian	Socially conscious	Growth and arbitrage
Investment roles	Traders, administrators	Analysts, strategists, economists	Research directors, client relationship specialists	Researchers, brokers, hedge fund managers
Examples	Zweig, Dreman	Buffett, Munger	Diversity fund, Domini fund	Lynch
Possible weaknesses	Too rigid, clings to past, lacks flexibility	Too theoretical, lacks data	Too idealistic, lacks toughness	Too reckless, lacks patience
Communication style	Comparative	Conditionals	Metaphors	Anecdotes
Time orientation	Past	Infinite	Future	Present
Needs	Membership	Competency	Relationship	Freedom
Risk profile	Risk-averse	Risk-seeking if merited	Risk-neutral	Risk-seeking
Fears	Losing control	Being judged incompetent	Being rejected	Being constrained
Financial propensity	To save, hoard	To take, wrest	To give, divest	To spend, dissipate

TABLE 6.3 Emphases of the Four Investment Cultures as Leaders

		Four Temperaments		
	Guardian	Rationalist	Communalist	Adventurist
Core values	Efficiency, hard work, duty	Competence, winning, excellence	Teamwork, openness, trust	Freedom, innovation, risk-taking
Definition of success	Excellent systems, smooth operations	Excellent track record and reputation for expertise	Happy employees, a great place to work	Innovative products and services on the cutting edge
Leadership	Stabilizing and reliable	Conceptual and strategic	Facilitative and visionary	Entrepreneurial and risk-taking
Core business	Index funds, traditional bank and insurance investment operations	Active managers: quant, value, growth	Retail and high net worth: client service is critical	Hedge funds and day traders, where risk and transaction levels are high
Examples	Vanguard, Allstate Investments	Wellington, Brandes	Edward Jones, A.G. Edwards	Hedge funds, day traders
Main focus	Processes	Performance	People	Pioneering

MEASURING CULTURE: CAT SCAN

The CAT Scan is designed to measure the culture of a firm, using the framework just discussed. Though each of the temperaments contributes something important to an organization, our goal is to assess the reality of a firm's culture—not what they think it *should* be. From this vantage point, we can better assess whether the culture supports the company's strategic mission.

For example, one large investment firm determined that it needed to be more entrepreneurial and innovative, despite the fact that its culture was heavily Guardian. They called in consultants to help them brainstorm and devise new, riskier strategies. Despite much time and money spent on this initiative, very little changed at this firm. Why? There was simply too much Guardian energy in their culture. The leaders' natural instincts were to stabilize, economize, and create processes for all aspects of the work. Every time they reached a critical action point, instead of following the new initiative, they would instinctively cut expenses, usually by doing another round of layoffs. The lack of awareness about their culture led to much confusion and conflict. To this day, the firm's results are mediocre, and it continues to lose talented people.

As part of identifying the culture of a firm, we use the CAT Scan to see if leaders and employees share the same perception of the environment in which they work. If the CAT Scan results for a leadership team show very different perceptions, we know that something is amiss. A culture should be strong enough that employees can clearly identify it. If this is not so, the leaders have failed to do their job of establishing clear values and the company ways of doing things.

Again referring to my experience working for Gary Brinson, the cultural norms were clear, regardless of whether you liked his way of doing things. Clarity and focus are important elements of success in investing. Investment firms are increasingly aware of this fact. "Alignment around business strategy" was rated the top factor by investment firms in the *Competitive Challenges Survey* (produced by Capital Resources Advisors after surveying more than 100 large firms).[6] A fragmented, poorly aligned culture spells failure.

Having thus laid out a framework for analyzing culture, we can now look at the results of our survey for investment firms.

CULTURE SURVEY RESULTS

Leaders from nearly 100 investment firms returned our survey, so we have a fairly robust database. Responses came from small shops with fewer than 10 employees as well as from huge global firms with thousands of employees. All were investment firms in the business of managing individual or institutional assets. Figure 6.1 shows the results for all the firms averaged together.

The Processes (Guardian) quadrant, with its emphasis on processes and procedures, was the most dominant (17.66). This finding is not surprising. The Guardian temperament is attracted to the financial career, with its traditional emphasis on numbers and precision. Also, Guardians by nature tend to be economically minded. They care about money and finance more than, say, the Communalist.

Tensions and Tendencies

Firms that are heavy on Process tend to be light on Pioneering, the entrepreneurial characteristics. There is a natural tension between these poles. Firms that are into process, six sigma, quality control, zero defects, and so on tend to have cultures that are very different from those that are into creativity and the next new thing. (Dean LeBaron at Batterymarch, a very innovative firm, didn't even prepare budgets!) So it is with investment firms. Ontario Teachers Pension Plan, in Toronto, has leaders like Bob Bertram and Leo De Bever, who are naturally creative and work to make it true of their organization's culture as well. Their CAT Scan is shown in Figure 6.2. Teachers was one of the few firms in our survey that showed high innovative tendencies. Most others were more in keeping with the traditional idea of a financial firm: prudent, conservative, and low-risk.

The tradeoff on the other axis—between People and Performance—was less skewed in our survey. Slightly more emphasis was given to the attitude of "People first" than the Performance attitude of "Get the job done." All-star Capital's CAT Scan, as mentioned at the beginning of this chapter,

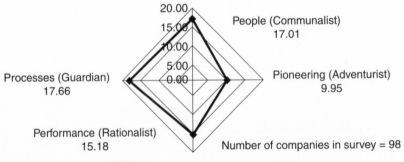

FIGURE 6.1　Average Investment Culture

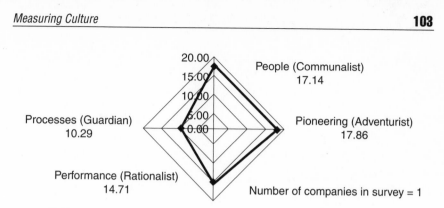

FIGURE 6.2   Ontario Teachers Pension Plan: An Innovative Organization

showed a clear preference for values such as "performance," "competition," "get the job done." People values were rated very low. Allstar's CAT Scan appears in Figure 6.3.

Allstar's culture results suggest that the firm's long-term success is in jeopardy, unless it focuses on the People practices necessary to retain top talent. Chapter 8 takes a closer look at some of those skills and probes the areas in which Allstar was lacking.

Big and Small Firms

The general results of the study revealed one sharp cultural difference between big and small firms (defined as having more than 50 employees or fewer than 50 employees, respectively). Figure 6.4 shows the culture of the big firms.

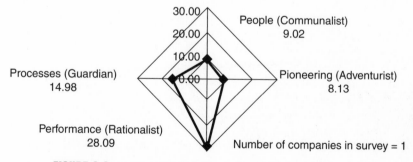

FIGURE 6.3   Allstar Capital: Heavy Emphasis on Performance

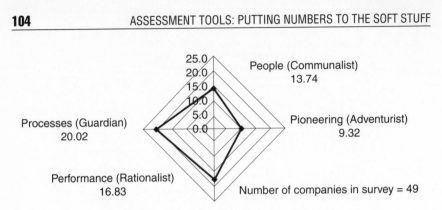

FIGURE 6.4   Big Firms (More than 50 Employees)

Big firms were heavy on Processes and Performance and significantly lighter on People and Pioneering. This is not surprising either, given that much of the financial world consists of Guardians and Rationalists. For example, nearly all of the investment leaders with whom our firm works are one of the two. Therefore, it makes perfect sense that these leaders would emphasize what they believe is most important: good processes and good performance.

Another factor in big firms' having this type of culture is the life cycle of companies. Big firms are more mature, by definition. They need leaders who can manage complex operations and provide organizational structure. For example, one of our clients is making the transition from being a small, entrepreneurial shop to being a global concern that employs more than 200 people. It is difficult for the president to give up control of day-to-day operations, but that is what must happen in the next phase of the company's growth. Hence, at this point an emphasis on processes and structure is appropriate and necessary.

Furthermore, many of the large firms in our survey are publicly traded, which explains their emphasis on performance. Wall Street is not interested in a firm's people or processes, except to the extent that they contribute to the all-important bottom line. A case in point is Global Investments, the firm discussed in Chapter 2. After a full day of discussing and debating the issue of values, they reached consensus on the five values that were most important to them. However, the value entitled "Results" was not one of the final five. During a break, the leader called us aside and said, "I'm going to insist that 'Results' be one of our core values, because at the end of the day that's what matters." When the group reconvened, he announced his decision and explained his rationale. The group accepted it and today they operate with six core values. The point, for our purposes, is simply that the high ranking of Performance by leaders of publicly traded firms is not surprising, and we found it amply demonstrated in our survey of big investment firms.

Small firms, in contrast, had very different cultures, as Figure 6.5 shows. Processes and Performance, heavily emphasized by the big firms, were less important, while Pioneering and especially People were given much more weight. It was surprising to us that *any* investment cultures—large or small—would place such heavy emphasis on People. Investment professionals tend to be tough-minded rather than tender-hearted, as measured by the MBTI. (More than 80 percent of the investors we've surveyed are Thinkers; that is, tough-minded.) Our experience in working with investment leaders has proven that they are resoundingly *not* touchy-feely types (no group hugs for this bunch!). Therefore, it was surprising to find that in the smaller firms, the tough-minded investment leaders chose relationships with their colleagues over Performance or Processes as most important.

A quality-of-life factor may explain this difference. Smaller firms are typically started by seasoned investment professionals who choose their partners on the basis of both competence and friendship—skill *and* fit. Quality of life is often part of the reason for the founding of the new firm in the first place. Also, the people who leave the big firms to work in these smaller shops have experienced the "big firm" culture described earlier and are choosing to create something different for themselves.

Furthermore, in contrast to the big-firm life cycle, the life cycle of a

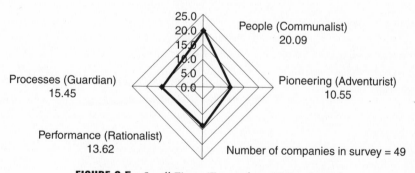

FIGURE 6.5 Small Firms (Fewer than 50 Employees)

small firm does not require lots of processes and procedures to provide structure. One dynamic leader can motivate and manage a handful of people. Finally, because none of these small firms is publicly traded, the demand for performance from Wall Street is not present.

Though we examined such factors as different asset types (bonds vs. stocks vs. real estate, etc.), different client types (individual vs. institutional), and different geographical emphasis (regional vs. national vs. global), this disparity between big and small firms was by far the most pronounced difference in cultures that we found. That's why we now turn to the all-important question: Is there a common culture for successful firms?

SUCCESSFUL INVESTMENT CULTURES

Obviously, there is an element of subjectivity when we explore successful investment cultures. *Successful* by whose standards? In our survey, we asked two questions related to successful investment cultures:

1. Relative to your internal goals, was your firm successful over the past few years?
2. Overall, has your firm's culture contributed to your success?

In the first question we were simply trying to measure whether the firm had succeeded relative to its own goals. This seemed a more appropriate measure than some industry metric such as growth in assets, return on capital, performance relative to your benchmark, or one of a myriad others. Our rationale was that in the investment industry, as in few others, it is horrendously difficult to make apples-to-apples comparisons of firms. For example, during the dot-com craze, value managers performed poorly compared with growth managers. Nevertheless, some value managers, by internal standards, performed admirably during this period. (One value manager we know did not lose a single client during that time period, even though performance was way below market averages.) Therefore, we asked the question in this subjective way to allow respondents to make their own mental adjustments based on their firms' situations. We assumed that respondents would answer honestly, as there was no incentive for inflating the score.

The second question was an attempt to isolate culture as a variable. In other words, a firm could have answered the first question with a resounding yes (a 5 on a scale of 1 to 5), but given the second question a score of only, say, 3. This would suggest that other factors—rather than culture, as defined earlier—contributed to the firm's success (e.g., individual brilliance, market timing, clever marketing, luck, etc.). We were very interested in examining the cultures that got "5" ratings to see if there was a pattern. Did these successful cultures have anything in common, or did they vary randomly? How did the best cultures rate on the first question, pertaining to success? Maybe many successful firms (ratings of 5) did not associate culture with their success, but rather attributed success to other factors.

When we examined the data, we found a clear pattern in the cultures that were rated as contributors to firm success. Likewise, the cultures that did not contribute to success also looked alike. Figure 6.6 shows the average culture of firms that answered the second question with a low rating (1 or 2).

Cultures that didn't support success were heavy on Process and Performance. The heavy emphasis on Process (23.89) implies a bureaucratic environment. Many studies, including a classic *Harvard Business Review* article,[7] suggest that rules and procedures are strong demotivators. The investment business thrives when intelligent, creative, individualistic professionals are given the freedom to perform at their highest level. The same *HBR* article, plus AIMR studies, show that achievement is a key motivator— but bureaucratic regimes often kill this motivation. Hence, it is understandable why high-Process cultures did not correlate with investment success.

What about Performance cultures? Doesn't a heavy emphasis on results and competition help achieve the desired performance? As Collins and Porras pointed out in *Built to Last*, preoccupation with results (read: *money*) was not associated with long-term success.[8] The best-performing companies acknowledged the need for fair profits, but not for squeezing every last

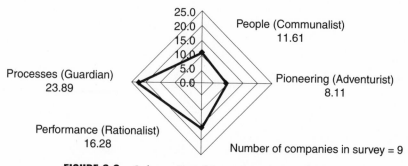

FIGURE 6.6   Cultures Rated Least Supportive of Success

nickel out. To quote the original mission statement of A.G. Edwards, a firm that earned a J.D. Powers rating as the best full-service broker:

> *Our purpose is to furnish financial services of value to our clients. We should act as their agents, putting their interests before our own.*
>   *We are confident that if we do our jobs well and give value for what we charge, not only will mutual trust and respect develop, but satisfaction and a fair reward will result.*[9]

Notice the emphasis on "fair reward" rather than "maximum profit." The recent examples of Enron and Andersen offer powerful evidence that too much drive for profit, at the expense of the other Ps, can ruin a company.

In the war for talent, firms like A.G. Edwards are the ones that attract and retain the best talent, because they provide an excellent work environment (A.G. Edwards spent seven consecutive years on the *Fortune* "Top 100 Places to Work" list) with challenging assignments, opportunities for development and learning, fairness, and similar People-oriented characteristics. As in professional sports, the team with the best talent usually wins.

In fact, this is exactly what we see in the cultures rated "Most Supportive of Success." The leaders of these firms emphasize People over Performance and Pioneering over Process, as shown in Figure 6.7. Apparently, cultures that provide an excellent working environment and promote innovation perform better than their counterparts who stress Process and Performance.

Can this really be true? Perhaps the ratings for success are not significantly different for these two groups. Maybe the firms with cultures rated

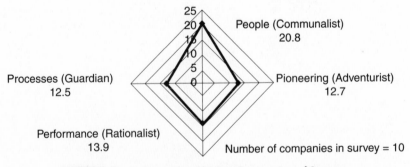

FIGURE 6.7   Cultures Rated Most Supportive of Success

"poor" still performed well, but for reasons other than culture. Well, see for yourself: The average ratings for success for the two groups are given in Table 6.4.

The numbers in Table 6.4 support the findings of Kotter and Heskett that positive cultures and success go hand-in-hand.[10] Furthermore, the graph of the "positive" culture indicates that leaders who emphasize People and Pioneering have greater success than those who concentrate on Process and Performance. The reason for this is probably the inescapable fact that winning investment firms must attract and retain the best talent and must encourage thought leadership and innovation.

IMPLICATIONS FOR INVESTMENT FIRMS

The assessment tools described in this chapter provide a framework for discussing leadership and culture with senior management. We sometimes post the culture graph on the wall to provide a visual reference during the discussion of values, beliefs, mission, strategy, and implementation. Participants will point to the charts to highlight or support insights about what they believe and why they act as they do. Never underestimate the power of visuals during a discussion! The simple diamond chart acts as a good reference point for any discussion of firm culture.

SUMMARY

The CAT Scan tool is one way to measure the dominant culture of an organization. It can be filled out by the leadership body, employees at random,

TABLE 6.4 Average Success Ratings

	Culture Rating (1–5)	Success Rating (1–5)	Number of Firms
Highest-rated cultures	5.0	4.4	N = 10
Lowest-rated cultures	1.0 or 2.0	2.6	N = 9

or the entire firm (if practical). Once the surveys are returned and processed, look for the following:

- *The dominant culture in your firm.* Does it make sense, given your mission and strategic focus?
- *Significant imbalance among the four basic cultures.* A clear warning sign is a heavy weighting in only one of the four cultures. Time and again, firms that show such an imbalance are also struggling with performance. Action steps should be designed to achieve greater balance.
- *The score for the People portion of the survey.* One clear finding in our study was that the high-performing firms place heavy emphasis on their people. This result aligns with Robert Levering's study of the 100 best places to work.[11] Have you paid enough attention to creating a great place to work?

SURVEY

Instructions: If you work for a large national or global firm, answer the survey as it relates to your immediate work environment.

The survey consists of six questions. Each question has four alternatives. Divide 10 points among these four alternatives depending on the extent to which each alternative is similar to your own organization. Give a higher number of points to the alternative that is most similar to your organization. Just make sure the total equals 10 for each question.

1. Criteria for Success	Score
A. The firm defines success in terms of its people, creating a great place to work.	
B. The firm defines success in terms of innovative products and service that are cutting-edge in the industry.	
C. The firm defines success in terms of its reputation and track record for expertise in the industry.	
D. The firm defines success in terms of efficiency; its processes and systems are the best in the industry.	
Total	**10**

2. Firm Leadership	
A. The leadership in our firm is best characterized as collaborative and visionary.	

B. The leadership in our firm is best characterized as entrepreneurial and risk-taking.
C. The leadership in our firm is best characterized as conceptual and strategic.
D. The leadership in our firm is best characterized as stabilizing and reliable.

Total	10

3. Strong Suit

A. The primary strength of our firm is our ability to develop high levels of trust, loyalty, and satisfaction in our employees and clients.
B. The primary strength of our firm is our ability to take risks, innovate, and put plans into action.
C. The primary strength of our firm is our ability to plan strategically and execute competently.
D. The primary strength of our firm is our ability to develop excellent processes that make for efficient work flow.

Total	10

4. Top Values

A. The top values in the firm are teamwork, openness, and trust.
B. The top values in the firm are freedom, innovation, and risk-taking.
C. The top values in the firm are competence, winning, and excellence.
D. The top values in the firm are efficiency, hard work, and duty.

Total	10

5. Strategic Vision

A. Our firm's vision involves excellent client service and a chance for employees to develop to their full potential.
B. Our firm's vision involves creating products and services that are entrepreneurial and exciting.
C. Our firm's vision involves a product or service that dominates the market and demonstrates our expertise at solving complex problems for people.

	Score
D. Our firm's vision involves a product or service that provides dependable, practical usefulness to people.	
Total	**10**

6. Possible Weaknesses

A. A possible weakness of our firm's culture is that we are too friendly and informal.
B. A possible weakness of our firm's culture is that we are too quick to act.
C. A possible weakness of our firm's culture is that we are too competitive.
D. A possible weakness of our firm's culture is that we are too bureaucratic

Total	**10**

Indicate your agreement with the statements below using the following key:

  1 = strongly disagree
  2 = disagree
  3 = neutral
  4 = agree
  5 = strongly agree

1. The culture of our firm supports good employee relationships and high morale.   _____
2. The culture of our firm supports entrepreneurial risk-taking.   _____
3. The culture of our firm supports competence and expertise.   _____
4. The culture of our firm supports efficiency through good processes.   _____
5. Relative to our internal goals, our firm has succeeded over the past few years.   _____
6. Overall, our firm's culture has contributed to our success.   _____

Results

Total for all question As   _____

Total for all question Bs   _____

Total for all question Cs   _____

Total for all question Ds   _____

CHAPTER 7

Diagnosing Culture by Measuring Values

We talk a great deal about values and vision.
—David Fisher, Chairman, Capital Group Companies[1]

Culture doesn't have to be invisible. By measuring your firm's beliefs about culture, you can decide where to invest precious resources for improvements. In this chapter, you will learn:

- How to determine the true core values of your firm, based on people's behaviors.

- How your firm's people-based needs and interests can be quantified quickly.

- How to see differences between what your staff wants in the firm's culture and what they have right now.

- Specific opportunities for growth and improvement.

I had just finished a talk on investment culture to a group of CFAs in Kansas City. When I asked for questions, an earnest-looking man at the front table said, "Okay, so how do we get started? What are some first steps?"

Fair question.

The CAT Scan diagnostic described in Chapter 6 is a good place to start. It gives people a context for talking about an intangible topic. Beyond that, there is a tool that goes directly to the heart of the question, namely, "What are your firm's core values?" Even if your firm has identified values and plastered them on plaques, posters, and mouse pads all over the office, you may still benefit from a survey to discover the real values of your department or organization. (Remember the discussion of Enron in Chapter 2.) In firms where people *don't* talk "a great deal about values and vision" (in contrast to Capital Group, whose chairman provided the opening quotation for this chapter), the old, dusty list of values hanging on the wall of a hallway may not capture the current reality.

The diagnostic tool that we use is an excellent way to further the discussion of culture. It has the benefit of being straightforward and understandable, but it also has a remarkably profound ability to reveal the health or disease within a culture. It's a good place to start because it provides a snapshot of where the culture is currently and how the culture should change for it to become optimal. The current snapshot is a bit like a medical x-ray. The doctor can tell fairly quickly (if not at a glance) whether the patient is healthy or if more lab work has to be done. The values tool also suggests clear action steps that a company's leaders need to take to address any issues, or—in what we hope is the case—simply to improve an already good situation. For those of you who like some evidence that this tool is viable, accepted in the field, and up to snuff, know that McKinsey & Company rated it tops against similar diagnostic instruments. They are using it globally to support their performance leadership work in major corporations.

VALUES ASSESSMENT TOOL

The tool was developed by Richard Barrett, and is described in detail in his book, *Liberating the Corporate Soul.*[2] For the purposes of this book, we first describe the theory briefly and then show how we have applied it to investment organizations.

Barrett's culture assessment starts with an elegantly simple process: a survey of personal, current, and desired values and behaviors for employees. All employees are shown a list of about 100 values (such as "honesty," "client service," and so forth) that have been customized for their industry and specific organization. (Values such as "thought leadership" and "fund performance" would be added for investment firms.) Employees then circle (or click on, if they're doing the assessment online) 10 words that describe their personal values; 10 words that describe their current environment, and 10 words that they believe will allow their firm to achieve long-term success. This exercise takes about 15 minutes and is done individually, not as a work group or department. The results are aggregated to determine the values of a work group or department.

The survey yields a values ranking. The values/behaviors that got the most votes for personal, current, and preferred work environment are listed in order. As you will see in some of the examples, this information by itself offers great insight and suggestions for action steps. Barrett takes it a step further, though, and assigns each value and behavior to a different level of organizational development. Borrowing and expanding on an idea from Abraham Maslow's hierarchy of human needs, Barrett suggests that organizations go through a similar hierarchy during development. Both individuals and organizations move from the lowest level of needs (survival) to the highest (self-actualization).

At the lowest rung of the ladder, both individuals and organizations must meet their physical needs. Individuals must have food, water, air, and shelter. Organizations must have safe facilities, equipment, and cash flow to operate. It is normal and healthy for new or struggling enterprises to be preoccupied with these survival needs. It becomes unhealthy for organizations when these needs become excessive and fear-driven; the resulting behaviors include turf protection, exploitation, and overcontrol.

The second level of development involves relationships. Values such as "open communication" and "customer service" are assigned to this level. The focus is healthy relationships between employees and customers. Going back to our earlier discussion of the four basic investment cultures, we often find lots of these values highly rated in Communalist companies. Underlying insecurities at this level show up in behaviors like blame, conflict, and manipulation.

The third level in Barrett's hierarchy corresponds to Maslow's level of self-esteem. Individuals who have met their survival and relationship needs naturally look for ways in which they can distinguish themselves through achievement. Similarly, organizations that are profitable and have solid, functional relationships look to become the best. They tend to focus on best practices, quality systems, efficiency, and excellent processes. Of the four basic investment cultures, Guardian companies tend to choose lots of these values in their assessments. If the emphasis on efficiency is overdone, however, bureaucracy and complacency can result.

At the fourth level of development, individuals and firms shift from a focus on self to a focus on the greater good. Maslow described it this way for individuals: "Self-actualizing people are, without one single exception, involved in a cause outside of themselves. They are devoted, working at something [that] is very precious to them—some calling or vocation."[3] The same phenomenon occurs with companies. As organizations meet their needs on the first three levels, they begin to focus on the needs of the firm in general, of the community, and of society.

At first we were a bit skeptical about making this assertion with regard to the investment industry. After all, the myth is that money is everything and, as Gordon Gekko said in the movie *Wall Street,* "Greed is good!" Why would firms shift from a "What's in it for me?" attitude to a more selfless interest in the common good? Nevertheless, our experience shows that they do. Firms such as Ferguson Wellman, Ariel Capital, Northwater Capital, American Century, and many others are marvelous examples of financial success and extraordinary generosity and service. The list of great investors who later established philanthropic organizations further supports this notion: John Templeton, George Soros, Gary Brinson, and quite a few others.

In Barrett's model, self-actualization for organizations is divided into several levels. The fourth level in the hierarchy (the first level of self-actualization) is called *Transformation.* Companies operating at this level have eliminated most of the fear-driven behaviors and are successful and fun places to work. Values that typically show up on their assessment results are "learning," "diversity," "empowerment," and "employee participation." Barrett does not assign any negative or, as he calls them, "limiting" behaviors to these higher realms of development. Fear is the cause of limiting behaviors, and at this stage it has largely been driven out of these firms.

The fifth level of the hierarchy is about organizational cohesion. This level relates directly to our earlier chapters about values and vision. Organizations that are driven by solid vision and value principles choose words assigned to this level: "trust," "integrity," "honesty," "fairness."

Level six involves deepening the sense of connectedness within the organization and to the outside community. It highlights values such as "leadership development," "coaching," "mentoring," "partnering," "community involvement," and "making a difference."

The seventh (highest) level includes values such as "wisdom," "vision," "ethics," "global perspective," and "future generations." The concern at this level is the whole of humanity.

Figure 7.1 shows the seven levels of organizational values, with a summary of the significance of each level.

Table 7.1 connects this discussion of hierarchy to the earlier discussion of vision statements. A company's mission statement often reveals the level of the hierarchy at which it is operating.

In Chapter 3, when we described Allstar's vision, we mentioned that they were in survival mode at that time. This is the first level in Barrett's framework. Human nature demands that basic needs be addressed before higher-level interests are considered. However, your staff members, in seeking ultimate professional satisfaction, will look for a firm whose level closely matches their own. For example, the people at Allstar wanted to focus more on level 4 work (continuous improvement) but were forced by

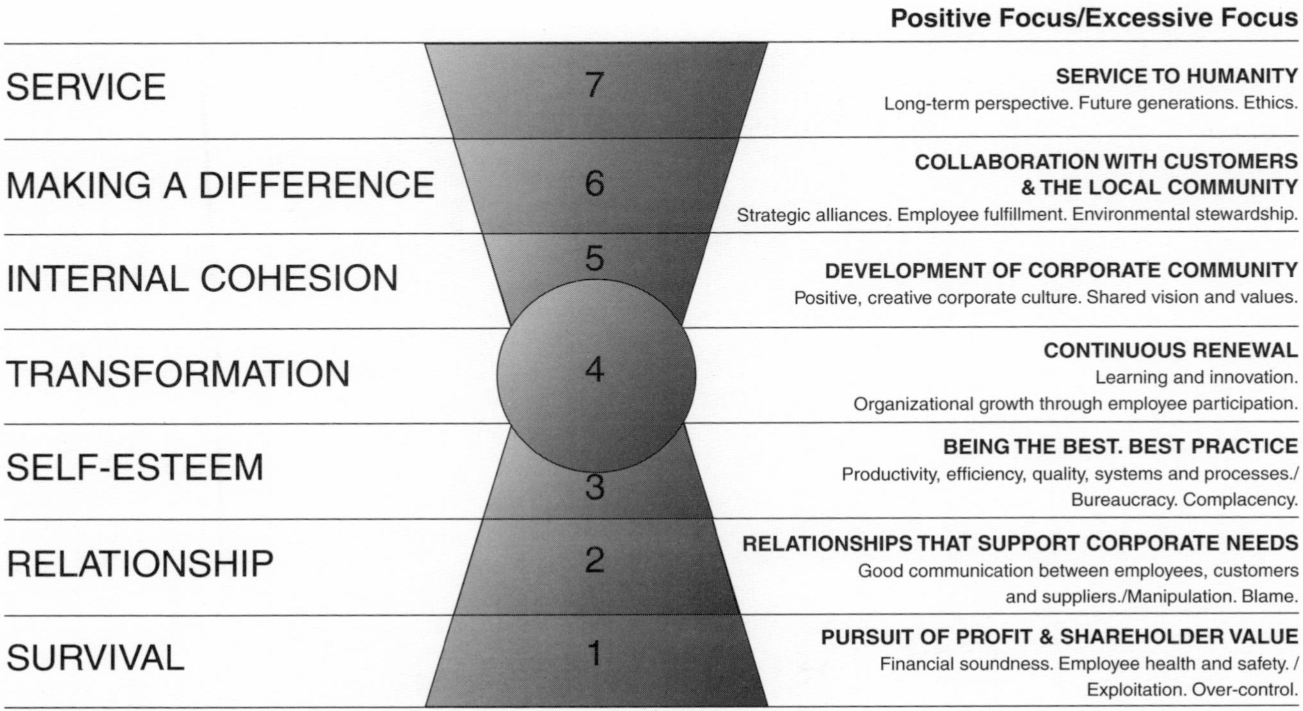

Positive Focus/Excessive Focus

7 — SERVICE TO HUMANITY
Long-term perspective. Future generations. Ethics.

6 — COLLABORATION WITH CUSTOMERS & THE LOCAL COMMUNITY
Strategic alliances. Employee fulfillment. Environmental stewardship.

5 — DEVELOPMENT OF CORPORATE COMMUNITY
Positive, creative corporate culture. Shared vision and values.

4 — CONTINUOUS RENEWAL
Learning and innovation.
Organizational growth through employee participation.

3 — BEING THE BEST. BEST PRACTICE
Productivity, efficiency, quality, systems and processes./
Bureaucracy. Complacency.

2 — RELATIONSHIPS THAT SUPPORT CORPORATE NEEDS
Good communication between employees, customers
and suppliers./Manipulation. Blame.

1 — PURSUIT OF PROFIT & SHAREHOLDER VALUE
Financial soundness. Employee health and safety. /
Exploitation. Over-control.

SERVICE

MAKING A DIFFERENCE

INTERNAL COHESION

TRANSFORMATION

SELF-ESTEEM

RELATIONSHIP

SURVIVAL

FIGURE 7.1 The Seven Levels of Values. (Reprinted with permission: Richard Barrett, Corporate Transformation Tools®, www.corptools.com.)

TABLE 7.1 Vision/Hierarchy Correlation

Motivation/Level Audience	Company	Vision Statement
Service—Level 7 Audience: Society	Merck	We are in the business of preserving and improving human life
	Hewlett-Packard	Our main task is to design, develop, and manufacture the finest electronic equipment for the advancement of science and the welfare of humanity.
Making a Difference—Level 6 Audience: Customers and community	Steelcase	Helping people work more effectively.
Meaning—Level 5 Audience: Employees	Sony	Respect and encourage each individual's ability and creativity.
Transformation—Level 4 Audience: Employees	Motorola	Continuous self-renewal.
Self-Esteem—Level 3 Audience: Employees	Georgia Pacific	Being the best at everything we do.
Relationship—Level 2 Audience: Customers	A. G. Edwards	We are dedicated to building a one-on-one relationship between an investor and a professional financial consultant.
Survival/Growth—Level 1 Audience: Stockholders	Kellogg	Profitable growth is our primary purpose.

the circumstances to concentrate on level 1 (fiscal health). Understandably, they were frustrated.

By now, those of you who are practical-minded (and that would be *all* of you!) are wondering how this hierarchy helps to evaluate the health of a firm's culture. Knowing where your firm is developmentally helps you in several ways:

1. *Identifying limiting behaviors.* Are a number of them present in your current-culture snapshot? These behaviors, such as blame and buck-passing, only limit a firm's potential. By clarifying what limiting behavior is occurring within the firm, the leadership has the opportunity to do some problem solving to correct the situation.
2. *Displaying a full spectrum of values.* The healthiest firms display a relatively full spectrum of values. That is, values rated highly by employees tend to be in each of the seven levels, rather than clustered in just one. This distribution for a corporation equates to being a well-rounded person. Whatever levels are highlighted by the results, leadership can see clearly where the firm is now and where people want to go, based on the desired-culture responses.
3. *Matching of positive values in the current and desired cultures.* The most successful firms tend to be close to their desired state already. Therefore, there is a strong overlap between the values in the current environment and those in the desired environment. Even in the very best of environments, though, leaders garner information about the specific improvements people would like so that they can continue to do their best work.
4. *Identifying and defining the values and behaviors* from the "desired culture" results to make decisions about directions for improvement.

Fundamentally, Barrett's approach is to use the intelligence that exists in the system (organization) at all levels to define what should be done to improve the overall performance of the company.

To show how this works in practice, let's look at the results from several investment firms. To simplify the analysis, we've eliminated the "personal" values aspect of the report and focused on the current versus desired culture, as identified by employees. First, we'll consider some healthy firms, then some unhealthy ones.

Aronson+Johnson+Ortiz, LP: Example of a Healthy Culture

Many professional investors are familiar with Ted Aronson, who founded Aronson Partners (now Aronson+Johnson+Ortiz or AJO). The firm, founded in Philadelphia in 1984, has grown to 60 clients representing just under $10 billion in assets under management. There are 7 principals and 27 employees total. The firm is heavily quant-oriented. All of the employees filled out the culture survey. The results are shown in Figure 7.2.

Current Culture Values

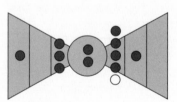

1. *Client satisfaction*
2. *Humor/fun*
3. *Continuous improvement*
4. Ethics
5. *Professionalism*
6. Excellence
7. Generosity
8. *Integrity*
9. *Quality*
10. Competence
11. Long hours (L)
12. *Teamwork*

Desired Culture Values

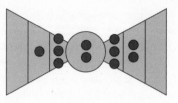

1. *Client satisfaction*
2. *Humor/fun*
3. *Teamwork*
4. Commitment
5. *Continuous improvement*
6. Open communication
7. Efficiency
8. *Integrity*
9. *Professionalism*
10. Employee fulfillment
11. *Quality*

Legend

Bold and italics = Current Culture and Desired Culture match
L = Potentially Limiting (hollow dots)

FIGURE 7.2 Aronson+Johnson+Ortiz, LP. (Reprinted with permission: Richard Barrett, Corporate Transformation Tools®, www.corptools.com.)

Based on the criteria discussed earlier in this section, the first thing we noticed in AJO's results was an absence of limiting values. Well, almost. One limiting value—long hours—was identified, but with mitigating circumstances: The long hours are spent in an environment of "humor/fun" (the value rated second highest). Most of us would *like* to spend long hours in a humorous, fun environment. Comedy clubs thrive on this premise. Those of you who know Ted Aronson know that he is hilarious. He regularly sends cartoons and jokes out to all his clients, friends, and acquaintances. (I made this remark to an audience during a presentation and one of the attendees came up afterward, removed a cartoon from his pocket, unfolded it, and said, "Ted sent this to me yesterday!")

Second, the values represent five of the seven levels. The absence of a value in the lowest level—survival—is often the case with *Built to Last* companies. They are performing so well and focusing so effectively on their core business that profitability takes care of itself. The heavy representation of values at level 3 (Self-Esteem, which translates into efficiency/Process) is right in line with expectations. AJO is a quant shop with emphasis on excellent trading practices, so they have to pay attention to systems and processes. We don't see a clustering of values at the fourth level, because there is no strong need for this organization to transform itself. It is already functioning at a high level. Companies that are ready to evolve—that is, change their culture—often show lots of values in the fourth level.

Third, the health of AJO is shown in the high number of matching values between current and ideal. There are seven value matches, including an exact match for the top two of "client satisfaction" and "humor/fun." This is an organization that knows who it is and likes it.

Leaders at AJO should be proud of the culture that they have created and preserved over time. Of course, a logical and fair question from professional investors is: "Okay, but has it paid off for them in financial success?" Table 7.2 represents results in three critical areas. As you can see, AJO has been hugely successful.

TABLE 7.2 AJO Results Record

	Record
AUM growth (10 years)	34.9%
Performance (10 years)	14.8% vs. 11.3%
	(Small cap vs. R2000)
Staff turnover	None

Ferguson Wellman: Small but Beautiful

Founded in Portland, Oregon, in 1975 by H. Joseph Ferguson and Norbert J. Wellman, Ferguson Wellman (FW) manages more than $2 billion for a variety of institutional and individual clients, and has grown to a team of 33 with 20 employee-owners. The company hosts an offsite retreat for all employees each year, for which we were asked to design the program; this included performing a culture assessment and presenting the findings at the retreat. This was important work for FW. It was even then a successful firm with a strong culture, but its values had never been clearly defined. As a growing firm, it needed this clarification for recruiting and evaluating staff. The results for FW are shown in Figure 7.3.

Notice that FW's current culture, like AJO's, is virtually wart-free. Six of the twenty-nine respondents indicated that the environment was hierarchical. This presents an opportunity for improvement, but certainly is no cause for alarm. Leaders at this firm have established levels of trust that allow them to explore this further with employees. They should start by finding out what the six respondents meant by the word *hierarchical* and how it manifests and limits their success.

As with AJO, there are seven matches between the values for the current and the desired cultures. The high number of matches means that FW does not have far to go to reach its desired state. FW is operating at a high level. A close look at the differences between the current and desired states gives leaders an excellent blueprint for continuous improvement. First, employees are saying that even more attention might be given to developing excellent teamwork. Second, they are highlighting "clear performance goals" as a place to focus and improve. During our work with FW, we talked to employees who gave examples of where performance goals could be sharpened. Importantly, despite the great survey results, the staff gave senior leadership the information it needed on where to go next. This direction is critical to avoid complacency and keep everyone moving ahead.

As in the case of AJO, results for FW are strong (see Table 7.3). The firm

TABLE 7.3   FW Results Record

	Record
AUM growth (3 years)	26.0
Performance (3 years)	Top quartile (Small cap vs. R2000)
Staff turnover	None

Current Culture Values

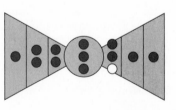

1. *Client satisfaction*
2. Community involvement
3. Client collaboration
4. *Professionalism*
5. *Integrity*
6. *Teamwork*
7. Humor/fun
8. Quality
9. *Balance (home/work)*
10. *Continuous improvement*
11. Ethics
12. *Financial stability*
13. Hierarchical (L)

Desired Culture Values

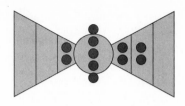

1. *Client satisfaction*
2. *Teamwork*
3. *Integrity*
4. *Continuous improvement*
5. Clear performance goals
6. Empowerment
7. *Professionalism*
8. Accountability
9. *Balance (home/work)*
10. *Financial stability*
11. Open communication
12. Passion

Legend

Bold and italics = Current Culture and Desired Culture match

L = Potentially Limiting (hollow dots)

FIGURE 7.3 Ferguson Wellman. (Reprinted with permission: Richard Barrett, Corporate Transformation Tools®, www.corptools.com.)

beautifully meets the full-spectrum criterion, showing values in each of the seven levels. From "financial stability" all the way up to "integrity," "ethics," and "community involvement," FW is covering each level of development. Much of the attention at the top end of the spectrum is generated by James Rudd, CEO. He has been so active in community affairs that the United Way has named its highest service award after him.

Brandes: Solid Culture, Solid Performance

Founded in 1974 by Charles Brandes, this firm has grown to more than 400 employees and nearly $80 billion in assets. Brandes is headquartered in San Diego and adheres strictly to Graham-and-Dodd principles of investing, which is no surprise: its entire senior management team of five individuals is Rationalist, with one Guardian to keep them honest. Rationalists are born to be active portfolio managers. Charles hand-selected his four senior cronies from his high school class. They are not only colleagues but also good friends. It's no wonder that the firm's culture is so cohesive (see Figure 7.4).

1. No limiting values at all are evident.
2. There are seven matches between the current and desired cultures. Brandes is close to realizing its desired culture. The top-rated value of "client satisfaction" is also in line with other outstanding firms.
3. There is a full spectrum of values, except for the lowest level. As Collins and Porras found, the *Built to Last* firms are not focused primarily on profit. When "profit/finances" does not appear on the values list, it is usually a sign that there are no issues. This is certainly true of the firms reviewed here.
4. Brandes leaders identified "professional growth" as an important focus area for the future. Attracting and retaining the very best people will require Brandes to offer the very best professional growth options.

It is also no wonder that the value of "teamwork" is highly rated. This organization values teamwork so much that a senior committee of 11 people decides collectively which stocks to buy and sell. When asked about the decision-making method (one person has final authority? majority rule?), they astonished us by saying that the group of 11 must reach consensus before action is taken. When I pushed Glenn Carlson, co-CEO, on this point, he said that he couldn't remember a time when the group had not been able to finally reach consensus. (Most of the investment teams we know have trouble agreeing on the day of the week, let alone complex buy-and-sell decisions!)

Current Culture Values

1. *Client satisfaction*
2. *Balance (home/work)*
3. *Vision*
4. *Open communication*
5. *Teamwork*
6. *Employee fulfillment*
7. Excellence
8. *Quality*
9. Values awareness
10. Global leadership
11. Professionalism

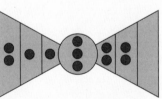

Desired Culture Values

1. *Client satisfaction*
2. *Balance (home/work)*
3. *Teamwork*
4. *Employee fulfillment*
5. Professional growth
6. *Open communication*
7. Integrity
8. Trust
9. Leader development
10. Continuous improvement
11. *Vision*
12. *Quality*
13. Financial stability
14. Humor/fun

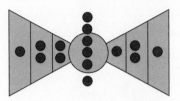

Legend

Bold and italics = Current Culture and Desired Culture match

L = Potentially Limiting (hollow dots)

FIGURE 7.4 Brandes. (Reprinted with permission: Richard Barrett, Corporate Transformation Tools®, www.corptools.com.)

TABLE 7.4 Brandes Results Record

	Record
AUM growth (5 years)	34.2%
Performance (20 years)	19.21% vs. 12.78% (Global equity vs. MSCI)
Staff turnover (5 years)	2 senior portfolio managers

What is the evidence that the leaders at Brandes truly value their culture? Simple. As Carlson put it, "We don't sell out." The offers are there, but these leaders love their work and the culture they have created.

Does culture translate into results? Take a look at its record (Table 7.4). The fund performance is not a typo: This is the best global equity fund in the world. Assets have grown rapidly and the firm rarely loses a key investment professional.

BIG AND, WELL, ALMOST BEAUTIFUL

Figure 7.5 displays the survey results for one of the 10 largest investment firms (more than $500 billion in assets). Results were pretty much as expected for "Global Firm": good but not great.

1. *Limiting values.* The limiting values for this firm are "bureaucracy," "slow-moving," and "risk-averse." These results should not surprise anyone. With more than 3,000 employees, this investment department reflects the conservative values of its parent company, a bank. As stated before, this information about limiting values gives leadership a chance to focus on problems and try to alleviate them as much as possible.
2. *Matches.* There are only two, but they're important ones. Again, "client satisfaction" heads the list. Time and again, this seems to be the biggest determinant of success. Is a firm's top focus on client satisfaction? If so, you have a winner. Perhaps now you don't think that Turner Investments is so crazy to write a mission statement about being of service.
3. *Full spectrum.* Yes, values have been chosen from every level but one.
4. *Areas for improvement.* This large firm received excellent feedback about where it can improve:
   —Accountability.
   —Clear performance goals.
   —Continuous improvement.
   —Leadership development.

Current Culture Values

1. *Client satisfaction*
2. Consensus
3. *Ethics*
4. Balance (home/work)
5. Bureaucracy (L)
6. Commitment
7. Financial stability
8. Risk-averse (L)
9. Slow-moving (L)

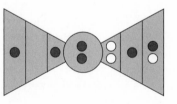

Desired Culture Values

1. *Client satisfaction*
2. Accountability
3. Clear performance goals
4. Continuous improvement
5. Leadership development
6. *Ethics*

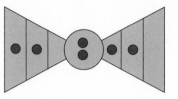

Legend

Bold and italics = Current Culture and Desired Culture match

L = Potentially Limiting (hollow dots)

FIGURE 7.5 Global Firm. (Reprinted with permission: Richard Barrett, Corporate Transformation Tools®, www.corptools.com.)

This firm's leaders must first define what each of these words means. Then they can brainstorm with employees about ways to improve in each area. This should go a long way toward improving the situation with limiting values.

Leaders can do a lot with the results of this inventory. In Global Firm's case, leadership knows that it must focus on clear performance goals to improve bureaucratic tendencies in the company. Perhaps even more interesting, employees are saying that "leadership development" is a way to solve the problems of bureaucracy, risk aversion, and slow movement. This large firm already has clearly established values, printed on a postcard-sized, laminated paper. The CIO is clear about the four top strategic goals. This culture is pretty healthy, though there is room for some improvement. Results (shown in Table 7.5) support this assessment: Asset growth is twice the industry average, and turnover is half the industry average. Performance is a tad better than the benchmark.

Private Equity Firm: Adding Another Dimension of Personal Values

For the final firm that we analyze with the values survey, we add the "Personal" component discussed at the outset of the chapter. We excluded it in the preceding results to simplify the analysis and presentation. The rationale for this addition is straightforward: When the things that are important to you personally are also valued in your workplace, you tend to feel better about work and are more productive. The days of leaving one's private self at the office door are long gone. Companies realize that they want the whole person—head, heart, and hands—on the job.

Therefore, when taking the values assessment, you can choose to include the personal values dimension. A large private equity firm (PEF) chose this option. PEF is one of the largest managers of private equity partnership

TABLE 7.5   Global Firm Results Record

	Record
AUM growth (10 years)	19.9%
Performance (10 years)	11.97% vs. 11.78% (Large cap vs. R1000)
Staff turnover (1 year)	18 (less than 5%)

investments in the United States and has one of the longest histories. Together with its predecessor organizations, PEF has been investing in private equity partnerships since 1979 and has been managing direct investments in private equity since 1972. PEF is well known internationally for its continuous commitment to, and deep understanding of, the private equity industry. In 2000, PEF was inducted into the Private Equity Hall of Fame.

Influenced heavily by its former parent company, even after being spun off, PEF was acutely aware of the importance of a well-defined, strong culture. When its leaders asked us to do the value survey, it was like a young, healthy adult going for a physical checkup. The firm was running smoothly, morale was good, and financial results were excellent. If anything was a problem, it was the one we'd all like to face: too much growth! The firm had expanded from a small, tightly knit group of professionals into an international organization with 65 employees and offices in the United States and Britain. Its CEO and human resources director had discussed the need to assess this larger organization. Were the members of this larger team still on the same page? What were the core values of the group? Were there differences in values between the European and American employees? Between the partners and the staff? They wanted to address these questions and see what steps they should be taking.

All employees filled out the assessment, including the personal values piece. The results are shown in Figure 7.6.

1. *Limiting values.* There are no serious limiting values (that is, they did not show up in the top 10 vote). The limiting values that did appear, only slightly, were "blame," "internal politics," "risk-averse," and "caution."
2. *Matches.* Two matches ("integrity" and "balance") are present in all three hierarchies, and there are four matches between current and desired: "client satisfaction," "integrity," "balance," "teamwork." This result shows that the company is operating from a solid base of shared values.
3. *Full spectrum.* Both the personal and current values charts have representation of the full spectrum for PEF. The desired culture shows a heavy emphasis on values in the transformation level. The interpretation of this data is that PEF as a whole, with its heavy personal emphasis on level 5 values (meaning and purpose), wants to transform its current culture into an even more cohesive and strong culture. This is a good sign.
4. *Areas for further improvement.* In the discussion that follows, we provide a much more detailed look at areas for improvement and action steps. This last is, in part, to answer the pragmatist reader, who is probably asking, "What do I do with this information? What conclusions do I draw from it? What steps do I take?"

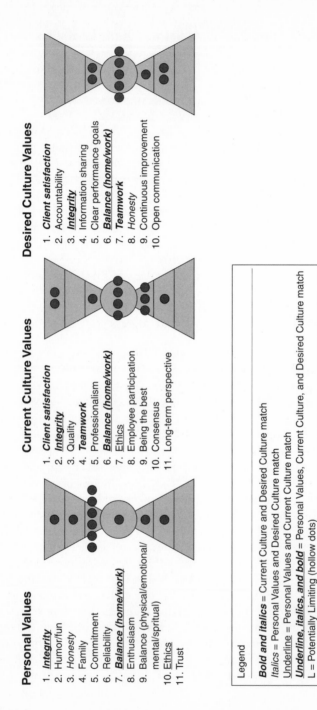

Personal Values

1. *Integrity*
2. Humor/fun
3. *Honesty*
4. Family
5. Commitment
6. Reliability
7. ***Balance (home/work)***
8. Enthusiasm
9. Balance (physical/emotional/mental/spritual)
10. Ethics
11. Trust

Current Culture Values

1. ***Client satisfaction***
2. *Integrity*
3. Quality
4. **Teamwork**
5. Professionalism
6. ***Balance (home/work)***
7. Ethics
8. Employee participation
9. Being the best
10. Consensus
11. Long-term perspective

Desired Culture Values

1. ***Client satisfaction***
2. Accountability
3. *Integrity*
4. Information sharing
5. Clear performance goals
6. ***Balance (home/work)***
7. **Teamwork**
8. Honesty
9. Continuous improvement
10. Open communication

Legend

Bold and italics = Current Culture and Desired Culture match
Italics = Personal Values and Desired Culture match
Underline = Personal Values and Current Culture match
Underline, italics, and bold = Personal Values, Current Culture, and Desired Culture match
L = Potentially Limiting (hollow dots)

FIGURE 7.6 Private Equity Firm (PEF). (Reprinted with permission: Richard Barrett, Corporate Transformation Tools®, www.corptools.com.)

DETERMINING THE CORE VALUES

The senior leadership had a well-developed appreciation for articulating the firm's values long before we met them. They had created their "guiding principles" with great enthusiasm and had effectively communicated them throughout the firm. The only problem was length: They had anywhere from 15 to 18 values. Central to the strategy of setting your values is keeping the number strictly limited. People have to be able to remember them easily. In three minutes or less, everyone at your firm should be able to answer: "What do we believe is important here?" Therefore, these leaders used the values assessment results to ascertain what the most important, or *core*, values were.

After a lively exchange, the leaders decided on these five values—and their definitions—as core for their firm:

- Client satisfaction.
- Quality.
- Teamwork.
- Integrity.
- Balance.

Note that these five values are virtually the same as those identified in the survey's current-culture portion. This is fine, as it indicates that the leaders are quite in sync with the employees; that is, they are all experiencing the same reality.

The next step was to define these words more carefully. Too often clients finish the hard work of agreeing on five or fewer core values, wipe their hands, pat themselves on the back, and say, "Great, now let's get back to work!" Big mistake. An important part of the values exercise is understanding your colleagues. It is more than an intellectual exercise about how *Webster's* defines certain words. One serious Swiss investment professional commented, after they finished the definitions exercise, "At first, I thought it was taking too long, but now I realize that the conversation was an important part of the exercise, not just the end result." Even in the difficult case of Allstar Capital, this exercise eased the tensions and began to restore trust and rapport.

In facilitating this exercise, we push for specifics. When a team member says, "*Integrity* means open and honest communication," we ask for an example. Tell us about a recent conversation with a colleague that was open and honest. What behaviors made you believe that he was being open and honest? "He looked me in the eye. He used direct language, without sugar coating. He took a risk and told me something I might not have liked." We also ask for an example of a conversation that did not seem to be open and honest. What behaviors were associated with that exchange? The benefit of these discussions for a team is that each member learns the expectations of her teammates. If you listen carefully, you will hear the guidelines for how to behave with them.

The downfall of most teams is that they simply assume what it means to, say, be respectful, when in fact they may have very different expectations. On my first business trip, my boss and I shared a suite of rooms in New York. When dinner time approached, I knocked on his door to see what the plan was for the evening. For this innocent action, I got a thorough chewing out. "In my house," he said, "when a person's door is closed it means they don't want to be disturbed!" Well, excuuuuuuuse me. How was I to know this custom and his expectations? Only one way: talk it out.

When we finished the discussion of values with the PEF team, they added these definitional bullets to their original five words:

Client satisfaction
> *Investment performance*
> *Communications*
> *Responsiveness*
> *Trusted advisor*

Quality
> *Professional*
> *Accurate*
> *Relevant*
> *Consistent*

Balance
> *Sustained stimulating and energetic environment*

Teamwork
> *Shares information*
> *Collaborative*
> *Positive attitude*
> *Meets commitments*

Integrity
> *Sound judgment*
> *Clients first*
> *"Walk the talk"*
> *Open and honest*

After thus defining the values more carefully, we established a baseline measure for each of these values. Measurement allows your team to set priorities as to which values are most in need of attention, given current goals at your firm. The bars in Figure 7.7 show current levels and levels needed to achieve the firm's objectives.

The benefit of a rating exercise like this is that it ties values into the strategic goals of the firm. By specifically asking, "How important is this value to achieving your goal?" you connect the two. In PEF's case, the largest gap was for "teamwork." In this way, you can use the information from the desired-culture survey to guide improvements, as the following sections show.

PLANNING FOR IMPROVEMENT

After they had agreed on the firm's values, the diagnostic information helped guide PEF's next steps, both for its strategic plan and for actionable next steps that could be taken right away. Here are the key elements from the results of the values assessment:

Current Strengths of PEF

- The PEF people are an exceptionally honorable group, as shown by their Personal Values of **honesty, integrity, ethics,** and **trust.** Their values

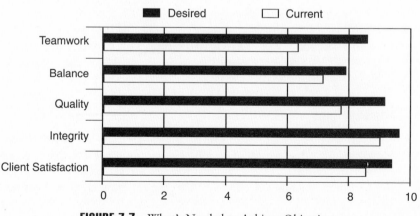

FIGURE 7.7 What's Needed to Achieve Objectives

of **humor/fun** and **enthusiasm** reveal that they are dynamic and upbeat. These are people who can be counted on to do what they say they are going to do, as demonstrated by **commitment** and **reliability**. Their outside lives are important to them, as seen with **family** and **balance (home/work)**. They understand the importance of taking care of themselves with **balance (physical/emotional/mental/spiritual)**.

- This is an organization that has a primary focus on meeting the needs of their customers, as depicted by the number one Current Culture value of **client satisfaction**.
- The people work to a high set of standards, as reflected by **integrity** and **ethics**.
- PEF is a working environment that invites and respects the contribution of all with **teamwork, employee participation** and **consensus**.
- Its values of **quality, professionalism** and **being the best** depict its commitment to excellence.
- There is little difference in values between the leaders and the staff.

Key Opportunities for PEF

- The people want a culture with stronger lines of communication, as shown by their Desired Culture values of **information sharing, honesty** and **open communication**.
- The employees want a working environment where people take responsibility for their actions, as depicted by the Desired Culture value of **accountability**.
- The value of **clear performance goals** indicates a need for defined directions for all.
- The employees would like focus placed on **continuous improvement**.
- Accounting/Operations (note: shown in separate breakouts) is hindered by the dynamics of **blame** and **internal politics**. The Direct Investment department may be adversely affected by **risk-averse**. London may be held back by the value of **caution**.

Recommendations

- Find out what the employees mean by the values of **information sharing, honesty,** and **open communication**. How would these values appear in everyday behaviors? Ask what obstacles are standing in the way of these efforts. Then begin processes that would implement and support these values.

- Decide on how to create and provide **clear performance goals**. This is a value that every demographic group has listed.
- Hold small group discussions to ascertain what **accountability** means and how it would be seen in day-to-day life. Determine how this would be rewarded.

Possible Strategies

- Determine what are behind the potentially limiting values of **blame, internal politics, risk-averse** and **caution** and rectify. These are the problem areas that need initial attention. The antidotes to these may be found in each group's Desired Culture values. Ask the employees what they see as the causes and manifestations behind each value and the corrective actions that they or others might take. As well, you may want to do an analysis on what each is costing you in lost opportunity, productivity and employee satisfaction.
- Discuss ways to embrace and support **continuous improvement**.
- Look to see which groups or departments are already living a Desired Culture value to learn how they are accomplishing this.
- Determine how to strengthen the values of **integrity** and **balance (home/work)**.
- Become aware of what the similarities and differences are between each of the demographic groups and how to work with them.
- Note that the values of **honesty, integrity,** and **balance (home/work)** reflect the Personal and Desired Culture Values of the people. Find out how well current processes and systems are working to encourage or discourage these.

NEXT STEPS

With the results of this culture assessment, leaders should consider these next four steps, with a particular focus on implementation and follow-through:

1. Provide information on the results to all those who participated. It is important that employees know:
   a. that their voices have been heard (via the survey).
   b. the results and implications of the values work.
2. Develop a Strategy and Action Plan to address the key findings of the values assessment report. The participants should learn of your intentions in this respect as well.

3. Ensure that expectations are reflected in the firm's performance evaluation process.
4. Review all means of regular communication to ensure that everyone is updated on progress made, from an individual level through to firm-wide progress on strategic goals.

SUMMARY

A values assessment is a very quick way to find out about your staff's alignment. You can quantify what behaviors your staff believes are being rewarded. Contrast this with what behaviors they believe *should* be rewarded to reach your goals. In this way, specific and measurable steps can be taken to foster the kind of culture that will ensure results.

TEST YOURSELF

Ask yourself the following yes/no questions. This test assumes that you have a set of specific values or guiding principles. (If not, revisit Chapter 2!)

Yes   No

1. Have you ever conducted a rating of the values?
2. Do your strategic goals or annual plans include improvements based on your values?
3. Do you have a means by which you can evaluate your firm's performance against your values?
4. Do you have a means by which you can tell how you should be performing against your values to achieve your goals?

CHAPTER 8

Leadership and Trust

Trust is our number one asset at Vanguard. We recognize you can't buy trust with advertising or salesmanship; you have to earn it—by always acting in the best interests of customers.
—Jack Brennan, CEO, Vanguard[1]

If a firm's leadership has credibility and trust, the organization is likely to have a strong culture and sense of purpose.
—Paul Schaeffer, SEI Investments (formerly of
Capital Resource Advisors)[2]

Leadership, trust, and sustainable cultures are inherently intertwined. In this chapter, you will learn:

- The three core elements of trust and effective leadership.
- How you can evaluate trust levels at your firm.
- How trust and leadership affect your firm's quantifiable results.
- How to improve trust levels.

Sally is pursued relentlessly by a previous employer in New York City. They fly to visit her in Houston, where she is working at another financial firm. They offer her lots of money and perks. They even contact her parents to see if they will try to influence her. Eventually, Sally relents and goes back to work in Manhattan with the old firm. At the end of the first year, she is the second highest producer in the mergers-and-acquisitions area. In the midst of this triumph, the firm fires her. The reason: firm-wide cost-cutting efforts.

The severance includes payment of an $80,000 bonus for her good results. A senior partner of the firm pulls her aside and says that he has seen the year-end bonus figures and that $80,000 is low by a factor of 10. Sally sues the firm and they settle out of court. The firm pays her $600,000, but insists that she sign a confidentiality agreement.

Do you trust the leadership at this firm?

The CIO repeatedly tells the director of research at a large Midwestern investment firm that the latter's salary is too low relative to McLagan data. This CIO tells the director that the situation will be "rectified in the near future." The CIO also hints at a promotion to deputy head of the department. Months go by and nothing changes. Eventually, someone outside the firm fills the deputy position. The director of research leaves to join another firm.

Do you trust this CIO?

John is an analyst with a mutual fund company specializing in growth stocks. He has been with the firm for five years. He is well liked, gregarious, and hard-working. He is studying for the CFA designation but has failed the first exam twice. His stock picks for the portfolio have underperformed in each of his five years. The director of research has calculated a Sharpe ratio for each analyst and John's is -1.9. John stays on at this firm.

Do you trust John to invest your money?

At Allstar, clients and staff are leaving. A senior staff member confides in us that he is leaving as well, he just hasn't decided when. We ask him what aspect of the situation forced his decision. He responds, "It's not the loss of clients or the bad performance or any of that, it's that I don't trust anyone here."

All of these stories are true. (John eventually did get fired and is now working as a tennis pro. The senior staff member at Allstar did leave.)

Trust is at the heart of the investment world. Investment counselors have a fiduciary responsibility to their clients. They are expected to put their own interests after those of the client. Most people realize this, which is why countless surveys of financial consumers show that trust is by far the most important factor in choosing a financial advisor. The average American is yearning for a square deal, a fair shake, a level playing field, and fewer clichés.

TRUST AND LEADERSHIP

You may be thinking, "Of course, trust is important to success. Tell me something I don't know!" In fact, trust seems to be so obvious a requirement for the leadership of great organizations that Jim Collins, in his excellent books on the topic, doesn't even discuss trust. It's as if Collins assumes that trust is necessary, in the same way we assume that oxygen is necessary for human life.

But current events paint a very different picture: the $1.4 billion Wall Street settlement; Enron, WorldCom, Andersen, Tyco; Philip Morris, which was hit with a $10.1 billion judgment for claiming, falsely, that "light" cigarettes were safer. These stories are putting trust to the test at whole new levels, both in the general business community and in the investments marketplace. The leadership teams in these scandal-ridden organizations operated on a double standard. They believed that they could show an ethical front to the public while operating unethically behind the scenes. They believed that being honest and being successful don't mix. Rather, they thought that competitive advantage is gained by flouting the rules and not getting caught. A *Wall Street Journal* article on Enron put it this way:

> *[Enron] became adept at giving technically correct answers rather than simply honest ones.*
>
> *One senior Wall Street official recalls recently asking Enron officials whether the company had retained bankruptcy counsel. He was told no. He later found out that while Enron hadn't formally retained such representation, it had met with bankruptcy lawyers. "If you don't ask the absolute right question, you don't get the right answer," he says. "Enron does that a lot."*
>
> *Yet public trust, above all, was what Enron had to have, in order to conduct its business as a trader and party to thousands of contracts.*[3]

The Wall Street brokerage settlement has not yet been completely resolved. "This is like World War II," said Columbia University securities law professor Jack Coffee. "Wall Street is fighting on four or five different fronts."[4]

Regulators blame Wall Street firms for blocking a final deal. In mid-2003, the state of New Jersey was locked in a tense war of words with the firm it investigated, Bear Stearns, and its top outside counsel, Dennis Block of Cadwalader Wickersham & Taft. Though all three parties declined comment, people close to the situation say Bear Stearns returned a New Jersey draft settlement document with most of the wrongdoing charges crossed out. Basically, Bear Stearns was continuing to deny that its analysts hyped stocks to win lucrative investment banking business.

Similarly, as of the same time, Massachusetts had been in a public battle with Swiss bank Credit Suisse First Boston for months. Knowledgeable sources said that the Massachusetts Secretary of State, William Galvin, was fed up with CSFB's attempts to delete the word *fraud* from a final settlement document. Galvin could not be reached; CSFB declined comment.[5]

BOILING FROGS

How do companies end up so far astray? Marianne Jennings, a professor of legal and ethical studies at Arizona State University, uses the term *ethics creep* to explain this phenomenon. Leaders take small steps over the ethics line until gradually they are way into the territory labeled "corruption." This is analogous to the well-known study in which frogs are placed in a pot of water. Heat is applied very slowly, until the water starts to boil, but the frogs never jump out, because the increase in temperature is so gradual. Eventually the frogs boil to death. Likewise, leaders who get scalded in their own ethical waters often express disbelief at what has happened. "How did it go this far?" they wonder. Same way: a very gradual increase in temperature. (Those of us watching our waistlines can certainly relate to "creep" as it applies to overeating: a sliver, a slice, a slab, a slob!)

Actually, the ethical debacles in business make the case for trust better than any piece of academic research ever could. Investors watched nearly $200 billion of market value evaporate as the truth about Enron and World-Com surfaced. It's impossible to ignore calamities of that magnitude. Now, even the most profit-driven bosses are taking steps to make sure that their businesses are clean. Values, ethics, and trust are becoming a hot topic as Wall Street struggles to regain credibility and Washington clamps down with tougher sanctions on white-collar crime.

This proves that trust and business practices are inextricably entwined, but what does the research show about trust and leadership? Is trust critical to effective leadership?

The Center for Creative Leadership, in Greensboro, North Carolina, has been researching the topic of leadership for decades, and has concluded that the best, most accurate predictor of success in an organization is leadership that behaves with integrity and honesty. In addition to these two core traits, three other related traits were identified: "loyalty, trustworthiness, and pride."[6]

Alfred Decrane Jr., chairman of Texaco Inc., reached a similar conclusion from his own experience in business:

> *Real leaders are fair and honest, and not just because of laws and regulations; they are ethical, open, and trustworthy. These basic roots of character, perhaps more than any others, garner the respect that is*

needed in order for an individual to be called a leader. I've been in business long enough to see that short-term "wins" can be achieved without these qualities, but I've also seen that lasting leadership and success—at whatever level—is impossible without them.[7]

QUANTIFYING TRUST

More evidence of the importance of trust comes from a study performed by Bruce Pfau at Watson Wyatt Worldwide. He and his colleagues studied 750 North American and European companies to discover the relationship between various human resource practices and stock prices.[8] The study by Watson Wyatt showed that "leaders play a key role in the establishment of a collegial company culture. Improving the trust and integrity associated with company leadership builds shareholder value by 2.3%."[9]

Hmmm . . . 2.3 percent doesn't sound like much, you might say. Well, pick a company at random; say, Allstate Insurance Company. Its market value is around $30 billion. A 2.3 percent increase represents a dollar gain of $690 million. That will pay for a few bent fenders.

Another piece of evidence is provided, indirectly, by Collins and Porras in *Built to Last*. Collins and Porras don't examine trust explicitly, but they do name "consistency" between core values and actions as one of the characteristics of visionary companies.[10] Trust is the by-product of companies that are consistent in this way, companies that "walk their talk." In fact, this consistency is the most dramatic difference between the visionary companies and the list of comparison companies that Collins and Porras chose in the study. Thirteen of the visionary companies (out of 18 selected) met this criterion, whereas none of the 18 comparison companies met it.

An example of integrity is the visionary company Johnson & Johnson. Its response to the Tylenol poisoning crisis in the 1980s was completely consistent with its values. When it was discovered that a few bottles of Tylenol had been tampered with, J&J pulled *all* the bottles off the shelves, despite the high cost. Another, more recent example of integrity is Baxter. Some of its kidney dialysis machines malfunctioned and caused the death of several patients. Baxter's CEO, Harry Kraemer, immediately assumed responsibility, shut down all production of the machines, and set up a relief fund for the victims. (While Baxter was taking these actions, the leaders of Arthur Andersen were saying, "We didn't do anything wrong," with straight faces.) Given that Baxter had only recently acquired the company that actually produced the faulty dialysis machines, Kraemer could have excused himself and Baxter and blamed it all on the new subsidiary. Instead, he didn't even mention that fact, taking full responsibility for the harm.

TRUST IN THE INVESTMENT INDUSTRY

Now it's time to focus specifically on the investment industry. The data represented in Figure 8.1 is from the International Association of Financial Planners.[11] Typically, a roomful of financial advisors readily agrees that trust is critical to their business, above any other factor. Given that trust is so important to their success, it makes sense to assume that financial advisors have a clear working definition of *trust*. After all, how can you practice being trustworthy if you don't know what it means? Interestingly, though, very few financial analysts have a ready definition at their fingertips. Rather, they rely on the old test for obscenity: "I know it when I see it."

Trust can be a tricky business, though, and we prefer to work with a definition that breaks it into three components. (We are indebted to Robert Bruce Shaw, author of *Trust in the Balance,* for this approach.[12]) These three components are:

1. CONGRUENCE: aligning words and actions *"I'll have the report ready for your next visit." (And you do!)*
2. COMPETENCE: demonstrating skills and abilities to do the job *"I have a CFP and a CFA designation."*

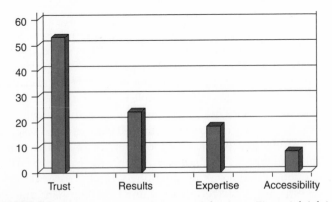

FIGURE 8.1 Most Important Factor in Selecting a Financial Advisor

3. CARING: Showing sincere concern for others *"I treat clients as I would family or friends."*

Violating or ignoring any one of these components can cause people to see you as untrustworthy. Revisit the stories at the beginning of this chapter and ask yourself which of the three components was violated in each one. (In some cases it could be more than one.)

The first case, with Sally, involves the third component: caring. At no time did the firm promise her lifelong employment, nor did it promise her a certain level of bonus. In this sense, no promises were broken. However, the message to Sally was clear: *Our interests come before yours. Never mind that you relocated back to New York, worked hard, got results, and trusted us to do the right thing. We're going to lay you off and chisel you out of a well-deserved bonus.* The only way Sally got her fair deal was by threatening a lawsuit. The firm's requirement that she keep the story confidential was a screaming confession of guilt. Consistency is good, but this firm was consistently sleazy. (Sally, by the way, had a bitter taste in her mouth after this experience on Wall Street and is now raising her kids on Main Street.)

For many, the concepts of compassion and investing don't mix. Compassion is a topic for ministers and rabbis; investing is a topic for hardened traders and shrewd strategists. Okay, then, take this quiz. Read the following quote:

> *We must open our hearts to greater love than we have ever imagined. Hold our families even tighter, appreciate our colleagues even more, show our neighbors even more respect; and honor all of those whom we meet along the road of life, from the highest to the humblest, even with a single gesture or a simple kindness.*[13]

Now, guess which of the following persons said it:

- Martin Luther King Jr.
- Mahatma Gandhi.
- The Dalai Lama.
- Jack Bogle.

Right. Jack Bogle. Surprised? We might have been, too, at the beginning of our research, but the more leaders we interviewed, the more we found an incredible depth of compassion and heartfelt concern for others. As Claude Rosenberg Jr., author of many books on investing and a leader at RCM Capital Management, said, "Empathy and humility are required for properly managing the people in the investment management industry."[14]

Patrick O'Donnell once told me that he believed his role was to "nurture" the analysts, and he quickly added, "I make no apology for using the word 'nurture.' If you don't want to nurture talent, you shouldn't be in the role." The lesson is that leaders who build trust do so with open hearts.

The second case was a fairly straightforward instance of promises made, promises broken. When my friend told me this story, I was careful to question him about whether the CIO had just dangled vague carrots in front of him, or had made solid promises. He said it was definitely the latter. My friend was not the only person who left this investment firm under these circumstances. This CIO, within a year of stepping into that job, had alienated nearly everyone on the staff. He told the real estate department members that their jobs were secure and then sold the portfolio and fired the staff over the next 18 months. This CIO was guilty of violating the caring component as well. Staff picked up on the fact that he was primarily interested in looking good to the CEO, not in looking out for his people. My friend left of his own accord and is now a CIO himself, running a $50 billion organization.

Honesty is a continuing problem in certain sectors of the investment world. In 1995, the Securities Industry Association commissioned a study on integrity, and one of the questions asked was, "Is honesty important in your job?"[15] Table 8.1 shows the results.

A separate study, done in July 1996 by a private market-research group, investigated the sales practices of 21 major brokerage firms. The ratings for "professional integrity" were "consistently mediocre, averaging a score of 73.5 of a possible 100. The best-performing firm, Smith Barney, scored only 75.1, a C in any professor's book."[16] Too many brokers' ethics resemble those skewered in a *New Yorker* cartoon mentioned earlier, in which a boss, at the head of a conference table, says to his team, "Honesty is the best policy. Okay, let's call that option A." Simple as it may seem, words and actions must align to build trust.

The third case involves the competency component. Most of us would trust John in the sense that he's a good guy and wouldn't lie to us. But would we trust him to lead us into battle? If our lives were on the line, would we want a captain who had repeatedly demonstrated weak judgment? Probably not. Often a case like John's is the hardest to deal with, because there is nothing malicious or devious about him. He wants to do well, and tries hard, but just can't seem to get the results. Most organizations will work with such a person to improve his or her skills. Eventually, though, if he doesn't improve, he has to go. Not only trust is at stake, but also the team's morale. It's hard to feel like a proud Marine when you've got Homer Simpson on your team.

Occasionally, you encounter a case that involves all three components at

TABLE 8.1 Integrity Study Results

Industry	Percentage Answering "Yes" to the Question: "Is honesty important to your job?"
Insurance agents	88%
Used-car salesperson	82%
New-car salesperson	78%
Real-estate agents	75%
Appliance salesperson	54%
Stockbrokers	52%

once. Consider, for example, West Virginia Consolidated Investment Fund. This group of investment professionals

> *invested commingled municipal pension and other funds to profit from higher returns available from capital-market investments (versus, for example, bank certificates of deposits). The investment officers in West Virginia were neither experienced or sophisticated, however, nor did they have outside advisers. After losing $280 million in 1987 by making incorrect bets on interest rates—and being forced to raise taxes to cover the loss—they claimed they had been pressured and lured into inappropriate high-risk investments by irresponsible securities salesmen.*[17]

So, not only did they demonstrate their incompetence, but then they also lied and said it was somebody else's fault. Bingo! A hat-trick: incompetent, dishonest, and uncaring. Wouldn't their mothers be proud?

Returning to the survey results shown in Figure 8.1, let's use our new three-point definition to reinterpret them. Rather than saying that trust is one of many factors in choosing a financial advisor, we see *all* the factors in the chart as important to trust. Renaming the factors according to our new definition yields this new list:

- CONGRUENCE means "walking the talk" and is usually interpreted as integrity, honesty, or trust. If someone is not honest or consistent with you, you don't trust that person.
- COMPETENCE means experience and results and is an important aspect of trust. Someone may be very honest, but if she does not have the skills and abilities to do the job, you won't trust that person.
- CARING may be demonstrated by accessibility. People who genuinely care about you and your financial well-being will make time to see

you and communicate regularly. Additionally, a financial advisor who really cares about you will be interested in more than just the money he can make from the relationship. Trust is built by genuinely caring about the client, over and above how the relationship serves your self-interest.

Before we look at the ways in which trust in an investment firm can be measured and strengthened by the leadership team, let's delve a little further into the relationship between financial advisor and client. Whether the relationship is retail or institutional, building trust is important to its success. Time and again we've talked to plan sponsors who have fired their plan managers, not because of weak performance, but because of poor rapport—that is, lack of trust. This is certainly the case with individual investors as well.

TRUST BUILDERS: KEY MESSAGES FOR DIFFERENT TYPES

In Chapter 4 we outlined the four basic cultures in the investment world. It is useful, in dealing with clients, to understand the values, beliefs, and behaviors of the people in each of these cultures. When you understand a person's values and beliefs, you know better how to communicate with her: What is important to her? What areas should you stress? What areas should you avoid? The following descriptions are intended to act as trust builders. You can use them to that end because they help you communicate more effectively with colleagues and clients. The Myers-Briggs Personality Type Indicator tells you which of the four temperaments you are dealing with (see Chapter 6).

The Guardian

Guardians constitute about 45 percent of the population. Their core values include order and belonging. The animal that best represents them is the beaver: industrious and group-oriented. Guardians come into life fearing that they might be overwhelmed by all the stimuli in their environment. They protect themselves by ordering their surroundings. They like plans and agendas.

Someone once quipped, "The way to make God laugh is to tell Him your plans." Guardians do not find this funny. Plans are important, almost sacred. Weekends are governed by a to-do list. The great fear of Guardians is chaos. If you know that one of your clients is a Guardian, clean up your office. Straighten the pictures on the wall. Adjust your tie.

The Adventurist

The core values of Adventurists, who make up 38 percent of the population, include action and freedom. The animal that captures their spirit is the fox: cunning and adaptable. Adventurists come into life fearing that they might be understimulated; they are natural adrenaline junkies. They are the first in line for shows like *Survivor*. "Give me a challenge" is their motto. They want action and adventure. The old cartoon with the two vultures ("Patience, my ass, I'm gonna kill something!") is the essence of Adventurists, whose great fear is boredom. If your client is an Adventurist, keep it lively.

The Rationalist

The 7 percent of the population that is Rationalists values knowledge and competency, as the name implies. Their symbolic animal is the owl: high in the tree, seeing the big picture, wise and revered. Rationalists come into life fearing that they may be overnurtured. They want to prove that they can make it on their own, and they want to be seen as competent. They are naturally competitive and are used to winning. They don't root for the underdog, and they rather like dynasties. (The New York Yankees will do fine, thank you.)

Because we laugh at our own foibles the loudest, a Rationalist friend of mine nearly hospitalized himself at a Woody Allen film in which Allen played a financial advisor. When asked about his approach to managing money, Allen's character responds, "I invest people's money until there is nothing left." My friend, a money manager, just howled at this appalling line. If your client is a Rationalist, you must impress him with competence and knowledge. Let these clients know, one way or another, that you are a winner.

The Communalist

The 10 percent of the population that is Communalist values relationships and harmony. Their animal is the dolphin, known to be highly intelligent and sensitive. Communalists come into life fearing that they may be undernurtured, or worse, abandoned. Therefore, they work hard to establish good relationships. They love harmony and abhor conflict. Often Communalists become mediators and counselors because they want to resolve conflict.

GUARDIAN	*Safety:* Focus on conservative, cautious approach. Give step-by-step instructions. Be practical. Talk about what has worked in the past.	**Beaver**
ADVENTURIST	*Excitement:* Focus on action and fun. Be brief. Use stories and humor to make your points.	**Fox**
RATIONALIST	*Performance:* Focus on excellence and results. Be logical. Show that your firm is a winner. Mention credentials and distinctions.	**Owl**
COMMUNALIST	*Relationship:* Avoid impersonal, bottom-line language. Take a personal interest in clients. Be authentic; don't "sell" them. Be casual and chatty.	**Dolphin**

FIGURE 8.2   Key Messages for Each Type of Client

They appreciate authenticity. A comedy scene involving an aspiring businessperson (played by Michael J. Fox) would amuse them. Fox's mentor advises him, "Above all, be honest." Fox's character responds, "No problem, I can fake that." Communalist clients don't want a slick sale. They want to have a genuine, heartfelt relationship with you. Casual and real is fine by them.

Key Messages for Clients

Figure 8.2 summarizes communication tips for each type. If you don't remember anything else about the four cultures, try to remember the key word associated with each one:

- Guardian: safety.
- Adventurist: excitement.
- Rationalist: performance.
- Communalist: relationship.

These key words can help you build trust because what they signify is at the core of each culture's basic personality. Remember them and you're less likely to step on an emotional land mine.

Our experience with investment cultures suggests that certain cultures are stronger on one component of trust than another. For example, Communalists tend to be naturally empathetic and send the message, "I care about you." Guardians tend to be honest and send the message, "My word is good." Rationalists and Adventurists are competitive and give people a sense that "you can trust me to get the results."

MEASURING TRUST LEVELS

To build trust, leaders must work on all three legs of the "trust stool":

1. Competence (helping the team achieve results).
2. Congruence (words and actions aligning).
3. Caring (showing empathy and a sense of being in this together).

Leaders can inventory themselves on these three scales. By surveying their colleagues and staff using the following list of statements, leaders get important feedback. Respondents should answer using a scale from 1 (strongly disagree) to 7 (strongly agree).

Competence/Results:

As a leader, I
1. *Articulate a clear strategic direction that will enable us to achieve our objectives.*
2. *Gain widespread agreement on necessary roles and accountabilities.*
3. *Make decisions on tough issues in a timely manner.*
4. *Hold people accountable to the highest standards of performance.*
5. *Create a sense of urgency and a drive to succeed.*

The second part of the trust inventory involves integrity. In this survey, leaders ask colleagues and staff to respond to the following:

Congruence/Integrity:

As a leader, I
1. *Act in a manner that is consistent with our organization's values and beliefs.*
2. *Am committed to a well-known strategic vision and set of values.*
3. *"Walk the talk" in following through on my commitments to others.*
4. *Hold people in the organization to the highest ethical standards.*
5. *Deal with reality as it exists, facing the hard truths.*

Finally, leaders must also show that they care for their associates. The simple image here is that of a captain and crew, where everyone is literally on the same boat. If the boat sinks, the captain and the crew all go down with it. This scenario fosters ultimate trust because it reminds everyone that their fates are tied together. Quite the opposite happens in many corporations. The Enron executives jumped off of that sinking ship with millions of dollars, leaving many of the crew financially devastated. There was no sense of caring; rather, it was every man for himself. (The same thing happens on ships, we might add. Bruce Ismay, owner of the *Titanic*, did not like the cluttered look created by 48 lifeboats on deck, so he ordered 28 of them removed. When the ship sank on its maiden voyage, there were not nearly enough lifeboats for the 2,228 passengers and crew—but owner Ismay found a seat on one of them.)

Remember the investment CEO on the West Coast, who was told by his board of directors to lay off 30 employees? That CEO agonized over the decision and, when he finally agreed, personally met with every one of the designated employees, explained the reason for the layoff, and apologized. We've since spoken with some of those employees and every one of them would like to work for that CEO again if they had the chance. Caring builds trust. The underlying attitude of caring is "We're all in this together."

The third part of the trust survey measures a leader's ability to empathize with employees:

Empathy/Caring:

As a leader, I
1. *Care about people and treat them as more than a means to an end.*
2. *Treat others as partners, sharing both risks and rewards of performance.*
3. *Believe that all people are capable of great accomplishments, and empower them to act.*

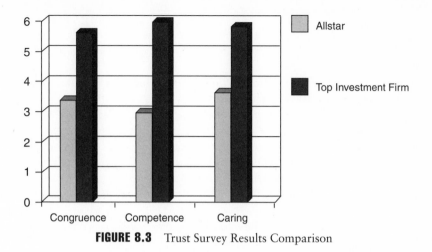

FIGURE 8.3 Trust Survey Results Comparison

4. *Strive to provide the support (training, advice, etc.) needed for others to be successful.*
5. *Remain accessible to people and open to discuss key business issues.*

Using Allstar Capital (a firm where trust had deteriorated sharply) as an example, we can graphically display poor trust levels compared to those of an average of seven firms we used as comparisons (see Figure 8.3). If we could use only one assessment tool to gauge a firm's solidity or dysfunctionality, we'd choose the trust survey, because it has the best chance of revealing the capabilities of the firm's leadership and overall firm health.

MOVING FROM DISTRUST TO TRUST

For some people, the need to produce results conflicts with mandates of consistency and integrity. Therefore, leadership must strike a balance between employee autonomy (so as to produce results) and control of employees (so as to sustain consistency). In GE's investment group, a trader was charged with engaging in fraudulent practices in the interest of gaining results. So GE put in controls where needed, without changing its fundamental practice of allowing autonomy to achieve outcomes. The following is GE's leadership model, which helps to balance results and values.[18]

GE's Four Types of Leaders

1. *One who delivers on commitments—financial or otherwise—and shares the values of our Company. His or her future is an easy call: onward and upward.*
2. *One who does not meet commitments and does not share our values. Not a pleasant call, but equally easy.*
3. *One who misses commitments but shares our values. He or she usually gets a second chance, preferably in a different environment.*
4. *One who delivers on commitments, makes all the numbers, but doesn't share the values we all must have. This is the most difficult for us to deal with. Too often we look the other way [and tolerate] these Type 4s because "they always deliver," at least in the short term.*

Type 4s require development or removal. Inaction will do serious harm and potentially undermine everything else the firm stands for.

Overcoming distrust requires tenacity and courage. Skepticism is natural to the investment industry. When trust issues develop, the people you

TABLE 8.2　Trust Corrections

Issue	Action Steps
Strategic mistakes	Take responsibility for the problem.
	Learn from the experience.
	Enforce accountability across all levels.
	Demonstrate immediate progress.
Ethical violations	Take immediate action.
	Conduct an organizational audit.
	Establish appropriate controls.
Brute-force management	Act on values and operating principles.
	Develop a culture in which people matter.
	Emphasize development and growth.
Downsizing	Focus on clients and markets.
	Act boldly.
	Communicate directly and truthfully.
	Provide ample support.
Reengineering/Restructuring	Focus on meeting client needs.
	Use high-involvement approaches.

count on to be skeptics turn up the intensity. What can you do to begin to move forward? Table 8.2 summarizes actions that can help.[19]

TEST YOURSELF

Ask your staff to work with you on the following:

1. Have your senior team take the inventory that appears at the end of this chapter. Compare your results with those of the top firms.
2. Have your staff evaluate the senior leader on the same inventory. Compare their results with those of the leadership team and the industry's top firms.
3. Where are your strengths and weaknesses? What action steps can you take?

Use the following scale to rate the statements below.

1	2	3	4	5	6	7
strongly disagree	disagree	disagree somewhat	neutral	somewhat agree	agree	strongly agree

As a team, we . . . [for the staff, it would be, "our leadership team members…"]

Congruence (Top firms' average = 5.6)

1. Openly share our perspective with people at all levels (even if opposing others' beliefs/values). _____
2. Hold each other to the highest ethical standards. _____
3. Act in a manner that is consistent with our expressed values/beliefs. _____
4. "Walk the talk" in following through on our commitments to others. _____
5. Deal with reality as it exists, facing the hard truths about our business, products, and ourselves. _____
6. Create an environment where we can, without fear, deal with issues openly and honestly. _____
7. Reveal our true motivations and avoid any form of manipulation in our interactions with others. _____
8. Are committed to a well-known strategic vision and set of values. _____
9. Deal fairly with others when problems or issues arise. _____

Competence (Top firms' average = 5.95)

10. Invest in and personally support the development and education of others. _____
11. Help others focus on a few key business priorities and clearly stated goals. _____
12. Recognize/reward successes and take action (feedback, development, or removal) on problems. _____
13. Gain widespread agreement on necessary roles and accountabilities. _____
14. Hold ourselves accountable to the highest standards of performance. _____
15. Create a sense of urgency and a drive to succeed. _____
16. Make decisions on tough issues in a timely manner. _____
17. Have articulated a clear strategic direction that will enable us to win in the marketplace. _____
18. Have the resources and autonomy we need to be successful. _____

Caring (Top firms' average = 5.8)

19. Remain accessible to each other, are willing to engage in dialogue about key business issues. _____
20. Have the flexibility we need to balance the competing demands we face. _____
21. Believe that all people are capable of great accomplishments, and empower each other to act. _____
22. Seek to understand others' point of view and the challenges they face. _____
23. Strive to provide the support (training, job opportunities, advice, etc.) needed to be successful. _____
24. Treat others as partners in the business, sharing both the risks and rewards of performance. _____
25. Work to create a common vision and a shared sense of purpose. _____
26. Expect each other to get results in a way that is consistent with our values. _____
27. Care about people and treat them as more than a means to an end. _____

PART Three

Getting Practical: Specific Tools for Improvement

CHAPTER **9**

Ambitious Goals
and Implementation

MFS's rapid rise in the pension world has been extraordinary.
—Rich Blake, institutional investor[1]

Collaborative goal setting is the natural next step after the identification of values, vision, and a distinct culture to keep your firm moving forward. In this chapter, you will learn:

- The specific components of large goals that will energize your people.
- The difference between personal and firm-wide focus.
- What it takes to bring goals to life.

The president of Allstar Capital sat across from us in the conference room adjoining his office. Two of his senior team had joined us for a debriefing on the results of the offsite retreat.

"Basically, it went well," he said. "In fact, we have already made progress on a number of the issues we touched on." He then ran down, item by item, the recommendations we had put together from their discussions, updating us on actions the group had taken. He was pleasantly surprised that his group had already made headway on a number of the next steps they had committed to. "I've heard some good feedback from our people. It does help to get away from the office and sort these things out. Of course, the most important thing is performance. If the numbers don't improve, all this teambuilding won't matter. We've got to hit our goal of 50 basis points over the benchmark."

Beth leaned toward him and said, "Remember that the work on values and vision, culture, strengths and weaknesses, etc., needs to be integrated with goals and action plans. The power of getting everyone on the same page, recommitting to a common vision and set of values, and getting reenergized is lost if there is no follow-through." Beth was alluding to the fact that the specific goal setting and action planning would only be as good as the follow-through. She asked the following series of questions:

"When are you getting together again to check on your progress?"
"How will you communicate about these plans to those who weren't here for the retreat?"
"How often do you plan to compare your progress relative to your expected timeline?"
"For every objective, who's going to do what by when?"
"Do your anticipated timeframes take into account prior commitments?"

When Beth finished, the president looked a little bewildered and said, "Yes, of course, all of those are key questions, I understand that," with a look that convinced us absolutely that he did *not* understand. Many leaders make this same mistake: They take the time to go offsite and work "on" the business rather than "in" the business (i.e., the day-to-day stuff). They are happy with the results. The staff is happy, too. They bask in the glow of some time well spent away from the trenches. They may wordsmith the values and vision statement. They may even hold a follow-up meeting with the entire firm to discuss it. And then, with all this wonderful momentum built up, they let it dissipate. They are swallowed up by the day-to-day battles. They strap on their helmets, fix their bayonets, and turn on their monitors. The analogy that came to mind was of the person who goes to a health resort for the weekend. She eats well, runs each morning, hits the weight machines, stretches in the yoga class, steams in the saunas. By Sunday night she feels like a new person. She commits to feeling this well all the time by continuing the healthy routine. By Wednesday evening, of course, she is sprawled on the couch, fast-food wrappers spread over the coffee table and floor, sipping a Coke and eating the last bite of a Dove bar. (Hmm. Maybe that suggestion from the health resort to find a personal trainer wasn't such a bad idea.)

We have seen the corporate version of this scenario play out many times. Therefore, it was no surprise when Allstar's president told us, "Thanks, you did a great job under difficult circumstances. We can take it from here." We responded that follow-through is absolutely essential to success and is usually where companies mess up. (One of the truisms of our field is that far too much emphasis is placed on strategic planning and far too little on follow-through.) The president looked at us with a smile, said, "We'll be fine," and escorted us out.

Well, bet you can guess how that story ends. In a moment, we'll consider a different leader and a different story with a very different ending.

BIG HAIRY AUDACIOUS GOALS

For now, let's stick with our approach of seeing how the *Built to Last* principles work in investment companies. In this case, we'll see if the top investment firms use what Collins and Porras call "BHAGs," short for Big Hairy Audacious Goals.[2] Then we'll look at the very practical nature of implementing goals and the questions that Beth raised with Allstar's president about follow-through.

Table 9.1 is the portion of the *Built to Last* scoresheet that deals with BHAGs. Table 9.2 shows the average scores for these criteria.

A famous example of a BHAG is the U.S. moon mission in the 1960s. At that time, the most optimistic scientific assessment of the mission's chances for success was 50–50, and most experts considered even that unrealistic. Nevertheless, President Kennedy's proclamation, on May 25, 1961, "that this Nation should commit itself to achieving the goal, before this decade is out, of landing a man on the moon and returning him safely to the earth" gave Congress the impetus it needed to appropriate $549 million and billions more over the next five years.[3] President Kennedy's goal statement had all the components needed to get people on board: It was clear. It was compelling. It was energizing. It was highly focused. And people "got it" right away. No lengthy build-up was required. No charts. No graphs. It was easily understood, meaningful in the context of its day, and definitely a BHAG. The characteristics of BHAGs are summarized in Table 9.3.[4]

Compelling goals are clear. "I've got to lose some weight" is not nearly as meaningful as "By July 4th, I will be 10 pounds lighter due to increased exercise and a healthy diet." You can ensure clarity by applying SMART criteria:

S: Specific
M: Measurable
A: Attainable
R: Relevant
T: Trackable

TABLE 9.1   BHAG Scoresheet

Category for scoring:	Score
II. Ambitious Goals	

Concept: Outstanding companies stimulate progress by setting ambitious goals. The core ideology described in part I provides stability for the company, whereas the ambitious goals stimulate change and motivate employees.

Use of ambitious goals to stimulate progress:	

+1	Significant evidence that the company repeatedly uses ambitious goals to stimulate progress.
0	Some evidence that ambitious goals are used, but inconsistently and less prominently.
−1	Little or no evidence that ambitious goals are used. Conservative strategies and certainty of results are emphasized.

Choice of truly "outrageous" goals:	

+1	Significant evidence that the ambitious goals were truly outrageously difficult and highly risky.
0	Some evidence that the goals were outrageous, but not as pronounced.
−1	Little or no evidence that the goals were outrageous.

Consistent usage of ambitious goals to stimulate progress:	

+1	Evidence that the company has used ambitious goals over time and through multiple generations of leadership.
0	Some evidence of the above.
−1	Little evidence that the company uses ambitious goals.

Score: Ambitious Goals	

TABLE 9.2 Average BHAG Scores

Success Criteria	*Built to Last* Average	Comparison Company Average
Use of ambitious goals to stimulate progress	.72	.17
Choice of truly "outrageous" goals	.72	0
Consistent usage of ambitious goals to stimulate progress	.06	−.56
Ambitious goals	1.50	−.73

TABLE 9.3 BHAG Characteristics

"Big Hairy Audacious Goals":

- Are so clear and compelling that they require little to no explanation, but still stir excitement in the listener.
- Fall well outside people's comfort zone. People should have some reason to make them try to pull off achievement of the BHAG and to make them believe that they can, even while they recognize that success will take more than they've done before.
- Are so bold and exciting in their own right that even if leadership changes before they're accomplished, they will keep moving the organization forward.
- Carry the risk of "we've arrived" complacency once they have been achieved. This requires planning of the next BHAG and complementary goals for other means of stimulating progress.
- Are consistent with the firm's identity.

For example, President Kennedy's moon mission statement not only fits both the BHAG and SMART criteria, it also includes a measure of success: "and return him safely to the earth." When goals are stated in this way, people can run with them.

CITICORP AND CHASE MANHATTAN: GOALS MAKE THE DIFFERENCE

Leaders can drive sustainable success by articulating these big goals. One of the company pairs studied by Collins and Porras was Citicorp and Chase. As

Collins and Porras pointed out, though both stumbled badly in the 1980s (as did most commercial banks at that time), Citibank successfully pulled out in front in the following decade. It did so on the strength of its goal setting and the inclusive nature of the process by which planning was done and accountabilities determined.

In the 1890s, City Bank (as Citicorp was known then) was made up of a president, a cashier, and a few employees. The president, James Stillman, stated that his goal was "to become a great national bank," and this drove the bank forward for generations. Frank Vanderlip, his successor, said in 1915 (when the bank had 8 vice presidents and fewer than 500 employees) that, "I am perfectly confident that it is open to us to become the most powerful, the most serviceable, the most far-reaching world financial institution that has ever been." George Moore, president from 1959 to 1967, sounded quite similar when he said, "Around 1960, [we decided that] we would seek to perform every useful financial service, anywhere in the world."[5] Eventually, after competing intensely for many years, Citicorp pulled out in front and became twice the size of Chase.

The key difference in the two banks' strategies was constant internal improvement (Citicorp) versus a primary focus on market and product strategies (Chase). Citicorp's leadership concentrated on management succession, management development, staff quality and training, whereas Chase focused on what the market was demanding right now.

Great companies set ambitious goals, then practice continuous improvement while reaching them. From our perspective, BHAGs of the type described by Citicorp's founders are not a far cry from the vision/mission framework we looked at in earlier chapters. BHAGs, though, go beyond just answering the important question, "What are we here to do?" Rather, they paint a dramatic picture of the completed goal.

BHAGs IN THE INVESTMENT WORLD

Of all the *Built to Last* principles, the practice of using BHAGs was the hardest to locate in the investment world. "Do you have some big, outrageous goals?" was the question that most often got the "Quayle in the headlights" reaction. Perhaps the most obvious BHAG for investment firms is simply a continuation of the Citicorp story. Under the leadership of Sandy Weill, Citigroup (once Citicorp) is making history with its attempt to be the world's greatest financial institution. When Citicorp and Travelers merged in April 1998, the deal was so "brash [that] its approval required an act of Congress and so big that both President Bill Clinton and Fed chairman Alan Greenspan [were] consulted beforehand. Citigroup, the company the merger gave birth to, threatened to dominate every aspect of financial services—from credit cards to stock brokerage, insurance to investment banking."[6]

The spirit of the BHAG clearly lives in Weill's bold attempt to form what he calls "the model financial institution of the future."[7] Though we salute his ambitious vision, we must caution that Weill defies nearly every principle in this book. He represents the antithesis of what we've written here, and as long as he succeeds you can justifiably question our approach. (Jeff Everett, CIO at Templeton, told us that Sandy Weill has been known to say, "What is culture but something you find in yogurt!") We agree with Samuel Hayes, professor of finance at Harvard Business School, who compares Citigroup's success "to the bumblebee, whose rotund body and tiny wings defy the physics of flight. Citi is the bumblebee that flew."[8] Nevertheless, Weill and his big dream are the stuff of BHAGs. (The latest developments in the Citigroup saga and Weill's decision to step down as CEO are the cover story of the June 2003 *Fortune* magazine: "Can Sally Save Citi?"[9])

Occasionally, investment leaders do refer to BHAGs. Bruce Bell, managing director at Oceanic Bank and Trust Limited, approached me after a presentation and said that he and his senior team had just returned from an offsite gathering specifically devoted to determining the firm's BHAG. Bell had read *Built to Last* and was intrigued with the idea of setting an outrageous goal for this team. When I asked what goal they had decided on, Bell responded with this: "We will be the premier provider of wealth management solutions from the Caribbean to a global client base by 2007."

Another example of a BHAG in the investment world comes from David Kundert, chairman and CEO of Bank One Investment Management Group. In 1992, the bank's then-chair, McCoy, asked Kundert and his team of 28 employees to create and build an asset management firm. Kundert applied the BHAG principle and stated that his group would not only survive in the asset management business, but would become a dominant player. A decade later, his group has grown to more than 500 employees managing $162 billion. They are the 16th largest mutual fund in the country. Kundert attributes much of this success to their culture. He says, "I'm a big believer that culture isn't easy to build. We got to build our own from scratch which seems easier than Jamie Dimon's job of changing a 75,000 person organization when he took over as CEO" of Bank One.

Bill Lyons, at American Century, said that his firm was close to adopting the BHAG of becoming the country's third largest mutual fund, after Vanguard and Fidelity. But the more they talked about it, the less enthusiastic they became. After all, one of the truths of the investment world is that clients rarely benefit from an active manager's growth. Many studies have shown that achieving positive outperformance simply gets harder as assets under management increase. For this reason, many firms that value client service close their funds when they reach a certain size. The typical goal of becoming bigger, then, just doesn't work in the investment business—at least not for everyone. Ariel Capital, in Chicago, has set some outrageous goals for itself, including becoming the number one small and mid-cap mutual fund in America. (We'll revisit this company and its goal setting later in the book.)

The quotation at the beginning of this chapter, from MFS, is a short statement about one of the most dramatic BHAG stories in the investment industry. Originally told by industry consultants that it should stay out of the institutional side of the business, MFS ignored their advice and took on the heavy hitters. The result? As an *Institutional Investor* article reported in December 2001:

> *[S]ince MFS plunged feet first into the institutional market nine years ago, it has amassed institutional assets of $31 billion. Even more startling, MFS pulled in $6.4 billion in new institutional accounts in the first 11 months of this year. (One notable trophy client: Frank Russell Investment Management Co.) And over the past couple of years, MFS has also raked in some $10 billion in defined contribution money.*[10]

Aside from MFS and Ariel (see Chapter 13), we found few examples of BHAGs in the investment world. There are at least two ways to interpret the industry's lack of interest in BHAGs. First, we could assume that the concept simply doesn't work well for investment firms, with the notable exception of the companies just mentioned. Perhaps because of the size issue, or for some other reason, BHAGs just aren't as useful.

A second interpretation suggests opportunity. Possibly BHAGs could be an additional tool to use in gaining a competitive advantage in financial markets. This may have been what Bruce Bell had in mind when his group went on retreat. It has certainly paid off for MFS, in its bold initiative to enter the institutional market, and for Ariel, in the small and mid-cap mutual fund market. In any event, we continue to monitor this element of sustainable success to see if more evidence presents itself.

GLOBAL INVESTMENT INC. AND GOAL SETTING

As we saw in the opening story, Allstar's leadership decided to skip the goal-setting and follow-through steps after the offsite retreat. The pain had temporarily lessened and they were glad to get back to business as usual. Many leaders do this, but not all.

In contrast, when the managing director of Global Investors' Asset Allocation and Risk Management division contacted us, there was a note of urgency in his voice. He and his team assist in the quantitative job of running one of the largest asset pools in the world. He had been charged with combining three different firms on four continents into a seamless team and achieving a very ambitious set of goals in a matter of months. From our first conversation, this leader made it clear that follow-through must be part of the consulting proposal. He had worked with facilitators who ran good offsite sessions and then disappeared. He wanted to make sure that we were in it for the long haul. We assured him that we were singing from the same hymn book.

At the offsite, the leader and his team capably answered the "who we are" and "what we stand for" questions with a clear articulation of values and vision. After some exploration of strengths, weaknesses, opportunities, and threats (basic SWOT analysis), we moved to collaborative goal setting. It doesn't matter whether you call this phase of firm leadership *strategic planning* or *action planning* or *determining strategic imperatives* or *long-term planning*. What does matter is ensuring that your firm participates in the regular exercise of defining and following through on "who will do what by when" for your internal and external improvements.

The goal the Global team agreed on was "To use cross-functional and cross-regional communication in order to achieve global process alignment and resource sharing." This goal falls well short of a big, hairy, audacious one, but it was still very ambitious given the circumstances and time constraints.

With their goal in mind, we used some basic project management techniques to help them design their action plan. The group had to come up with the specific steps that would lead to timely achievement of the goal. This is where people often fall into the how-to trap. They undertake a challenge they've never faced before and, naturally and justifiably, don't have a clue about exactly how they're going to get it done. Even asking "how" is a stopper. Instead, envision the achievement of the goal and then tell the story of what happened to create that success. Instead of asking "how"—that is, instead of starting from where we are—we ask the group to anticipate the successful attainment of their goal and have them answer as though looking back in time: "What did you do to make that happen?" The answers fly! Often we get so many answers that we have to work hard to pare them down to a truly realistic list of seven or fewer objectives. Why limit the number of objectives? Because people's plates are already full; goal setting works only if it's realistic.

The group then determines who will be responsible for each objective. That person oversees the drafting of a list of action items. When all the action items are roughed out, a timeline is created. Here is where a good understanding of project management helps, as people have a natural tendency to figure the timeline from start to finish. A better technique is to work backward, from the finish to the start. By working backward, the group is forced to answer the question "What must we have finished just before we work on this activity?" (This is the equivalent of planning your trip departure by saying, "To get to the airport by seven, I have to leave by six, which means I need to be in the shower by five-thirty, which means I need to be up by five.") The group plans the project while acknowledging and allowing for all the other predictable events that will vie for their time, such as conferences or performance evaluations. As we worked on the action plan, one member of the team thought he had at least six months before the project would actually have to start. After constructing the timeline backward, he realized that his group had to begin the following week!

The final plan included success measures, accountabilities, and timeframes that the group members would expect from each other. A number of their activities stemmed from the values rating you read about in Chapter 2. For example, they decided on a set of communication-type objectives, to improve teamwork. Again, being realistic is key. We had the group chart the activities on a wall-sized calendar to get a feel for real time. This turned out to be the only way they could see a three-week conflict that stood in their way: a standing commitment to complete performance evaluations. They had to work around this, but they made adjustments accordingly and proactively.

Getting agreement and closure on the "who does what by when" issues is three-fourths of the battle. The final part is a clear answer to "When do we talk about this again?" A sure formula for failure is to take the wonderful summary booklet, full of great insights and actionable ideas, and set it confidently on the shelf, thinking, "Surely we'll get to these ideas soon." If you do this, *it never happens*. You must schedule regular times to work on the goals. The Global Investors group decided to make its commitments a standing agenda item for the monthly meeting. They did, and they got their results: the timely achievement of most of their key milestones. They are now tying the accountabilities laid out in the action plans to their performance evaluation system. This will help ensure thorough communication and excellent integrity, as people get assessed on their performance relative to their commitments.

As an aside, one of the best goal setters we've ever seen is John Ward at ServiceMaster. During an offsite session in which he was first getting to know his senior staff, we watched as he relentlessly followed up every discussion with, "What's the action item?" and "When will you have it done?"

One of the powerful benefits of goal planning is that it shifts the onus away from you, the leader. The goals themselves, discussed and agreed upon by the whole team, become the focal point. You gain the leverage of your group's consensus about priorities and accountabilities. Also, as your firm's leadership changes over time, the focus on goals and the process for renewing them becomes the constant. It's true that what people focus on grows. At Allstar, people focused on the problems—and sure enough, they grew. The values, vision, and goals process described in this book places the focus on positive change. Despite all the possibilities for conflict in the Global case, there was relatively little dissension. As the team racked up more and more successes, the incidence of conflict was reduced even further. The habits of progress become ingrained. Accountability improves and the pride of ownership and belonging grows with it.

FOCUSING FORWARD

An important, and expected, effect of goal planning is the difference it will make in your group's attitude and motivation. Shared goals and a common understanding of the current challenge create a very positive foundation for day-to-day work. Particularly for investors, who are by nature pretty driven, having specific targets is critical. (Increasingly, we see "clear performance goals" surfacing as a top priority for investment firms.) You already have your business targets, of course, but if you add objectives that pertain to your values and the cultural elements outlined in Chapter 4, you will add to your capacity for sustainability. Although BHAGs capture the imagination as far as large-scale goals, many professional service firms will find that moderate improvements on current systems and processes are the way to go. This is where the values assessment tool described in Chapter 7 is relevant, to help your firm decide which internal improvements to concentrate on. When your staff people have described their view of the best environment, they can focus on making it happen.

ACCOUNTABILITIES: WHO DOES WHAT BY WHEN?

Deciding on your strategies and doing the action planning for implementation is a bottom-up process. The same people who are going to be responsible for the results should create the plans, the measures of success, the timeframes, and the consequences of success and failure. Maister calls the role of leadership in this regard that of "friendly skeptics," who will ask the challenging questions and help guide the process through to final approval of a plan.

The action plans get the bulk of the attention. Implementation and follow-through are the hard challenges, as these ideas are above and beyond the intense daily workload that people are already managing. Great ideas may be abundant, but resources are not. A quick way to deflate a group's enthusiasm and trust is to shortchange them on resources after they have committed. Leadership as a shared responsibility is exemplified in this process.

PERSONAL FOCUS VERSUS FIRM-WIDE FOCUS

At Allstar, we saw the result of personalizing the current state of the business. The primary focal points were demonstrated by a combination of questions like "Who's to blame? Who can we lean on to do better? When is he going to change? What's the matter with her?" There was no concentrated focus on shared ideas for improvements, only the offensive implication that if certain people hadn't been so wrong, we wouldn't be in this mess. This kind of personal negativity guarantees a downward spiral.

Particularly during rough times and times of change, people need a focal point outside themselves. By clearly answering—together—the question of "what do we want next?" your firm can unite in support of a shared plan of action. As they clarify roles and responsibilities, they can move quickly on their own toward their preferred future.

TEST YOURSELF

Ask yourself the following yes/no questions:

                                                                          Yes   No

1. Do you have a regular cycle of goal setting or short-term strategic planning?
2. Are the people who are responsible for the results also responsible for the planning?

Yes   No

3. For your high-level goals, does everyone understand who is responsible for what and by when?
4. Are the goals that you identify tied into your performance evaluation process?
5. Is leadership perceived as sharing in the goal-setting and alignment systems?
6. If asked, would people give high marks to the leadership's ability to guide the collaborative goal-setting process?
7. Do you have an accountability plan to keep yourselves advised about progress and obstacles?

8. What are your next steps in regard to collaborative goal setting?

CHAPTER 10

The Innovative Culture

There are several key success factors for asset managers in the future, and one of them is creating an innovative culture.
—Guy Moszkowski, Managing Director, Salomon Smith Barney[1]

The ability to innovate is a critical edge for *Built to Last* companies. In this chapter, you will learn:

- The characteristics of an environment that promotes innovation and creativity.
- The guidelines for creativity discussions.
- The three critical elements of creativity.
- How to assess the creativity styles present in your firm.
- How to influence people with different creativity styles.

The chief investment officer of a large global firm looked at the agenda for the two-day leadership offsite. It included time to discuss progress on various action plans, time to review results from asset classes, and time to examine the way that staff members are rewarded for performance. There was also some time set aside in the evenings for dinner and socializing.

"I want to do something different on the second day. I think we should have an expert on time management help us get our workloads under control."

I waited to see the reaction of the nine department heads around the table. They looked unconvinced. I said, "Well, we are experts on that topic. We have trained hundreds of groups over the years."

"Good," said the boss. "So you could put something together for us? Say a half day on efficiency skills?"

Beth, as usual, asked the right question: "What are the outcomes you would want?"

The group then spent a few minutes discussing the question and came back with ideas like, "doing more with less," "faster implementation of our plans," "ways to handle all the e-mails and phone calls." Beth nodded, making notes of these suggestions.

I waited a few minutes and then directed their attention to a page, in front of each of them, that contained the most recent values ratings. Before the meeting, Beth and I had discussed the fact that the largest gap between current and desired ratings for their values was the one called "Thought Leadership." This group had discovered their five values in a previous offsite session, defined them, and baselined the ratings. Over the next 18 months, the values for four of the five had steadily improved; the only laggard was Thought Leadership. This was the value that incorporated innovation, coming up with unique insights and proprietary investment processes.

"The biggest gap on your values rating," I said, "is for Thought Leadership. We believe that might be a good place to concentrate." I added that my first book dealt with creativity in the investment industry and that we had worked with many clients on these skills.

One department head immediately chimed in. "Great. Could we do something with creativity? I know workload management is an issue, but we all agree that thought leadership is something we need right now."

The conversation wandered for a few minutes with no resolution as to how to handle the special topic. Eventually, one of the department heads forced the issue again: "So, can we do some work on creativity?"

The CIO looked at me and said, "Can we do something in the time we have available?"

"Yes, and we should include some prework so we can hit the ground running."

"All right," he said. "But I want the outcome to be very practical, not some theoretical discussion. And I'm not singing *Kumbaya* after the group hug." The group around the table laughed.

We finished up our planning and the meeting adjourned.

CREATIVITY AS A CULTURAL ISSUE

This CIO's view of creativity is like that of many we've encountered in the investment world. Creativity, they believe, is absolutely critical to investment success. As active managers, they must add unconventional ideas to their portfolios. They cannot simply follow the crowd. They have to encourage their team to think differently from other professional investors. Art Zeikel, formerly of Merrill Lynch, makes the same point: "[P]rofessional investors go to the same schools, read the same books and reports, and follow the same valuation guidelines, so it's no wonder that they tend to reach the same conclusions—and tend to get the same mediocre results."[2]

These same CIOs who believe in the importance of creativity also believe that there is a recipe for implementing it. In the sample case that begins this chapter, the CIO was saying, in essence, "[T]ake half a day, teach us the formula, and then we'll go do it and be done with it."

This is where creativity and culture come together. Creativity, like trust, integrity, or discipline, is not a formula. Rather, it's an attitude and a series of behaviors that are encouraged (or discouraged) in the culture. Returning to a premise of this book, the best investment professionals have earned that distinction because their mental models are superior. The road maps in their brains can guide them skillfully through more (and more varied) terrain than the average person's can. The problem, as Michael Mauboussin at CSFB correctly points out, is that "mental models require upfront investments of time and energy. At first, there is no quick payoff. It's only after a while that you get the dividends." Mauboussin agreed with us that the diagnostics and tools discussed in this chapter for enhancing creativity work—but they work only if they are practiced and become habitual. The need for unique insights in the investment business has reached the point where many individuals and firms are taking creativity work seriously.

The ongoing need for new and improved products and ways to do business is why many of the *Built to Last* companies include creativity in their core values (see Table 10.1).

In more than half of the *Built to Last* companies, creativity (or its more practical sister, *innovation*) is specifically stated as part of the culture; that is, it is specifically recognized as being important to their success. The seven *Built to Last* companies that did not include creativity as a core value had clearly decided that it was not critical to their business success, or that creativity was subsumed by another value, such as "continuous improvement" (which is a stated value for four of the seven). In any event, leaders must protect and exemplify the values of the organization. Therefore, if they have chosen creativity as a core value, then it is their charge to see that it lives within their firms.

In Chapter 2, when we discussed values, we emphasized the importance of congruence. When there is congruence, the values really reflect the truth of the firm and its people. Enron was cited as an example of incongruence. In the area of creativity, we know of a large financial firm that had similar problems with incongruence. One of the firm's core values was innovation.

TABLE 10.1   Companies' Inclusion of "Creativity" Value

Company	Creativity in Core Value
Motorola	Tapping the "latent creative power within us."
Sony	To experience the sheer joy that comes from the advancement, application, and innovation of technology.
Wal-Mart	Swim upstream, buck conventional wisdom.
Walt Disney	Continuous progress via creativity, dreams, and imagination.
3M	Innovation: "Thou shalt not kill a new product idea."
Citicorp	Being out front—such as biggest, best, most innovative, most profitable.
General Electric	Improving the quality of life through technology and innovation.
Johnson & Johnson	Decentralization = Creativity = Productivity.
Merck	Science-based innovation, not imitation.

The choice of "innovation" as a core value was unusual, because this firm was in the commodity end of the insurance business. Nothing about its business suggested that they needed to be on the cutting edge, nor had they distinguished themselves in this area. Further, the culture was decidedly Guardian. These leaders and their employees were steady, solid, dutiful, and precise. Many of them were CPAs and actuaries. To be fair, one of their leaders, a capable and bright guy, told us that he thought "Innovation" for them was spelled with a little "i."

We were surprised, then, when this firm underwent a massive brainstorming exercise. The top 100 officers in the company were called into this effort; guest speakers like Gary Hamel addressed these sober Guardians about breakthrough thinking from his book, *Leading the Revolution*.[3] (That must have been a little like watching Shirley Maclaine address a group of Southern Baptists on the finer points of reincarnation.) All participants received crystal globes with the inscription, "Big ideas can change the world."

After all this hoopla, and months of meetings and brainstorming, we wondered if anything had substantially changed within the company. I called the "little-i" leader mentioned earlier and asked him what changes had resulted. He laughed and said, "Well, we've got a new brochure on safe driving." That was the upshot of this push for "big ideas."

What happened? Why did this effort flop?

The company was sincere in its efforts to promote innovation. It got all the senior people involved. It gave them resources. It certainly spent a ton of money, time, and effort on this initiative. Why, then, were there no fruits from the labors?

In our opinion, the answer lies in the little-i leader's view of innovation, and in their culture. Guardian cultures are usually strong in little-i creativity. They are very good at working within existing frameworks and models. Continuous improvement is their mantra. Total Quality Management initiatives fit them perfectly. They are great tweakers of existing products, models, or processes. They are not naturally given to breakthrough thinking. They prefer steady and rather linear improvement, firmly rooted in the success of the past.

The other three cultures that we described earlier—Adventurist, Rationalist, and Communalist—are all more likely to embrace Innovation with a capital "I". The investment leaders we know fit neatly into one of these two camps: little i or big I. Jack Brennan, Parker Hall, and Gary Brinson are process-oriented, very much little-i people. Dean LeBaron, Ralph Wanger, and Rob Arnott are breakthrough thinkers. They enjoy figuring out the new paradigm and discarding the old one. When asked about his creative process, Arnott gave this answer:

> *I'm an ENFP, but also a curmudgeonly questioner of conventional thinking. When something is a widely held belief, I just naturally wonder, "Gosh, has anyone actually tested that idea?" Often, the answer is no. It's a bit like Aristotle, with his bits of wisdom passed on for 1,500 years, and accepted as gospel until Galileo dropped two weights from the top of the leaning tower. Two-thirds of Aristotle's intuitions were brilliant and correct. One-third were intuitively reasonable but wildly incorrect. I don't want to suggest that I'm anything like Galileo, only that he and I share a willingness to test already-accepted ideas.*[4]

BIG "I" OR LITTLE "I"?

What's to be done, then, in practical terms, about this difference between the two types of creativity? How do investment leaders use this information to run a more creative shop?

First, consider these four questions:

1. What type of creativity is necessary for you to succeed?
2. Do you need breakthrough ideas?
3. Are you in a business that requires you to be on the leading edge?
4. Have you got the right people for the kind of thinking you need?

Index funds and trust departments may decide that they don't need (or want) breakthrough thinking. They want to continually refine and improve their current process and, if necessary, copy a good idea from a competitor from time to time. Thomas Edison said, "Make it a practice to keep on the lookout for novel and interesting ideas that others have used successfully. Your idea has to be original only in its adaptation to the problem you're working on."[5] Active managers, in contrast, had better think seriously about whether they can add value by borrowing ideas or tweaking existing ones. Our guess is not.

The question then becomes whether you have the right people for the job. Is their creative style appropriate for your investment objectives? To address this question, we created an assessment tool that measures your creativity style (see Figure 10.1).

Your score on this test will range from a low of 8 to a high of 40. For the sake of simplicity, we break the continuum into three broad categories: Adaptors, Balancers, and Innovators. The lists of common strengths and weaknesses shown in Table 10.2 were developed from focus groups conducted with people in each category.[6]

When we use this assessment with a professional team, we print out the continuum so that members can see where they fall on the continuum relative to their teammates. If there is a heavy emphasis on privacy with a team, it's fine just to print the number of people who fall into each category. Here, for example, is the distribution for the insurance company that was pursuing "big ideas":

Adaptors: 13	Balancers: 5	Innovators: 1

The important point in all of this is to recognize the different creative styles and to understand the effects of the difference. In the insurance company example, nearly every officer was an Adaptor, with a few Balancers thrown in, yet the company was calling on this group to do the very things that are identified as their weaknesses! To use a basketball analogy, imagine the futility—not to mention the frustration—of assembling a professional basketball team of players who are all less than six feet tall. No matter how

Instructions: For each of the two columns (A and B), decide which of the two statements is a better description of you. Then, using the scale below, place a number in the box between the two columns:

1 = Agree strongly with "A"
2 = Agree somewhat with "A"
3 = Balanced between "A" and "B"
4 = Agree somewhat with "B"
5 = Agree strongly with "B"

Personal descriptions

COLUMN "A"	SCORE: 1–5	COLUMN "B"
I am characterized by precision, reliability, efficiency, and prudence.		I am seen as a spontaneous, tangential thinker, and novel in my approach.
I am concerned with resolving problems rather than finding them.		I am concerned with discovering problems and new solutions.
I seek solutions to problems in tried and understood ways.		I question underlying assumptions and often reframe problems.
I am seen as sound and dependable.		I am seen as imaginative and daring.
I tend to like structured situations.		I tend to like unstructured situations.
I am able to maintain high accuracy in long sessions of detail work.		I work in short bursts and prefer to delegate routine tasks.
I rarely challenge the rules, and only then with strong support.		I often challenge the rules and am often irreverent toward norms.
When collaborating, I supply stability, order, continuity.		When collaborating, I supply a willingness to risk and break the mold.

Total score: _____

FIGURE 10.1 Creativity Style Assessment

TABLE 10.2 Creativity Style Assessment Interpretation

Score Range	Adaptors	
	Strengths	**Weaknesses**
8–21	Analytical	Too practical, no theory
	Solutions fit current	Intense, highly focused structure
	Good in emergencies	Seems unapproachable
	Stable and practical	Overanalyzes
	Good "team player"	Needs all the facts
	Task-oriented	Close-minded, "my way"
	Conscientious	Lacks originality
	Very efficient	Low profile
	Maximizes available resources	Resistant to change
22–26	**Balancers**	
	Reliable	Emphasizes utility over novelty
	Finds solutions quickly	Slows down new approaches
	Can see both sides	Not enough risk taking
	Goal-oriented	Stagnating
	Versatile	Too flexible, moves too easily from one project to another
	Calculated risk taker	Bored easily
	Tolerant of extremes	Own needs often ignored
	Fingers in many pies	Sometimes caught in middle
27–40	**Innovators**	
	Innovative ideas also are practical	Impatient, bored easily
	Will work day and night on stimulating problem	Will work day and night to detriment of other relationships
	High energy, easy generation of ideas	Hates structure and red tape
	Welcomes complex problems	Hates to be "managed"
	Improvises readily	Ideas aren't realistic

hard they practice or how much heart they bring to the court, they just aren't going to beat many pro teams. In the basketball case, the frustration is lessened by the fact that everyone can immediately see why the team loses. With creativity styles, the differences are invisible. No one can tell your style by appearance. That's why this assessment is useful.

Does it accurately predict the big-idea people? Pretty closely, yes. This assessment tool is largely based on the Myers-Briggs factors, using the Sensing-versus-Intuitive preference that distinguishes between practical, detail-type people and big-picture, theoretical types. In a study conducted with professionals in four fields of expertise (mathematics, science, journalism, and architecture), employees were asked to nominate coworkers whom they considered "very creative." Of the 105 who were eventually selected, fully 102 showed a preference for Intuitive on the MBTI. This is just the result you'd expect. (The three Sensing types who were considered highly creative correspond to the rare athlete who's less than six feet tall but succeeds in the NBA anyway. It does happen, but the odds are stacked against it.)

Is the point, then, that Adaptors are not creative? No, not at all. They can be very creative, but usually not in the break-the-mold-and-start-fresh sense. They tend to excel at tweaking existing products or processes. If you were running an index fund or a trading desk, you would probably do well to have an excess of this thinking style. Quant shops and active managers, in contrast, had better get some Innovators on the team.

Here is the result for the global investment team that we discussed at the very beginning of this chapter:

Adaptors: 3	Balancers: 3	Innovators: 4

Given that this investment organization is a combination of index funds, active management, retail and institutional clients, all different asset classes, and quant methods, it didn't surprise us to find this balance. In fact, balance can be a great asset to an investment organization. Each of the creativity styles is valuable when used in the right setting. The problem with most organizations is that the difference in style becomes a source of conflict rather than a source of strength. Adaptors see the Innovators as mad scientists who can't remember where they parked their cars, and Innovators perceive the Adaptors as overcautious bureaucrats with green eyeshades and freshly sharpened pencils. It's not long until lines in the sand are being drawn.

For this reason, it's worth identifying and understanding the difference in creative styles, and learning how to speak the language of the other style. Table 10.3 sets out a brief set of rules for translating your thoughts into their language.[7]

TABLE 10.3   Recommendations for Influencing Adaptors and Innovators

When Influencing High Adaptors:	When Influencing High Innovators:
Provide a detailed agenda.	Give the big picture.
Show how the idea builds on established best practices.	Show benefits of radically new direction.
While presenting, be organized and precise, with a script to back it up.	Identify the cutting-edge elements; back up with summary in bullet points.
Provide checkpoints and an evaluation plan; emphasize need for careful approach to implementation.	Identify future trends and show how the idea sets the pace.
Provide information in advance; don't spring new ideas on them and expect immediate support.	When adaptation is needed to support an innovative initiative, state the case for each need; don't expect immediate support.
Do your homework; make sure you are thoroughly prepared with details.	Recognize breakthrough thinking; provide opportunities for building on new ideas.
Emphasize that innovative creativity changes the paradigm for the better and show how.	Relate the idea to emerging issues that are unique and exciting.
Underscore the need for innovative thinking in certain parts of grand adaptive plans.	Emphasize that precision and efficiency are needed to develop and implement innovative ideas.

These tips are designed to improve the effectiveness of your investment team as it strives for more creativity. The global team that we worked with found it useful to identify any brainstormed idea as "big C" or "little c." In other words, for each idea, they asked whether they were going for a breakthrough idea or a bit of improvement.

For the analysts and stock pickers reading this book, we will digress for just a moment to say that many a company has been undone by not recognizing the role—and power—of the two different styles. Clayton Christensen, mentioned earlier, wrote a best-selling book on this topic, called *The Innovator's Dilemma*.[8] In it, he shows the value of each type of thinking. For most companies, Adaptors are useful for the role of continuous improvement, making the small tweaks that keep them up with the competitors. A good example would be an automobile company. There haven't been any major paradigm shifts in the car business recently . . . improvements here and there, but nothing revolutionary. Not so with the laser printing industry. The laser printer, which used to be head and shoulders above the inkjet printer, has lost its advantage. The inkjet represents what Christensen called a "disruptive" technology; that is, one that displaces the current standard. Christensen cites example after example of premier companies whose management followed best practices in the industry only to lose out to a new, disruptive technology that wasn't even on the radar screen. A current example is the writable CD and the old magnetic floppy disk. Dell Computer announced that it will no longer even make hardware for the floppy. With its limited 1.44-megabyte memory, it cannot compete with a 700-megabyte CD. Customers were happy with the floppy right up until they saw the CD next to it on the shelf and said, "Whoa, this is *much* better!"

ASSESSING YOUR CULTURE FOR CREATIVITY

Regardless of one's creative style—tweaks or thunderclaps—the organizational culture plays a major role in overall creativity. Collins and Porras recognize this and identify the factors in Table 10.4 as important.[9] Table 10.5 shows the average scores for the *Built to Last* and comparison companies.

Although the *Built to Last* factors shown in Table 10.5 are a useful way to monitor creativity within an organization, we also like to draw from the work of Teresa Amabile (Harvard), who has been researching the topic for more than 20 years. The outcome of all her work is a survey called KEYS, which has been adopted by the Center for Creative Leadership (ranked number one by *Business Week* magazine for educational excellence) as its official culture survey for creativity. We like to borrow from the best, à la Edison, and are quite sure that the elements of the KEYS survey accurately assess the creativity within an organization.

KEYS assesses six management practices that support the work environment:

1. *Organizational Encouragement.* Top management support for creative risk-taking, an open atmosphere for idea exchange, and recognition of creative work.
2. *Supervisory Encouragement.* Giving support to direct reports, communicating effectively, and setting clear expectations and goals.
3. *Work Group Supports.* Skill diversity, teamwork, mutual trust and support, and commitment to work.
4. *Sufficient Resources.* Access to appropriate facilities, equipment, and information.

5. *Challenging Work.* The importance of the work combined with the difficulty of achieving the goal.
6. *Freedom.* The sense of control staff have over developing new ideas, deciding how to accomplish tasks, and developing new and effective processes.

TABLE 10.4   Assessment of Creativity and Adaptability

Category for scoring:	Score
IV. Creativity and Adaptability	
Concept: Top companies are careful not to stagnate. They create an environment where employees try many things and then see what works. This requires management to trust the employees and not micromanage them. Management uses different rewards and techniques for stimulating creativity and initiative.	
Consciously using an evolutionary process	
+1 Evidence of consciously using an evolutionary process of variation and selection (a conscious version of Darwinian evolution). Strategic shifts resulted from it.	
0 Some evidence of the use of conscious evolution.	
−1 Little or no evidence of using an evolutionary process.	
Employee autonomy: empowering "hands off" management	
+1 Evidence of high employee autonomy. Employees have wide personal discretion in how to fulfill their responsibilities.	
0 Some evidence that the company historically has encouraged and practiced employee autonomy.	
−1 Little or no evidence that the company empowers its employees.	
Rewards for stimulating autonomy and evolution	
+1 Significant evidence that the company uses a variety of ways (other than the above) to stimulate autonomy: rewards for creativity, safe to make mistakes, incentives for discovering new opportunities.	
0 Some evidence for stimulating employee autonomy in the above ways.	
−1 Little or no evidence that the company has a history of using different methods to stimulate autonomy.	
Score: Creativity and Adaptability	

TABLE 10.5 Average Creativity Scores Compared

Criteria	*Built to Last* Average	Comparison Company Average
Consciously using an evolutionary process	.44	−.17
Employee autonomy	.39	−.39
Rewards for stimulating autonomy and evolution	.83	−.72
IV. Creativity and Adaptability	1.66	−1.28

In addition, KEYS looks at two management practices that inhibit the work environment:

1. *Organizational Impediments.* Destructive criticism, turfism (turf protection and kingdom building), rigidity, and resistance to change.
2. *Workload Pressure.* Unrealistic expectations, insufficient time, and too many distractions.[10]

The original KEYS survey contains 78 questions, all of which relate to one of these 10 items. We have simplified these 78 questions down to 20 (almost a literal example of the 80/20 rule), which we believe do an adequate job in pinpointing a culture's strengths and weaknesses relating to creativity.

The modified Creative Culture Assessment is shown in Figure 10.2.

The global investment team from our example story filled out this survey during their two-day retreat and found the following strengths (highest rated factors) and weaknesses (lowest):

Strengths:
  Challenging and important work.
  Recognized and rewarded employees.
  Trust and openness.
  Leader interacts well with team members.

Weaknesses:
  Distractions.
  Too much work.

The first step in reacting to these survey results is, of course, to define what is meant by each of these terms. Fortunately for this group, one of their strengths is that the leader interacts well with the team and builds trust,

Instructions: For each statement, give a score of 1–5 based on the scale below:

1 = Strongly disagree
2 = Disagree somewhat
3 = Neutral
4 = Agree somewhat
5 = Strongly agree

_____ 1. I have a great deal of freedom in deciding what projects I work on and how I do them.

_____ 2. I believe that my work is challenging and important.

_____ 3. I have access to the materials, information, and resources that I need to carry out my projects.

_____ 4. My leader sets clear and consistent goals for me.

_____ 5. My leader interacts well with us and values our different talents and abilities.

_____ 6. My leader supports our workgroup and provides constructive feed-back.

_____ 7. My workgroup demonstrates good teamwork; there is trust and open-ness to new ideas, and it values diversity.

_____ 8. Our workgroup encourages people to take risks and solve problems creatively.

_____ 9. Performance evaluations for our workgroup are fair, and there is room to "fail constructively."

_____ 10. People are recognized and rewarded for creative work.

_____ 11. There is an open atmosphere and lively flow of ideas in our work-group.

_____ 12. There are few political problems in our workgroup.

_____ 13. Negative criticism is NOT a problem in our workgroup.

_____ 14. Leaders are open to doing things in new ways.

_____ 15. Policies and structures are not TOO formal or constricting in our workgroup.

_____ 16. I do NOT feel that there is too much work and too little time to do it.

_____ 17. There are NOT too many distractions from my work in this workgroup.

_____ 18. Overall, my workgroup is conducive to my own creativity.

_____ 19. Overall, my workgroup is productive.

_____ 20. Overall, my workgroup is efficient.

FIGURE 10.2 Creativity: Organizational Assessment

which leads to openness. To probe further into the group's creative strengths and weaknesses, we used a technique developed at the Center for Creative Leadership (CCL), called Visual Explorer.[11] It uses imagery to get partici-pants out of their logical, left brains and into their creative, right brains. The technique can be used for any type of brainstorming. It is particularly effec-tive for analytical types who spend much of their time in the logical, linear mode. Our goal was to get a deeper sense of the team's creative strengths and weaknesses.

The simplicity of this technique is part of its appeal. We asked the global investment team members to browse through the 200 photos that we had placed on tables around the room. Images ranged from abstract to black-and-white photos to 19th-century paintings. They were selected by two instructors at CCL for their ability to stimulate a range of thoughts and emotions.

The group used these pictures in two exercises.

1. Each group member selected an image that characterized a time when the group was very creative. Then each person explained why he or she had chosen that particular image, and received some feedback from the other group members.
2. They repeated the first exercise, but this time with images that represented obstacles to their best creativity.

Having done debriefings with groups for many years, we can say with certainty that using the photos makes the discussions much richer. The key to success is to create safety in the room, so that people feel comfortable being open, and to encourage dialogue rather than debate. Entire books have been written on this subject, but the main point can be summed up briefly: In debate, you hold on tightly to your position and try to discredit the other position. Debate is a win/lose proposition that involves a competitive attitude. In dialogue, you release your hold on your positions and examine where they came from in the first place. You attempt to think as a collective. Dialogue is a mutually constructive process that requires a cooperative attitude. The average person has a difficult time with dialogue because it is seen so infrequently in our society. In the United States, the entire political and legal systems are based on debate.

The global investment team brainstormed next steps after completing the Visual Explorer exercise. They arrived at several key action steps that would help them strengthen the creativity in their culture. They also addressed one of the weaknesses by agreeing to address time management at their next retreat.

PRACTICAL TAKEAWAYS

Teams that we have worked with find the following two items very useful in enhancing creativity. As Alison Winter at Northern Trust noted, "Effective

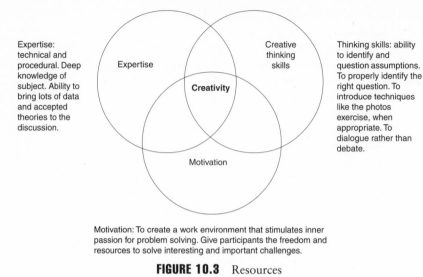

Expertise: technical and procedural. Deep knowledge of subject. Ability to bring lots of data and accepted theories to the discussion.

Thinking skills: ability to identify and question assumptions. To properly identify the right question. To introduce techniques like the photos exercise, when appropriate. To dialogue rather than debate.

Motivation: To create a work environment that stimulates inner passion for problem solving. Give participants the freedom and resources to solve interesting and important challenges.

FIGURE 10.3   Resources

leaders try to give creative people the time and tools they need to be creative."[12] Here are some specific ideas for doing this.

Creativity Keys

Examine the "three keys to creativity" (Figure 10.3) and discuss the group's strengths and weaknesses with regard to each area. Are there steps that should be taken to improve one of the areas? (For example, if you are brainstorming in the area of behavioral finance, should participants read a few books on the topic to strengthen their expertise?) Is one of these areas in particular causing the group's creative efforts to bog down? (For example, is senior management micromanaging, thus killing motivation?)[13]

COMPLEX QUESTION WORKSHEET

Use the following worksheet to address the critical issue of asking the right question. Einstein said, "If I had an hour to solve a problem, I would spend 55 minutes on the definition and 5 minutes on the solution."[14]

Worksheet for Framing a Complex Question

Definition of "Complex Problem":

A complex problem defies existing approaches or solutions. Because of its importance, it demands decisive action. But, because the team or individual is not sure what to do, there is a need to slow down and carefully reflect on the problem, so as to develop a sustainable solution.

A complex problem involves some or all of the following:

- You feel "stuck," and the problem is a source of real pain. Prior attempts at resolution have misfired.
- The problem seems outside the current of proposed approaches. Existing frameworks and formulas don't fit. You may not be sure exactly how to talk about the problem.
- The problem involves a clash of basic assumptions, worldviews, or departments. People disagree about the nature of the problem and what should be done.

Take a few minutes to reflect on the topic that has been selected for our brainstorming session:

Write what comes to mind when you think of the designated challenge.

Describe a key episode, typical example, or image that captures much of what the challenge is about?

Our goal in framing the problem is to allow as much creativity as possible. Below are five ways to reframe problem statements so that they invite a broader range of potential solutions. Read the five examples and then return to your problem statement above. Do these examples suggest ways in which you could reframe the problem?

Generalize the Problem Statement:
- Sample problem statement: "How to improve the aluminum beverage can."
- Reframed: "How to design a functional beverage packaging system."

Question Boundary Assumptions:
- Sample problem statement: "How to increase the speed of baseball players in reaching first base."
- Reframed: "Why speed? Maybe it is also a problem of lightness of equipment? Maybe better reaction time could make a difference? Why baseball players? Is this a problem for players of rugby, soccer, or football? Why first base? Is there not a problem in quickness in stealing bases, running for fly balls, and other tasks demanding speed?"

Catalog the Components of the Problem:
- Sample problem statement: "How to eliminate the tardiness of plant employees."
- Reframed:
  —"How to motivate employees to arrive on time."
  —"How to make it easy to arrive on time."
  —"How to express the importance of punctuality."

Ask "What Is the REAL Problem?"
- Sample problem statement: "How to redesign a fund-raising program for a university."
- Reframed:
  —"How to convince graduates that money is needed."
  —"How to make money for the university."
  —"How to get rid of the current fund-raising committee."

Play "I Wish…" (assume an ideal world with no constraints):
- Sample problem statement: "How to reduce the costs of the benefits program without reducing the benefits."
- Reframed:
  —"I wish benefits didn't cost so much."
  —"I wish we could manage the program without an administrative staff."
  —"I wish our people were healthier."
  —"I wish our insurance premiums didn't cost so much."

SUMMARY

This chapter was intended to provide techniques for assessing and improving the creativity of your culture. The emphasis was on the environment, not on specific techniques for enhancing creativity.[15] Collins and Porras identified the top firms as having cultures that promoted creativity and adaptability.

TEST YOURSELF

1. How does your firm score on the *Built to Last* items? Where can you improve?
2. What are the creative styles of your senior management team? How many Adaptors? Balancers? Innovators?
3. Have your firm fill out the organizational creativity assessment. What are your strengths? Weaknesses?
4. Do you encourage dialogue, as well as debate, in your organization?
5. What steps can you take to improve the environment for creativity?

> *One of the most important leadership responsibilities in this tough business is creating excitement, which is probably best done by encouraging creativity and innovation.*
> —Claude Rosenberg Jr., RCM Capital Mangement[16]

> *An effective leader must understand that investment management is a creative business and creative people need to be managed accordingly.*
> —Alison Winter, Executive Vice President, The Northern Trust Company[17]

CHAPTER 11

Compensation and Ownership

Compensation ranks only fifth on the list of factors that contribute to positive feelings and job satisfaction.
—Luke Knecht and Richard Lannamann,
Russell Reynolds Associates[1]

Compensation speaks volumes about what's important in your firm. In this chapter you will learn:

- The real factors that attract and help retain your stellar professionals.
- Why compensation is a particularly thorny issue for investment professionals.
- Guidelines that can make your communications about compensation easier.
- The role of trust in compensation agreements.
- How shared ownership contributes to success.

"We should talk about compensation; we know people are unhappy with our current arrangement," said the president of Allstar Capital in the planning meeting for the offsite. Then he added, "But let's not. There's already enough tension without tossing that one on the table."

The director of research filled the ensuing silence with, "We are negotiating an increase for one of our key players so that he stays during this crunch period."

The president resumed, "We've been meaning to talk through these compensation issues but with the pressure that we're under, it would be a terrible time to try to have that discussion."

IT'S RARELY ABOUT THE MONEY

True to form, Allstar had committed two classic mistakes concerning compensation. First, they had avoided a careful and complete discussion with the team members about compensation philosophy. This discussion forces you to face two questions: Specifically, what do you value and reward at your firm? How do you translate those values into a compensation structure that motivates people to perform in the firm's best long-term interest?

Second, Allstar had started cutting side deals with various staff members to keep them happy. Its leaders were managing compensation on a case-by-case, ad hoc basis. In some instances, they were counteroffering bids from competitors. If there's one thing we've learned about compensation at the best firms, it is this: Don't get sucked into the counteroffer game! Statistics show that the people who successfully negotiate for a counteroffer leave the firm within 18 months anyway. Counteroffers don't work, because money isn't really the issue.

As we stated in Chapter 1, in the section about industry myths, *money is not everything*. Study after study confirms this. To cite just a few, let's look at a study by Russell Reynolds Associates, done in 1996. It asked, "What are the major factors influencing job satisfaction for professional investors?" The factors rated as shown in Table 11.1.[2]

Compensation was certainly a factor in employee satisfaction, but it wasn't in the top grouping.

A more recent survey comes from Capital Resource Advisors. They survey hundreds of major investment firms on various issues, including factors in employee satisfaction and commitment. The results for the summer of 2002 were as follows:[3]

Leadership credibility and trust	84.8%
Organizational culture and purpose	69.6%
Opportunity for growth and development	50.0%
Challenging, meaningful work	50.0%
Total compensation	50.0%
Relationships with coworkers, customers	39.1%
Work recognition	39.1%
Quality of life/work balance	28.3%
Ownership	24.4%

TABLE 11.1 Job Satisfaction Factors

Factor	Percent of Respondents Indicating That This Factor Was a "Positive" One
Professional achievement	86
Personal or professional growth	79
Work itself	78
Taking responsibility	77
Compensation	54
Career advancement	52
Recognition	52
Relationship with supervisor	40
Relationship with peers	40
Impact on personal life	35
Status	33
Security	30
Work conditions	23
Relationships with subordinates	21

Again, compensation was certainly a factor in employee satisfaction and commitment, but it was a distant fifth to the main topics of this book: leadership and culture, which rated first and second.

Another cut at this data specifically investigates why investment professionals leave their jobs. The name of the talent game is attracting and *retaining* top professionals, so this survey pertains directly to the question Allstar was facing: "How do we keep the top people on our staff?" This survey, conducted by Moss Adams LLP, asked investment professionals why they left their last jobs. The results are shown in Table 11.2.[4]

Notice that compensation hardly registered as a reason for leaving. Our experience confirms these findings. Compensation is often presented as the main problem, when actually it is not. One experience with a client showed this most profoundly. The staff of a private placement division felt bitter and resentful that they were being asked to perform in the top quartile, compared to their peer group, when they were being paid in the bottom quartile. Clearly, this was unfair. The staff fought the unfair arrangement and eventually did prevail in getting higher salaries. For a short while, there was celebration and improved morale, but a short time later, things were back to

TABLE 11.2   Reasons for Leaving Job

Reason for Leaving an Investment Firm	Percent of Respondents Citing This Reason
Terminated for poor performance	23
Better opportunity elsewhere	18
Incompatible with firm culture	14
Lifestyle change	14
Relocation	11
Terminated for cause	7
Retirement	7
Do not know	4
Insufficient compensation	3
Layoff/reduction in staff	2

usual. The staff was grousing again and relationships were strained. When we asked one of the staff why the raise in salaries hadn't done more good, we got this answer: "It's not really about the money. The issues are deeper than that." We pushed a bit to see what "deeper" meant and got: "We don't really trust the leaders and we don't feel respected by them." Whether people (on either side of the fence) realize it or not, as such stories and studies clearly show, it's rarely just about the money.

Another money story comes from a European colleague. Two of his friends worked at Goldman Sachs, a firm known for its outstanding culture. They liked the firm but resented their boss. Eventually, the two left Goldman for another well-known firm, thereby getting both more money and relief from the bad boss. Leaders at Goldman learned of this incident and fired the bad boss, while simultaneously contacting the two ex-employees and urging them to return. In the end, the two did return to Goldman, for more money than they were making before at Goldman but less than they were being paid by the new firm.

Why, then, do we hear so much about money in this particular industry? Money is a difficult topic in general, but it seems even thornier in the investment world. Three reasons may explain it:

1. Performance is difficult to measure. Attribution analysis is still more art than science. Is an analyst skillful or lucky? Many money managers are completely unwilling to face the statistical realities surrounding this

question. As Mark Hulbert, author of *Hulbert Financial Digest*, wrote, "[Y]ou would need 308 years of beating the market by 1 percent annually to satisfy a statistician at the 95 percent level."[5] So, of course, this brings up the next question: Could we ever evaluate performance in a person's lifetime? Well, yes, if the analyst could "beat the market by around 12 percent a year. In such a case, the statisticians would be satisfied after only a dozen years of beating the market."[6] Even Bill Miller's recent incredible record at Legg Mason falls short of this target!

2. Money is central to the investment professional's life. They deal with it every day. Many chose the profession because of a fascination with wealth and the accumulation of it. It doesn't work to say to these people, "You're really not upset about the money, but rather what the money represents: self-esteem, success, fairness." (If you did say this to them, there's a danger that they would hurt themselves laughing.)

3. Investors are highly competitive by nature. They are very interested in keeping score and winning. (In a game simulation called "The Prisoner's Dilemma," conducted at an AIMR conference, investment professionals distinguished themselves by being the *most* competitive group we'd ever seen! They were also the most creative group, cutting deals and creating third markets.) Compensation is an obvious metric for scoring and winning.

We found that the top leaders would basically agree with these points. People in the investment business probably are more interested in money—and keeping score—than the average person. It's a question of degree. Here the top leaders agreed that "we don't want people whose top concern is money. Better that they leave." Dave Coolidge at Blair even tells candidates, "[I]f you want the big Wall Street money, then go to New York. That's not what we're about." Jack Brennan at Vanguard is firm on the same point: "We don't counteroffer." In 2002, Langdon Wheeler of Numeric Investors L.P. said that he was getting several calls a month from highly paid Wall Street analysts who wanted to come work with him. Wheeler told these callers that he couldn't pay them the high salaries they were used to. Invariably, each of them said, "I don't care about the money. I just want to work in a place where it's enjoyable."

Leaders of the top firms would laugh at the idea that serious teamwork is a money issue. As Thomas Luddy, CIO at J.P. Morgan, said,

Teamwork is a cultural issue; it is an accumulation over a long time of many little things—things that give constant reinforcement to teamwork activities within the organization. And although a firm may have some

compensation incentives, if it does not have the constant cultural rein-
forcement and if it is not attracting people that are motivated by and
enjoy being part of a team, annual compensation incentives are not
going to foster teamwork.[7]

Our experience confirms this notion: You can't buy teamwork any more
than you can buy friendship.

IT'S ABOUT CLARITY AND FAIRNESS

The real question becomes "What does money mean?" With the median
total compensation for a seasoned investment professional at $245,000, not
many of them are starving to death.[8] So, what is important about money?
For David Maister, Harvard professor and consultant to professional service
firms, money is symbolic:

> *[A]t least as important as dollars and cents are the signals communi-*
> *cated, or at least perceived to have been communicated, through com-*
> *pensation decisions. These messages—about what gets rewarded and*
> *about the relative status and respect accorded to each partner—affect*
> *not only the firm's culture and atmosphere, but also, by influencing how*
> *partners choose to spend their time, its strategic direction.*[9]

The key to money's symbolic importance was summarized well by Deb
Brown of Russell Reynolds Associates, who partnered with AIMR to
conduct a large industry study of compensation. She told us, "People
need to believe that they are being paid fairly for their contribution to
investment performance and business results." *Fairness* is the key. Consider
this story from James Rothenberg, president of Capital Research and
Management:

> *If a firm wants fairness, generosity, and commitment organizationally,*
> *then the top of the organization must show the way. I learned this lesson*
> *early in my career at Capital. When I was first offered the opportunity*
> *to buy some stock in Capital, I was excited, and I bought the stock.*
> *Little did I know in 1973 that we were about to enter a very difficult*
> *period; it was one of the few times in my experience that the value of*
> *Capital stock, which is determined by a formula price, actually declined*
> *significantly in the following 12 months. Being a brash young analyst*

*at the time, I went to the research director and said, "It would be won-
derful if you would give me the opportunity to buy some more stock
and average down." A few weeks later, the chief financial officer walked
into my office and offered me an amount of stock equivalent to my
first purchase but at the lower price; the stock was sold to me by
the then-president of the company and the son of the founder. The lesson? Fairness, generosity, and commitment must come from the top of
the organization.*[10]

Leaders and compensation directors at investment firms around the
world echo the same sentiments. Fran Skinner of Focus Consulting, who
was the director of incentive measurement, competitive compensation, and
relative performance analysis for an organization with $80 billion of assets
under management, said that it must be "fair, equitable, and competitive."
Before establishing their market-based compensation plan, she and the compensation committee spent a lot of time developing the philosophy behind it.
For them, the driving force was to create fairness by tying all compensation
to an objective standard; they studiously avoided any case-by-case treatment. They have defined a peer group and use the McLagan data because
she believes that it enhances the credibility of their system.

Like Coolidge and Brennan, Skinner's previous firm makes it clear to
candidates that they could make top dollar elsewhere. Compensation expectations relative to the market are established upfront with all potential
new hires. In addition, the compensation philosophy and annual market
analysis process are periodically reviewed with employees at group meetings
led by Skinner (the director of compensation and incentive performance
measurement). Key to those group meetings is reinforcing:

- The alignment between performance expectations and incentive compensation opportunity.
- That an ongoing, thorough analysis is performed using a variety of
  sources to validate and ensure that the compensation opportunity re-
  mains competitive and in alignment with market performance.
- That the director is the investment professional's advocate, constantly
  working to ensure that the compensation and measurement process is
  fair to both the employee and the company.

The upshot of this commitment to fairness by the organization was solid
long-term track records and lower-than-average voluntary turnover—even
during the boom years of the late 1990s, when double-digit annual turnover

was common in many investment firms. The firm was committed to minimizing voluntary turnover, which translated into solid performance and expense savings by avoiding all the costs associated with new managers repositioning portfolios to their liking. The end result was employees who were able to achieve their compensation expectations when performance warranted, and a firm that could maintain reasonable yet competitive compensation levels.

In addition to cash compensation, Skinner's previous firm makes priorities of training, performance assessment conversations, and promotion from within, utilizing its succession planning process. Employees see that they can grow into greater roles and responsibilities if they take the training and leadership offered by senior staff and translate that into performance. This type of environment, combined with explicit market-based compensation expectations, is a formidable motivating force. Finally, the firm offers other valued benefits, such as work/family balance, onsite child care, a convenience store, and a health club, among other things.

An investment professional at a major Midwestern investment firm made many similar points when talking about compensation. This firm prides itself on providing a great work experience, as seen in its selection to the "Top 100 Places to Work" survey.[11] Compensation is team-based and competitive, but not necessarily top-dollar. People at this firm know they could make more money elsewhere, but they are part of the family and culture. New hires, for example, are assigned a welcoming committee that helps them figure out the basics of community life: public transportation, school systems, real estate tips, even restaurants and entertainment. What value do you place on that? Plan sponsors are thinking about this trade-off more seriously as resources get increasingly limited. What they cannot offer in terms of eye-popping salaries and bonuses, they can make up for with intangibles.

Employees who leave this firm looking for greener pastures and, presumably greener paychecks, often return to the fold. One investment professional told us,

> *In the last two years, more than 13 percent of newly hired employees are people who've left the company and returned. There's something that brings people back, something that can't easily be replicated elsewhere. It's got to be the culture. Since I've worked in this division . . . , six people have left voluntarily. Every single one of them came back within 2 years. I find that fascinating!*

At first, we did, too, given the strength and prevalence of the industry myth that money is everything. As we did more research, though, we found that a strong, positive culture definitely has an economic value, though it is hard to quantify.

COMMUNICATION AND EXPECTATIONS

Compensation is a difficult subject that should be tackled sooner rather than later. In fact, we recommend that firms doing foundational work—vision and values—include compensation in the agenda. (We brought in Fran Skinner to our firm for exactly this reason; the soft work of vision and values must be tied to the hard work of compensation and performance evaluations right from the start.) The following questions should be addressed:

- What is your compensation philosophy?
- How will your philosophy be tied to performance evaluations and merit increases?

Unfortunately, as we saw in the case of Allstar Capital, it's all too easy to avoid the conversation. Deb Brown says, "It's all about communication and setting expectations, and most firms don't do this well." Fran Skinner agrees: "You cannot stress the 'setting expectations' theme enough when talking about compensation. Absolute dollars of compensation are not as important as what people's expectations were relative to market compensation." Firms don't handle this area well for two reasons: First, because under any circumstances it's a tough conversation. Second, most firms haven't done the foundational work that we describe in the first few chapters of this book. David Maister, in his book on managing the professional service firm, explains why this foundational work is key: "In a firm divided over values and direction, no judiciary, elected or appointed, will ever be fully trusted. Strategy, governance, and compensation are inextricably intertwined, and lack of consensus in any one spills over into the others."[12]

MEASUREMENT VERSUS JUDGMENT

All this shows why, in trying to devise a good compensation system, leaders must be prepared to include the conversation as part of their foundational thinking. Alison Winter of Northern Trust said, "When building an incentive plan, management has to start by looking at what the incentive plan is trying to accomplish."[13] Leaders must tie the incentive plan to the vision and values of the firm—and they must aim for fairness as the key to keeping investment professionals satisfied. Bill Nutt, chairman of Affiliated Managers Group, agreed that compensation becomes secondary for investment professionals once they feel they are being treated fairly. Thereafter, the other factors listed in the surveys cited earlier become central to their happiness.

Further, leaders must accept that compensation will always be a judgment call rather than strictly a numbers game. As Patrick O'Donnell put it,

> *The basic reason that quantitative evaluation processes do not work entirely is that measuring an analyst's impact on an organization is complex, difficult, and often has unintended results. For instance, if we tell analysts that they are going to be paid on the basis of a year-end evaluation, and if those analysts have a wonderful first half of the year, we have created an incentive for them to coast for the second half of the year.*[14]

Maister agrees that quantitative systems are not optimal. He said: "Decisions about compensation must result from a judgment process, not a measurement process (although, to be sure, judgments should be formed with knowledge of whatever statistics are available). The ways to improve a measurement system are usually obvious. How does one improve a judgment system?"[15] In answering his own question, Maister went on to say that there must be a process in place that people have agreed is fair and works reasonably well. Using a judicial analogy, he identified the factors that result in the best possible process:[16]

- If the people being judged do not trust the judges, the system won't work.
- The laws governing the decision must be consistent and well understood.
- Judgments should not be made until a sincere effort has been made to collect all pertinent information, and the "defense" has been allowed to make its case.
- Judgments that are explained are more readily understood and accepted than those that are not.

As obvious as some of these factors may seem, it is remarkable how few firms follow them. Following these rules is imperative, though. As one investment professional said, his satisfaction with his compensation and that of others largely depended on his perception of the legitimacy and integrity of the group that made the compensation decisions.[17] Again, the *perception* of fairness is key. This is one reason why communication is so important. Staff should get clear descriptions of the process and the data so that there is no room for them to make up stories in the absence of information. Poor data is the single biggest reason for mistrust of compensation judges. Each investment professional should have a written copy of the criteria for success and a record of his or her performance relative to those criteria. Compensation discussions should be handled face-to-face. It's often helpful to use 360-degree feedback for the "intangible" part of the compensation; that is, colleagues should be solicited for input on their coworkers with questions like:

- Which of the professional staff have you worked with closely in the past year?
- For those you worked with, how would you rate their performance and contribution to the firm?
- In what ways does she or he excel?
- In what ways that we may not know about has she or he contributed to the firm's success?
- For what should this person be recognized and praised?
- If you were to encourage this person to do one thing differently, what would it be?

Brandes in San Diego compensates its analysts on the quantity and quality of their research, not on the performance of the stocks. Its compensation philosophy holds that the 11-person investment committee should be held accountable for stock performance. After all, it is their job to decide if the analyst has done good work and if the stock is undervalued. The analysts are thus freed up to dive into analysis and not become hypnotized by watching their recommended stocks move up and down with the market. This system also avoids the problem of analysts gaming the system, as mentioned earlier. The investment committee incorporates lots of feedback from coworkers in the evaluation of analysts.

After you have carefully thought through the compensation philosophy, gathered both objective and subjective data from coworkers, and evaluated this data using a formal analytic approach (to ensure fairness and the perception of fairness, as everyone is treated the same way), then you must communicate the decisions to all concerned. Part of the communication involves explaining the results, so that they will be accepted as fair. Even when an employee perceives that she has not been dealt with fairly, explanations can go a long way toward smoothing ruffled feathers.

In many instances when an employee becomes upset (we've witnessed quite a few), there is a misunderstanding on the part of the employee. For example, in one case an analyst was very put out about what seemed to him to be an unduly low bonus award. (No one's sense of fairness seems to extend to getting upset about being overpaid . . .) When the leader in this case showed the analyst all the personal calculations and reviewed the team and firm results with him, the tension dissipated. The analyst had performed so well that year that the modest bonus just didn't seem right. It wasn't until he saw the team's results and the firm's results, both of which were mediocre, that he accepted the amount he'd received.

Should leaders practice an open-book approach to compensation? Although some firms swear by this full-disclosure policy ("show everything to everyone"), it can invite problems. Only the person on the top of the heap will feel satisfied. Even if all the others feel that they were fairly treated—which is the goal—they may still feel unhappy about their relative status. That's why we recommend a fair and clear process that doesn't invite comparisons.

The ultimate test of whether the compensation system is working is whether it encourages the full range of behaviors needed for the firm's success. A good compensation system encourages alignment of individual, group, and firm interests.

OWNERSHIP

In the top firms, the old ways and notions of command and control have given way to more participatory forms of management. In the latter, everyone in the firm is encouraged to take ownership in the results. Patrick O'Donnell said, "We try to create a common sense of ownership in the department by having analysts supervise each other, by having analysts train each other, and by getting analysts involved in a wide variety of other things that would normally be thought of as governance."[18] Alison Winter, at Northern Trust, expressed a similar attitude about promoting a sense of ownership:

> We want to promote a proactive interchange of ideas and open-mindedness by encouraging portfolio managers to share successful ideas and talk about what they are doing. We want to promote a "shared destiny" concept among our portfolio managers and increase their ownership in the success of the organization and in our collective performance, not individual performance.[19]

When we asked Winter what she was most proud of as a leader, she said it was the way her team had hung together during the tough markets at the turn of the century. "Rather than turning on one another or blaming each other, they supported one another. It was truly inspiring, but not surprising. We've worked so hard at instilling the team mentality."

The strategies for spreading ownership through the firm are many, but the principle is the same: the deeper and wider the ownership, the better. For this reason, as we conducted our research, we were most impressed with firms like Turner Investments. Remember Bev, the receptionist who met us and took our coats, was an owner in the firm. Now *that's* deep and wide ownership.

Ownership is critical to preserving culture. I asked Glenn Carlson, co-CEO at Brandes, to give me the strongest argument he could that culture was crucial to their success. He responded immediately, "We haven't sold the firm." He continued, "If we sold the firm to some large global company, they would most likely screw up what we have created here." Research supports Carlson's claim. Tillinghast-Towers Perrin performed a survey of Forbes 500 CEOs and asked them to define the biggest pitfalls to successful mergers; their responses appear in Table 11.3.

Right at the top of the list is "incompatible cultures." Carlson and his senior leaders are reluctant to cash out because it would destroy the gem that they have created.

TABLE 11.3   Merger Pitfalls

Rank	
1	Incompatible cultures
2	Inability to manage target
3	Unable to implement change
4	Synergy nonexistent or overestimated
5	Did not anticipate foreseeable events
6	Clash of management style/egos
7	Acquirer paid too much
8	Acquired firm too unhealthy
9	Need to spin off or liquidate too much
10	Incompatible marketing systems

AFFILIATED MANAGERS GROUP: A STRATEGY FOR EFFECTIVE OWNERSHIP

Peggy Eisen, chair of the Institute for Financial Markets, describes a common problem with ownership in the investment business:

> *Here's the all too common scenario. Two to three guys found a firm and among themselves own 80%. The firm becomes very successful and they give ownership to a few employees. Then the founders reach age 55 or so. One decides he wants a lifestyle change and another wants out altogether. So they look at the other folks in the firm and decide they can't pay them what they think the firm is worth because they own so much. They then have to find a transaction which becomes the transition of both ownership and leadership. But wait, the problem becomes twofold: 1) the ownership was not widespread enough, and 2) no one was groomed for succession. So of course the transaction screws everything up! Believe me, I saw this scenario more than once!*[20]

Bill Nutt at AMG has also addressed this very problem. He has built a successful business through his understanding of how ownership supports culture. Recognizing the thorny issues surrounding firm ownership, Nutt devised a strategy for buying controlling interests in mid-sized asset management companies, thereby providing a partial buyout for the owners, while maintaining a "hands-off" policy toward their investment operations. The result for the 17 firms that constitute AMG is that they can spread the ownership of their firms, plan for succession, and maintain precisely the culture that created their initial success. Nutt is interested in long-term success records and especially in firms that "have been through terrible times and stuck together." Figure 11.1 shows the AMG investment structure. A clear sign of Nutt's belief in the importance of culture is his statement that the "big brokerage houses will never be successful over the long term because they don't have clear cultures." Nutt holds that culture is the key to future growth because human capital is a firm's most vital asset.

How have the 17 AMG firms fared? We find this another interesting piece of evidence supporting the superiority of strong-culture firms. Nutt selects his acquisition targets on the basis of many of the criteria that we've already discussed: clear vision and values, well-articulated investment philosophy, long-standing tenure of the investment team, and so on. Dropping AMG into the framework that we showed in Chapter 1 gives the following comparison for five-year investment returns:

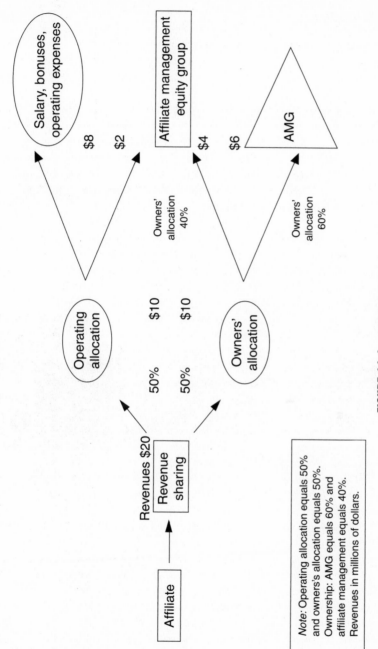

FIGURE 11.1 AMG Structure

Note: Operating allocation equals 50% and owners's allocation equals 50%. Ownership: AMG equals 60% and affiliate management equals 40%. Revenues in millions of dollars.

205

Total return:

Portfolio of top five investment firms:	49.8%
Portfolio of eight other investment firms:	20.7%
AMG investment (17 firms):	70.0%

BATTERYMARCH: BUCKING THE TREND

In the interest of full disclosure, we can report on one investment legend who sees ownership very differently. In our research on ownership, Dean LeBaron's name kept surfacing as someone unwilling to let go of the reins of control. We went right to the source and asked LeBaron why he chose that approach to ownership. His response:

Yes, I owned 100%, not to be greedy (I hope) but to see that we could explore deviant investment strategies (more risky to the manager's business than the investor . . . like buying [companies] priced for bankruptcy), to reduce to zero a tendency to spend a lot of time [on] business policy issues to which business school graduates are prone and to maintain a climate of change and insecurity that is essential for a change organization (edge of chaos).

To put it another way, the problem of self-organization is usually more one of implementation rather than acceptance of the theory. Visualize a boundary case of a company that has been driven close to collapse by a dominant and wrong leader. If you go to the board of directors or bankers of that company and say, "I have a new solution. Let's allow the [company] to be run by its emergent knowledge. Of course, I can't tell you what the outcome will be or the cost or the time schedule but it will all get worked out."

You are unlikely to be hired as a consultant to put in such a practice although privately each of the directors might think it is a good suggestion.

Why won't you be hired? Because this plan does not give the level of assurance promised by directed strategies, even when the chances are that the strategies are wrong.

My company, Batterymarch, could be different because it had a benign dictator (me) who never had a business plan, never a budget, induced change by moving people's locations regularly, never gave anyone security (but did give very large compensation) . . . and everyone individually hated it but agreed that it was the best collective strategy.

Fortunately I did not have to answer to anyone and could allow the company to run according to these principles. When I sold the company, the people who took over changed back to a standard organization chart with titles, planning meetings and all the stuff.

The individual human brain seems to strive for the pretense of certainty when the systems of existence are almost emergent. People drive away from the edge of chaos since it is uncomfortable. I was lucky enough to be able to hold people there where they could thrive . . . but they hated it.[21]

ARONSON+JOHNSON+ORTIZ, LP: DEEP AND WIDE OWNERSHIP

LeBaron's creativity aside, the more traditional approach to spreading ownership is seen at Aronson+Johnson+Ortiz, LP (AJO), founded by Ted Aronson. As a way of spreading the "psychic ownership" of the company, Aronson changed the name of the company from simply "Aronson+Partners" to include his two colleagues. (He tells us that the most fun part of that change was that he surprised them with it.) The financial ownership did not change: Aronson owns 60 percent, Johnson and Ortiz 15 percent each, three partners have 3 percent each, and one has 1 percent. Currently there are 12 partners in the firm, but in theory all 27 employees can become partners. The same is true with stock ownership. In the near future, new ownership will come out of Aronson's 60 percent share; in the farther future, it will come pro rata from the partners.

This arrangement seems to be working well for AJO. Unlike employees of LeBaron ("they hated it"), employees at AJO love the environment, which is evidenced by the fact that no one leaves. And performance is stunning, as we saw earlier in this book.

Of course, the larger a private firm is, the harder it is to spread the ownership. William Blair & Company is interesting in this respect, as it is truly a mid-sized investment firm that covers all five buckets: investment banking, asset management, equity research, institutional and private brokerage, and private capital. With 795 employees, WB&Co. is much larger than an AJO or a Turner, but it has still worked toward broad and deep ownership. Fully 167 employees are principals in the firm.

SUMMARY

Compensation and ownership are integral aspects of a firm's culture. Good leaders take the time and effort to forge consensus around key questions such as, "What is our compensation philosophy?" and "How do we define and manage ownership?" The benefit of getting everyone on the same page for these issues is seen in higher morale and increased effectiveness. Furthermore, top professionals will be less likely to leave a company that has its act together in this respect. Not incidentally, reduced turnover provides a steady pool of resources from which to pick and groom new leaders. This is the subject of Chapter 12.

TEST YOURSELF

Ask yourself the following yes/no questions:

Yes   No

1. Do you have evidence that your staff has a solid understanding of your compensation structure?
2. Do your compensation and bonus discussions go smoothly overall?
3. When people leave your firm, do you know why?
4. Have you attended to the top-rated factors for professional satisfaction?
5. Do you have specific opportunities for shared ownership in your firm?

6. What are your next steps regarding compensation and ownership?

Compensation must be aligned with what the firm is trying to accomplish and must reflect the immutable fact that people are the only assets in the business.
> —David Minella, when he was president of
> LGT Asset Management[22]

It's about communication and setting expectations.
—Deb Brown, Managing Partner, Russell Reynolds Associates

The best people simply will not stay with firms that do not provide some type of ownership.
> —Charles B. Burkhardt Jr., Founder, Rosemont
> Investment Partners, LLC[23]

CHAPTER 12

Homegrown Leadership

MFS stands for My Final Stop.
> —Lisa Jones, Executive Vice President, MFS

Change and fresh ideas need not come from the outside. Sustainable firms plan for succession and actively develop the talent that will lead into the future. In this chapter, you will learn:

- The link between homegrown talent and long-term success.
- The most meaningful activities for leadership development.
- Strategies for coaching your next generation of leaders.

"I heard your talk on investments and have a story for you about homegrown leadership," said the voice on the other end of the phone.

"Good one or bad one?" I joked.

"The worst one," she said, without a trace of amusement in her voice.

"Who is this?"

"I'll tell you, but only if you keep my name out of it."

After I agreed, she told me her name and a little about the investment firm she works with. The firm manages more than $50 billion (nearly all institutional money) and various asset classes: stocks, venture capital, bonds, real estate, some private placements. The firm employs about 220 people, of which approximately half are professional investment staff. The issue that concerned this lady was management succession.

She continued, "In 1996 our parent company got a new CEO and he was hell-bent on cutting $30 million out of our expense structure. He was

Chainsaw Al with a smile. As part of the belt tightening, he announced an early retirement program. Anyone over 50 could get full benefits and a good chunk of cash. Many employees jumped at it. Not our chief investment officer. Fred had been with the firm 14 years, and in the opinion of many colleagues and myself, had done a fine job. He was only 52 and wanted to stay on. He loved investing and people respected him. And, based on what you said in your talk about culture, he really knew the culture of the firm.

"So, he went to the new CEO and bargained for his job. Basically, he asked if he could stay on. The response he got was, 'Of course, you can stay on. But we really don't see a future for you in this organization.' Fred was bitter about being RIFed, but he packed up his Ibbotson Sinquefield chart and went home.

"As staff members, we discussed the possibilities among ourselves and decided to promote the deputy head of the department, a man named Bill. He had been with the firm 10 years and was not old enough to be considered in the RIF. As second in command, he had done a first-rate job bringing in talented people, setting a tone of fairness and honesty, training and developing new staff, running the asset allocation and strategic planning committees. While the CEO interviewed outside candidates for the CIO job, we circulated a petition to officers in the investment department asking if they would support Bill for the role of CIO. To a person, they signed off on it. Then another officer and I scheduled time with the CEO and presented the petition and our views on Bill. The CEO heaped a lot of praise on Bill: 'Oh yeah, he's a player and he's definitely being considered for the job.' We left the CEO's office absolutely certain that Bill would never be named CIO.

"And he wasn't. About two weeks later, the announcement came down that a guy from the East Coast had gotten the job. His background was fixed income at a major insurance firm. For months after arriving on the job, the rumor mill was in high gear: Is he here to cut more people? What is his strategic vision? Are we going to start down the acquisition trail? How am I going to fit into his new department? Or am I?

"He held a town hall meeting and proceeded to address the troops for 30 minutes and say virtually nothing, hence sending the rumor mill into even higher gear. By his third month into the job, we had lost three talented senior people. All of them had received calls from headhunters and decided, 'What the hell, now is as good a time as any to leave.' The new CIO made no serious attempts to counteroffer or otherwise keep these people on his team. Over the next six months we lost another key person per month. The statistics began to resemble the aftermath of a merger, where 25–50 percent of executives leave in the first year. Meantime, the CIO brought in a few of his own favorites from his old place of employment. By the end of his first year, we had lost nearly one-third of the professional staff, people that one year ago were considered talented performers. Asset-class performance was mediocre, assets under management were down slightly, and morale—as measured by a firm-wide opinion survey—stunk."

I had to agree with the caller, this was right in there with the worst of the succession stories. "Yeah, that's bad," I said to her.

"But there's more, you haven't heard the punch line," she said.

HOMEGROWN AT GE

Before we reveal the punch line, let's consider this story so far, because it illustrates an important point about the link between winning cultures and homegrown leaders. The best leader thoroughly understands the culture of the organization—and the only way this can occur is for the leader to be homegrown. That's why succession planning and leadership are so important.

Consider the case of Jack Welch. He was homegrown General Electric all the way. He started with GE after graduate school, when he was 24. The process by which he became CEO is remarkable. Seven years before Welch was named CEO, his predecessor—Reginald Jones—had developed a list of 96 possible candidates for the job, *all* of whom were GE insiders. (Contrast that with our example case!) Jones spent 2 years paring the list down to 12 contenders; then the list was further pruned down to 6. Each of the six was given a department to head, and reported directly to Jones. The evaluation process continued as the candidates competed in rigorous challenges, essay contests, and interviews, which included questions from Jones, such as, "You and I are flying in a company plane. It crashes. You and I are both killed. Who should be chairman of General Electric?"[1]

Seven years after the process started, Welch won the top job. The runner-up candidates went on to become presidents or CEOs of companies like GTE, Rubbermaid, Apollo Computer, and RCA.

The case of Welch at GE is not unusual for *Built to Last* companies. Collins and Porras showed that homegrown was the rule, not the exception. Table 12.1, from their study, shows the comparison between the 18 outstanding companies and the comparison companies.[2]

In choosing a new CEO, *Built to Last* companies went outside their own cultures only 3 percent of the time. The comparison companies were *six times* more likely to go outside and try to find a "savior" who would know how to fix the current problems. Only 2 of the 18 *Built to Last* companies,

TABLE 12.1   CEO Provenance Comparison

	Built to Last Companies	Comparison Companies
Number of CEOs in their collective history	121	158
Number of CEOs chosen from outside the company	4	31
Percentage	3.3%	19.62%
Average tenure as CEO	17.4 years	11.7 years

at some point in their history, went outside to find a CEO, versus 13 of the 18 comparison companies.

The *Built to Last* scoresheet for the "homegrown" component is shown in Table 12.2.[3] The average scores on these criteria, for both *Built to Last* and the comparison companies, are shown in Table 12.3.

If you've read this far in the book, you can appreciate the importance of choosing a CEO from within the ranks. Continuity of leadership is absolutely critical to preserving and protecting the values, vision, and culture of an organization. Remember that culture is invisible. It lives in the collective perception and behavior of every person in your organization. The minute you bring in an outsider, who is by definition foreign to the organization, you begin to redefine the culture. This point was made dramatically by many of the investment CEOs whom we interviewed. Glenn Carlson, co-CEO at Brandes in San Diego, said emphatically that the leadership team (and owners) would not sell the company because it would ruin the culture. New owners would become new leadership and would trash what Charles Brandes and his team have established over the past 20 years. This is where it becomes painfully obvious that there is more to running an investment firm than money. Brandes and his senior team could make a bundle selling out, but they love what they have created.

MFS: CULTURE DEFINES THE COMPANY

MFS in Boston is another firm that understands the importance of promoting from within. MFS believes that its culture is its competitive advantage. Here is the company's statement about culture:

At MFS, we believe that our culture is an integral part of our success. When you examine the inner layers of how people live and interact, you

TABLE 12.2 Homegrown Component Scoresheet

Category for scoring:	Score
V. Leadership Continuity	

Concept: Top companies spend a great deal of time developing and strengthening their culture, so they want to preserve it over time. Hence, they carefully train and develop future leaders so that the new CEO can be homegrown. Evidence supports the contention that internal succession (skillfully done) provides far better results than bringing in an outside CEO to rescue the firm (the savior syndrome).

Leadership continuity: "Promote from within"	
+1 Significant evidence that the CEO is selected from within the company.	
0 Evidence that the CEO is usually selected from within the company, with one or two exceptions.	
−1 Evidence that the company has deviated from the "promote from within" strategy for CEOs more than twice.	
Absence of charismatic leaders: No savior syndrome	
+1 No evidence that the company cannot find a highly qualified successor or is looking outside to find a savior to help in troubled times.	
0 Evidence that the company has experienced the above at least once in its history.	
−1 Evidence that the company has experienced the above at least twice in its history.	
Leadership training: "Homegrown"	
+1 Significant evidence that the company develops leaders through training, rotation of jobs, and mentoring, and carefully grooms future leaders.	
0 Some evidence that the company develops leaders as described above.	
−1 Little or no evidence that the company develops future leaders.	
Succession planning	
+1 Significant evidence that company has a history of careful succession planning and formal CEO grooming.	
0 Less evidence of the above.	
−1 Little or no evidence that the company has a history of careful CEO succession planning.	
Score: Leadership Continuity	

TABLE 12.3   Average Leadership Continuity Scores

Characteristic	Built to Last Companies' Average	Comparison Companies' Average
Leadership continuity: "Promote from within"	.83	−.06
Absence of charismatic leaders	.67	−.11
Leadership training: "Homegrown"	.39	−.33
Succession planning	.33	−.39
Leadership continuity	2.22	−.89

begin to understand the cultural essence of a place, an organization or, in our case, America's first and one of its most progressive mutual fund companies.

Our culture has enabled us to maintain a positive environment where all of our employees are encouraged to reach their full potential and where innovation and strong investment performance and service have been the results.

Teamwork is the hallmark of our culture, as seen most notably in MFS Original Research, a process in which our investment research analysts study companies inside and out, visiting thousands of businesses around the globe each year. They then pass their investment recommendations on to portfolio managers.

Emphasizing the free flow of information across all of our lines of business, our culture has allowed us to be internally cooperative and externally competitive.

It is a culture of opportunity that helps us develop talent from within and maintain a remarkable record of worker loyalty. We have carefully preserved our culture as our company has blossomed. And we believe it is one of the many traits that make us unique in the financial services world.[4]

Given this commitment to culture, it's not surprising that MFS is totally sold on homegrown leadership. The proof? The company's CEO, CIO, and CFO were analysts with MFS in the 1980s, moved up to portfolio management in the 1990s, and assumed their leadership roles at the turn of the century. They know the culture from the inside out and are speaking from personal deep belief when they endorse the company's statement claiming that culture is its competitive advantage. President John Ballen calls himself the "keeper of the culture," which is a primary responsibility of leadership.

Ballen spoke to us very openly and proudly of what they have established at MFS. At one point, we asked, "Given that culture is your competitive edge, why do you feel comfortable speaking so freely about yours?" The answer was obvious, in retrospect. Ballen said, "Culture takes years to build. It's not like the secret formula for Coke, which can be stolen and implemented in weeks. Culture must be carefully defined and implemented over years."

Evidence that MFS really has used homegrown management to build an exemplary culture is ample. When MFS made *Fortune*'s "Top 100 Places to Work" list in 2002, the article credited MFS's culture for its investment success:

> *MFS's corporate culture has been a big factor in its success. The firm prizes teamwork, dotes on youth and seems to inspire loyalty—a commodity that has always been rare in money management. In an industry where portfolio managers flit from pillar to post, just three investment professionals, out of 160, have left MFS over the past five years.*[5]

Another industry observer, Henry McVey at Morgan Stanley, agrees: "The strength of MFS is in its culture. People really seem to genuinely enjoy working at MFS. That's why they can attract and keep good people." The retention of good people, combined with excellent fund performance, has allowed MFS to succeed. "Pension funds like stability of personnel running money and consistent outperformance," says Salomon Smith Barney analyst Colin Devine. "MFS certainly has shown they can deliver that." To be precise, at the time of this writing, 77 percent of MFS's funds are outperforming their benchmarks for a 3-year period.

WILLIAM BLAIR: GROOMING LEADERS FOR THE TOP

Another investment firm that really understands the power of homegrown is William Blair & Company in Chicago. Founded in 1935 by William McCormick Blair, the firm shares the tradition of many *Built to Last* companies of having a founder who stayed in place for a long time. At *Built to Last* companies, the average tenure of the founder was 32.4 years. In Blair's case, he worked at the firm for 47 years, until his death in 1982 at the age of 97! (At the beginning of the 1980s, the Blair staff had become dispirited after living through a horrible decade of poor market returns. They asked Mr. Blair for a pep talk as they headed into the new decade. Mr. Blair responded, "The 80s? They're going to be great. They were last time!") In the tradition of their founder, Blair's chairman, Ned Jannotta, and CEO, Dave

Coolidge, have been at Blair for 44 and 34 years, respectively. When asked about his main objective in the firm right now, Coolidge said without hesitation that it was "to identify and develop the next generation of leaders." Coolidge told us that this goal is in keeping with what Mr. Blair told him in 1969 about the main mission: "I am trying to recruit people who will run this firm after the family is out." Jannotta and Coolidge agree that their most important task is to create an environment where the next generation can own and run the firm.

To this end, Blair identifies and promotes leaders who can step into the difficult role of running an investment firm. One such leader at Blair is Michelle Seitz. By her own admission, and that of Blair's senior leaders, she was thrown into a tough situation: becoming head of the investment management group (the largest division in the firm) during a market slump—and all that at the ripe old age of 35. Hard as it might have been, the combination of her investment and people skills earned her these endorsements from staff members:

> "An absolutely first-rate leader."
> "Michelle has stepped into a tough situation and has demonstrated great leadership characteristics."
> "She has been straightforward in communicating."
> "She has earned our confidence and respect."
> "She has made many important and difficult decisions."
> "She conveys confidence and inner strength, which are very important traits for your position."
> "She gets the highest marks from me with regard to her open and honest communication with the department."

Like Welch at GE, Seitz and other equally qualified individuals competed for the top jobs at Blair, with the goal being to preserve and strengthen the culture.

Like MFS, Blair lost some people during the high-flying tech bubble. Four young corporate finance professionals left to take senior positions at dot-com companies and get a piece of the action. By 2002, three had returned to Blair.

Do Blair's independence and strong culture lead to business success? As an article in *Forbes* from 2002 put it:

In the first half of this year Blair's profits rose 16% to an estimated $25 million on revenues of $150 million, as the overall industry's net income *fell 28%. While Blair has maintained its 21% return on equity through the current investment-banking downturn, the returns of Lehman Brothers and Goldman Sachs have fallen to 13% and 12%, respectively.*

Goldman did 51 M&A deals in the first half, 36% fewer than in the same period last year. Blair's corporate finance department, meanwhile, did 17 deals—only one less than it had done through June 30, 2001—worth $2.2 billion and generating an estimated $20 million in fee revenue.[6]

The foregoing experiences of Brandes, MFS, and Blair are examples of what is common practice in the best investment companies. At Vanguard, Jack Bogle, the founder, selected Jack Brennan as his successor and carefully groomed him for the top job. Likewise, at American Century, Jim Stowers, the founder, picked long-time employee Bill Lyons to take over the reins. At Franklin Portfolio Associates, John Nagorniak, the founder, passed the baton to John Cone, who worked with Nagorniak from the start and helped him develop the models that have made the company successful.

In light of the success of these companies, the story that opened this chapter seems even more ridiculous. "So, what is the punch line?" I asked, very curious as to how things could get much worse.

"It just happened again," my telephone informant said. "The CIO was moved to another position in the firm and the announcement just went out that we would look outside for another one. This guy has had six years to identify and develop a successor . . . SIX YEARS! And he hasn't done it. So now we get to start all over again. And you know, I think I *am* going to start over again, by looking for a healthier culture."

I felt genuine compassion for this woman. Clearly she was a good—and loyal—egg who had just had enough, and I told her so. The vision of our firm, as idealistic as it sounds, is to see our clients thriving in the challenge of their work. When the culture is riddled with dysfunction, it becomes impossible to enjoy the challenge of investment work. That person deserved to work at a Brandes, or an MFS, or a Blair, Vanguard, or American Century.

COACHING FOR LEADERS

Given the stunning track record of firms that promote from within, what can you do to coach those who have the potential to lead your firm into the future? Although inspirational vision statements and well-defined cultures help create strong work environments, nothing replaces one-on-one, highly personalized, closed-door counseling for motivating the next generation of leaders. This is the primary means of building close personal relationships, from the beginning, with strong rapport. To foster an atmosphere of dynamism, ambition, and professional development, coaches are always dropping by to ask, "How's it going?" A key talent of a good coach is to discern what motivates a particular individual. Status, recognition, money, challenging work, teaming, autonomy, rivalry, and many other stimuli may all be effective, but you have to know the individual. Good coaches don't dictate what should motivate people. They discover on a case-by-case basis what actually *does* motivate each individual whom they've targeted for potential promotions.

Coaching is continuous. Feedback and constructive criticism are best given in small doses, in as timely a fashion as possible. Feedback includes not just what could be improved, but also thoughts for action steps moving forward. Therefore, a good coach is both analytical and creative, a good listener and a skilled advisor.

Effective coaches go out of their way to celebrate during the journey. "Well done" and "thank you" are part of ongoing, sincere expressions of appreciation, even as they keep raising the bar to create stretch goals. As a coach, you want to be demanding, but you also realize the value of early wins and successes, giving people the confidence required to continue taking risks.

Jim Dethmer, lead coach for Focus Consulting, says that successful coaching has two primary functions:

> *First of all, a good coach helps identify the genius of the leader being coached. Far too many executives spend time doing things at which they are merely competent or even incompetent. Great leaders spend at least 80 percent of their time working out of their genius . . . those things that they love to do and that they do better than almost anyone else. Genius activity for the leader is activity that produces the highest ratio of productivity for time spent.*

The second primary function of a good coach, according to Dethmer, is to identify and help remove the critical blockage in a leader's development. Each person "has one key issue that, if identified and resolved, would enhance effectiveness and productivity significantly." Using tools like 360-degree feedback, assessment instruments, and personal interviews, coaches like Dethmer can identify the one key blockage. A great coach needs the skill to communicate the critical blockage in a way that creates openness rather than defensiveness in the leader.

TABLE 12.4 Career Events and Learning Opportunities Affecting Leadership Development

Type	Percentage
Job assignments	38%
Contact with other people	21%
Hardships endured	19%
Miscellaneous, including training	22% (9% course work)

LEADERSHIP DEVELOPMENT

The Center for Creative Leadership studied executives and what they considered to be the significant career events affecting their development. The results, shown in Table 12.4, clearly show that tough job assignments yielded the highest percentage of meaningful learning opportunities. Experience can be gained through new assignments at work and through leadership roles with volunteer organizations. Nevertheless, the best experience will only be as meaningful as your understanding of it when it's over; this is an important tie-in with coaching. Reflection is where the discoveries are made. Without reflection, experiences will not, by themselves, produce insights.[7]

The purpose of homegrown leadership is to perpetuate the values, the vision, and the processes you've built over time. As leader, you are the keeper of the culture. The best way to do that is to groom new leaders from within the culture.

TEST YOURSELF

Ask yourself the following yes/no questions:

Yes No

1. Did you rate well on the *Built to Last* scoresheet?
2. Do you have a leadership development program?
3. Have you rewarded and promoted the participants in this program?
4. Do you have a succession plan?
5. Have you clearly communicated the plan to the appropriate parties?

	Yes	No

6. Do you discuss coaching strategies regularly to learn from your experiences?

7. Do you recognize good work regularly and in a timely fashion?

8. What are your next steps in regard to succession?

PART
Four

Putting It All Together:
Case Study

CHAPTER 13

The Best of the Best:
Ariel Capital

Slow and steady wins the race.
—John W. Rogers Jr., Chairman and CEO, Ariel Capital

This chapter provides an in-depth look at Ariel Capital's strong culture. You will learn how to interpret and use:

- The Myers-Briggs Personality Type Indicator.
- The CAT Scan assessment.
- The trust assessment.
- The values measure.
- The innovation survey.
- The *Built to Last* scorecard.

This chapter takes all the elements of leadership and culture that we have discussed so far in the book and combines them for the analysis of one investment company. Having used Allstar Capital as a powerful example of what *not* to do to achieve long-term success, we thought we'd provide a positive example of a firm that has built an exceptionally strong culture. Selecting one firm from among the many excellent ones was not easy; in the end, we just went by the numbers. Based on our metrics for leadership and culture, Ariel Capital Management, Inc., eked out the top spot. With a turtle

mascot and a motto of "Slow and steady wins the race," Ariel Capital perfectly embodies the spirit of a book on long-term success.

As Dale and I prepared to leave for our meeting with Ariel's leaders, we
turned on *Good Morning America* on the television. The host was interviewing a woman named Mellody Hobson. I held up the current issue of
Newsweek and said to Dale, "Hey, she's on the cover of this week's issue."
Ordinarily it's no great coincidence for the same person to be on a morning
talk show and a weekly magazine cover. If it's your week in the limelight,
everyone features your story. What was coincidental, though, was that our
meeting that morning was with the same woman: Mellody Hobson, president of Ariel Capital, along with John W. Rogers Jr., the chairman and CEO.

We had interviewed a number of the senior team members at Ariel.
After a few rounds of interviews, we knew that we had found something
quite special. (When Peggy Eisen, chair of the Institute for Financial Markets, learned of our project, she said simply, "You must talk to Ariel.") For
one thing, all the people we met at Ariel seemed genuinely happy. Despite
the tough markets and the possibilities of war in Iraq, these people were
thrilled with the culture they had created. As president, Mellody oversees the
culture committee, which has specific responsibility for preserving and
strengthening the firm's culture.

Before we discuss the findings from Ariel, we want to make two things
very clear:

1. We have never done any work for Ariel, so we are not repaying them for
   favoring us with an assignment.
2. We cannot claim any credit for Ariel's excellence. We played no part in
   it whatsoever. (Importantly, though, Ariel did work with outside experts
   on vision, mission, values, strategy, culture formation, creativity, communication, and other areas of competency. They do planned offsite retreats each year, part of which are devoted solely to examining and discussing culture issues. This practice is common to the best firms.)

ARIEL'S RESULTS: AN ENVIABLE RECORD

Before we look at the leadership and cultural practices that earned Ariel the
top spot in our rating system, let's look at its financial performance. After
all, if we couldn't link excellent leadership and cultural practices to performance, the economic value of this book would be quite limited. The exciting aspect of all our research is the direct correlation between excellent
qualitative factors (leadership, culture, etc.) and good quantitative results

(fund performance, growth in assets, low employee turnover, etc.). After a while, our ability to predict a firm's excellent financial results just from examining its qualitative data became remarkably accurate.

Ariel's track record is outstanding. In our research we focused on three common measures:

1. Long-term fund performance.
2. Growth in assets under management.
3. Employee turnover.

Fund performance has been superior. Since Ariel's flagship fund was started in 1986, Lipper Analytical Services has rated it the best fund in its category. Not top quartile or top decile, but the best fund, period.

Assets under management have grown over the past 10 years at 23.3 percent annually. Total assets under management for Ariel at the end of 2002 were just over $10 billion. In 2002, Ariel was the second fastest growing mutual fund in the industry for the year.

As far as attracting and retaining good people, Ariel has lost only one key executive in the past five years. On September 30, 2002, Eric McKissack resigned from Ariel for personal reasons. He did not join another investment firm, nor did he start his own. McKissack is still friends with his colleagues at Ariel, and attended Rogers's wedding even after his departure. Aside from that one loss, Ariel's team is completely intact.

Finally, the University of Chicago Business School provided another interesting measure of success. Julie Morton, associate dean of MBA Career Services, told us that for three years running Ariel has had a 100 percent yield on offers for full-time employment. That is, *every* offer they made was accepted by the candidate. When I asked Julie to interpret this statistic, she said simply, "People really think highly of them and want to work there."

A LEADER'S CHARACTER AND VISION

Ariel's story starts even before its founding by John W. Rogers Jr. The story begins with the people who influenced his life and shaped his character. In our meeting, Rogers spoke respectfully of his father, Judge John W. Rogers, a Tuskeegee Airman during World War II and subsequently a juvenile court judge in Chicago. He said his father believed in "discipline, integrity, and hard work." His father's code of honor was "Always do what you say you will do" and "Tell the truth."

An equally strong influence on Rogers was his mother, Jewel Stradford

Lafontant. Also a lawyer, she held a number of influential positions, including one as a representative to the United Nations in 1972. Rogers remembers these lessons from his mother:

- "Anything is possible."
- "Never accept second best."
- "Do everything you do in a first-class way."

Another influence on Rogers's life was a character we met earlier in this book: Ned Jannotta, the much-admired leader at William Blair & Company. Jannotta hired Rogers at Blair and taught him that "the best way to build an excellent firm is to surround yourself with quality people and be willing to share the credit and the profits." Rogers has done both at Ariel. Note that the name of the firm he founded is not "Rogers Capital." He has worked to make it a true partnership and not "his" firm.

Much of what Rogers learned about teamwork came from his college basketball coach, Peter Carril, a basketball Hall-of-Famer. Like Jack Brennan at Vanguard, Carril was ruthless about subordinating personal egos to the good of the team. The same lessons were reinforced by John Johnson, founder of Johnson Publishing. Johnson preached the importance of not worrying about whether you are the center of attention. He also taught Rogers about patience: "If you did a good job consistently and were patient, others would recognize it and you would be rewarded."

These influences, then, were very much at the core of the man who founded Ariel in December 1982. Rogers wrote that

> *The name Ariel is one of my favorite names. It was derived from a character on the television show,* The Waltons. *When I was a teenager, I named my pet parrot Ariel. Originally, we had two logos. We used the turtle and hare on the Ariel newsletter and a gazelle on the company brochure (the gazelle was suggested by a PR firm). The gazelle's image of being swift and nimble on difficult terrain had some appeal, [but] in light of suggesting an ability to weather market turbulence, the turtle seemed to capture more of Ariel's essence.*[1]

From the outset Rogers was focused on the notion of "slow and steady wins the race." He has always valued patience. His vision has always been for Ariel to be the premier small and mid-cap value fund manager. The actual wording of the values and vision statement has changed over the years, as he and his senior team continue to sharpen and shape it, but the intention is the same. From its humble beginnings—less than $1 million under management by a handful of employees—Ariel has grown to 65 employees and more than $12 billion under management.

THE PERSONALITY OF LEADERSHIP

We often start with the Myers-Briggs Personality Type Indicator in assessing an investment firm's leadership and culture. This tool helps the senior team answer questions such as:

- How do we take in information?
- How do we process the information?
- How do we reach decisions?
- How do we communicate those decisions to others?
- How do we best leverage our differences?

We want to know the hard-wiring of the leaders so that we can look for strengths, weaknesses, and blind spots. Myers-Briggs tells us what people pay attention to, how they take in information, how they process it, how they make decisions, and how they communicate those decisions. Myers-Briggs also provides insights into values, beliefs, and behaviors. Table 13.1 reviews the Myers-Briggs preferences (that is, the possible ways in which humans prefer to use their brains) and shows where Rogers falls on each scale.

Rogers's type was fairly easy to identify just from meeting with him. He is very thoughtful and his energy seems inwardly focused. He did not process his thinking out loud, as would an Extrovert. The second preference was a bit harder to discern, but there were some clues, such as the name of the company. Intuitives like to deal with metaphors and visual images. The name *Ariel* and the myriad of turtle artifacts all around the office were signs that Rogers likes symbols. All the senior staff members told us that Rogers is very comfortable with the big picture. Like many master investors, though, Rogers has trained himself to be good with details as well. This combination is potent for investment success.

The third preference deals with decision making—Thinking vs. Feeling. More than 80 percent of the investors we've met and worked with have a preference for Thinking. Rogers is a rare turtle in this sense, as he prefers Feeling. In simple terms, Thinkers check their heads first and then consult their hearts; Rogers goes to the heart first and then consults his head.

At first we were surprised that the firm we had chosen to highlight was led by a Feeler, but after some reflection we realized that this made perfect sense. After all, we are highlighting the people side of the investment firm in

TABLE 13.1 MBTI Review (with Rogers's Scoring)

Extrovert (E): Breadth Do-think-do People, places, things	**Introvert (I):** Depth Think-do-think **ROGERS** Inner world of ideas
Sensing (S): Practical Observant Step-by-step	**Intuition (N):** Theoretical Creative **ROGERS** Leaps of intuition
Thinking (T): Objective Logical Tough-minded	**Feeling (F):** Subjective Values-based **ROGERS** Tender-hearted
Judging (J): Organized Decisive **ROGERS** Disciplined	**Perceiving (P):** Casual Open-ended Flexible

this book—and who better to do a brilliant job with people than a Feeler? Feelers naturally prefer harmony and good relationships, which is precisely what Rogers has created at Ariel. His desire for good working relationships extends to his policy of telling all employees that they can call him at home, at any hour, if they need to speak to him. This offers goes beyond just sounding good; many employees have taken him up on it. People who have a preference for Feeling typically have a warmth to them. And while we wouldn't describe John as gushing, he certainly is different from, say, a Donald Rumsfeld or a Lou Gerstner, neither of whom give off warm fuzzies. Rogers enjoys people and especially likes watching them grow and develop. Like Patrick O'Donnell, he did not hesitate to describe his role as "nurturing."

The final preference shows whether a person likes to be organized and plan things, or casual and flexible. Again, it was evident from meeting with John in his offices that he likes things organized and precise. His office would never be confused with Andy Rooney's.

The fact that Rogers is INFJ in the Myers-Briggs rating also tells us that his temperament is Communalist (based on the NF preferences). We were at first surprised that such an outstanding investment firm was founded by a Communalist, as they are fairly rare in the investment landscape. (The most notable Communalist whom we know personally is Rob Arnott, founder of First Quadrant and now editor in chief of the *Financial Analysts Journal*.) Leaders at successful investment firms most commonly are NTs rather than NFs.

Communalists are first and foremost interested in people and relationships. They are also interested in ethical behavior and values. Rogers began working on a statement of guiding principles before he even founded Ariel. Over the years, the mission and values have been revised and perfected. Now they are circulated with the firm's Tuesday status report so that each week all employees see the values. It's no surprise that one of the values of a Communalist is "community"! As you will see shortly, this value runs through the entire organization, starting with the founder.

How does the personality of the founder/leader relate to the temperament of the senior team? In our experience, working with many investment and nonfinancial companies, we have nearly always found a match between the leader and the team. In other words, it's true that birds of a feather flock together. Ariel is an interesting exception. Table 13.2 shows a fairly well-balanced team, with the exception of the final preference: way more Judgers (organized) than Perceivers (flexible). The senior team is a mirror of Rogers's own personality.

Given Rogers's preference for Introversion, Intuition, and Feeling, he has assembled a team that has fair representation in the other preferences (Extroversion, Sensing, and Thinking). This balance is extremely important, as each of the preferences brings its own strengths to the job.[2] We have seen many cases in which the preferences of the leader were so thoroughly mirrored in the team that there was little or no balance. (For example, a quant

TABLE 13.2 Balance of Ariel's Senior Team

Extrovert (E): Breadth		Introvert (I): Depth	
Do-think-do		Think-do-think	**ROGERS**
People, places, things	3	Inner world of ideas	5
Sensing (S): Practical		**Intuition (N): Theoretical**	
Observant		Creative	**ROGERS**
Step-by-step	4	Leaps of intuition	4
Thinking (T): Objective		**Feeling (F): Subjective**	
Logical		Values-based	**ROGERS**
Tough-minded	3	Tender-hearted	5
Judging (J): Organized		**Perceiving (P): Casual**	
Decisive	**ROGERS**	Open-ended	
Disciplined	8	Flexible	0

team from a major global firm was composed of nine Intuitives and only one Sensor. This team was wonderful at brainstorming, but weak at implementation.) Rogers's team, in contrast, has a good mix of the different thinking styles. Researchers Lu Hong and Scott Page have found that "cognitively diverse groups can locate solutions to difficult problems and that diverse groups tend to outperform groups of the individually best agents."[3] Michael Mauboussin at Credit Suisse First Boston has studied this research and agrees with us that "Myers-Briggs provides a useful and accessible way for an investment firm to measure its cognitive diversity."[4] In this regard, Rogers has assembled a diverse group based on the first three preferences. (As we will see shortly, another top value for Ariel is diversity, so the Myers-Briggs result is in keeping with this core value.)

But what about the 8–0 score on Judging versus Perceiving? Isn't that a gross violation of the diversity principle? In a word, yes. In defense of Ariel, though, we can say that the overwhelming majority of investment professionals is Judger, not Perceiver. They tend to like their world organized and their plans decisive. The senior team at Ariel must be careful not to get blindsided by this preference. Their desire to be precise and decisive may interfere with the need to react flexibly to the changing demands of the market. Marty Zweig, the famous technician, noted in this regard: "The problem with most people who play the market is that they are not flexible."[5] Furthermore, Judgers tend to be uncomfortable with loose ends. During brainstorming, for instance, they are the first to say, "Okay, we've got enough ideas out on the table, let's start to make some decisions." Any expert on creativity will tell you that the great ideas come in the second or third wave. Therefore, members of this senior team need to be conscious of these pitfalls in order to avoid them. They may have to learn to delay some decisions if they are to come up with the best solutions.

Although we chose to discuss the Myers-Briggs tool first, we want to emphasize that we're not necessarily stating that you *have* to use the MBTI to build your team. Our point is that this kind of data helps you understand the potential impact of style preferences, which cause conflict for some and too much homogeneity for others. Myers-Briggs can help you benefit from the diversity you have and figure out how to compensate for what may be missing, so that you and your team can do your best thinking.

The overall balance in thinking styles and values is also seen in the Culture Assessment Test (CAT) Scan for Ariel's senior team. The Myers-Briggs results for the senior team place them in the categories listed in Table 13.3.

The absence of Adventurists is not at all unusual for active investment managers. For the most part, Adventurists find traditional money management firms boring and want something more exciting, like day trading or

TABLE 13.3   Four Investment Cultures

	Number from Senior Team at Ariel			
	4	1	3	0
	Guardian	Rationalist	Communalist	Adventurist
Core values:	Efficiency, hard work, duty	Competence, winning, excellence	Teamwork, openness, trust	Freedom, innovation, risk-taking
Definition of success:	Excellent systems, smooth operations	Excellent track record and reputation for expertise	Happy employees, a great place to work	Innovative products and services on the cutting edge
Leadership is:	Stabilizing and reliable	Conceptual and strategic	Facilitative and visionary	Entrepreneurial and risk-taking
Core business:	Index funds, traditional bank and insurance investment operations	Active managers: quant, value, growth	Retail and high net worth: client service is critical	Hedge funds and day traders, where risk and transaction levels are high
Examples:	Vanguard, Allstate Investments	Wellington, Brandes	Ferguson Wellman	Hedge funds, day traders
Main focus:	Processes	Performance	People	Pioneering

hedge funds. Still, a firm devoid of Adventurists may lose some of the risk-taking energy that they provide. Ariel's CAT Scan (see Figure 13.1) correlates perfectly with the temperaments listed earlier—as they should, given that they are measuring the same thing. (For this reason, we often skip the CAT Scan if we have a team's Myers-Briggs results.) When using the CAT Scan, your team can find out:

- Does our senior team share the same view of our business?
- If not, what are reasons for our seeing the same business differently?
- Are we well balanced across the four quadrants? (the Balanced Scorecard approach to management)
- What are our strengths and weaknesses, relative to the four quadrants?

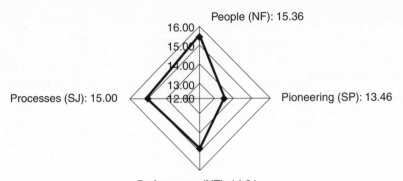

People (NF): 15.36

Processes (SJ): 15.00

Pioneering (SP): 13.46

Performance (NT): 14.91

FIGURE 13.2   Goal Balance in Culture Types: Ariel Capital

- What is the relationship between our preferences and the type of business we're in?
- What impact do our preferences have on our strategies for improvement?

Ariel's CAT Scan shows that there is reasonably good balance among the four types of cultures. In the spirit of the Balanced Scorecard, we expect to see this in the top companies. A strong imbalance usually means trouble: one or more of the key areas of the firm is not getting its due. In Ariel's case, the lowest score (13.46) is in the Pioneering quadrant, which reflects the absence of Adventurist energy. Because there is a natural and healthy tension between the Process people (Guardians) and the Pioneering people (Adventurists), you would not expect to see high scores for the latter in a firm that has four Guardians on the senior staff. Rather, we see that Process is the second highest score, after the understandably highest score for People, reflecting the values of Rogers, the founder, and his preference for people and community. In such a case (that is, when Myers-Briggs results are available), the CAT Scan acts as confirmation. It's also useful when debriefing results with the senior team, in that it gives a visual representation and therefore stimulates conversation.

Some readers may be thinking, "If Ariel is strongest in the People/community quadrant, then why isn't it more aligned with one-on-one advisory services? Why is Ariel an active manager of mutual funds?" Good question, because it is important for firms to align with their strengths. A heavy Process firm (index fund, for example) shouldn't try to swim in the same waters with highly creative and entrepreneurial teams; the Process firm will get eaten alive. Firms should play to their strong suits. In Ariel's case, an important value is client satisfaction. Educating investors and providing service are huge considerations. Their people skills are so tuned to the point that a doorman at the St. Regis Hotel in New York bought shares in their fund simply because of the way Ariel people interacted with him when they visited and stayed at the hotel. Excellent fund performance is seen as providing a service to the client, not as an end in itself.

This attitude is different from, say, the performance culture at Brandes, where co-CEO Glenn Carlson openly admitted, "We really enjoy kicking complete ass!" We just can't imagine Rogers saying that. Although very competitive, Rogers's main thrill seems to come from helping people build financial security. In this light, Ariel's presence—and success—as an active mutual fund manager makes perfect sense.

To summarize so far, Myers-Briggs and the related CAT Scan can help you determine the natural tendencies of your leaders. You can assess the balance of thinking styles on your team. You can determine where strengths can be leveraged. You can also assess whether the dominant culture in your organization is aligned with the proper business strategy. Are you playing to your organization's strength? Are there any severe imbalances that should be addressed? You should be concerned if one culture is grossly underrepresented. It comes as no surprise that Ariel, which has a stated value of "building a diverse and talented team," shows good balance in our diagnostics.

TRUST BUILDERS

Next, we look at how well this leadership team has built trust in the organization. Trust is the lubricant that allows the engine to run smoothly. In firms where trust levels are low, everything takes longer. Turnover goes up. Cycle times lengthen. There is less adherence to cultural norms, which usually means that the loudest voices (not necessarily the leaders) set the tone. Agreements must be negotiated and wordsmithed and signed. Lawyers are brought in. If trust is low enough, eventually everything comes to a standstill. The master investor Warren Buffett understands this principle. His acquisitions are done on a handshake with the owner. Buffett rightly points out that if you don't trust the other person, there's no point going into business together. No amount of lawyering can fix basic distrust.

A trust survey will help clarify issues such as:

- Do we have serious trust issues in our organization?
- If so, which of the three components of trust is most responsible?

- What can we do to address the weak areas?
- What specific behaviors are called for?

Ariel's senior leaders all mirror the founder's deep belief in integrity. The earlier quotations from Rogers's father and mother show what shaped him, and these values underlie his commitment to building trust within his organization. Fear is a major factor in distrust. Fear inhibits people from speaking openly and honestly. It interferes with the natural process of clearing up misunderstandings and admitting mistakes. It was evident from our visits that fear has largely been driven out of the firm at Ariel, but we asked the Ariel staff to complete the indicator discussed in the earlier chapter on trust, as a way of measuring trust levels. In Figure 13.2, Ariel's results are presented alongside those of other exemplary investment firms and those of Allstar Capital, where trust had largely disappeared.

Ariel's trust levels are exceptionally good. Each of the three legs of the "trust stool"—congruence, competence, and caring—displays high scores. Ordinarily, a firm's results suggest that one of the three legs needs work, and usually we can predict which it will be. For example, a highly competitive Rationalist/Performance culture may score well on the congruence and competence scales, but it often shows weakness in the caring department. Conversely, we have seen very friendly, warm Communalist/People cultures that score well on congruence and caring but need to work on their competence (bringing home the bacon).

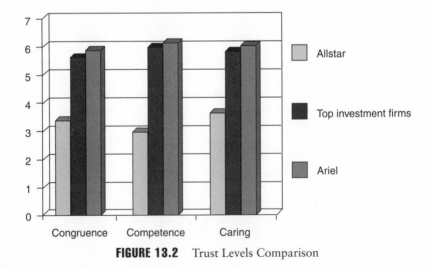

FIGURE 13.2 Trust Levels Comparison

The benefit of this trust survey is that it allows the leaders to analyze the responses and get down to the specific behaviors that are creating distrust. This level of detail is far and away more useful than some trust surveys we've seen, which basically ask, "Do you trust your coworkers?" The survey we've provided allows you first to break trust into three distinct components, and then to drill down into the weak component(s) and find out exactly what behaviors are causing the distrust. For example, in the Communalist/People firm we just mentioned, where competence was the weakest leg of the stool, the lowest score by far on the survey was for the statement, "Leadership helps people focus on a few key business priorities and clearly stated goals." In other words, trust was lacking in the area of results because the leaders were not stating and prioritizing clear goals. That sort of information is useful because leaders can address it and fix it.

In Ariel's case, areas for further improvement are "clear performance goals" and "accountability." This highlights opportunities to clarify roles and responsibilities. It also indicates that senior leaders can continue their efforts to create open and honest communication.

We move on, then, to looking at the values of the organization. Typically, after examining the Myers-Briggs, CAT Scan, and trust results, we can make some educated guesses about what we'll see in the values assessment. For example, given Ariel's excellent trust levels, we anticipate seeing all positive values in the results, with no limiting values or behaviors appearing because of distrust or fear.

VALUES ALIGNMENT

The values assessment tool[6] allows you to survey the entire firm, quickly and easily, to see if there is general recognition of and agreement on the most important values in the firm. Equally importantly, it also allows you to see which areas the employees are suggesting will yield opportunities for future improvement. Firms that have strong cultures and agreement around values are *coherent*. One of the reasons for Allstar Capital's collapse was an utter absence of coherence. When tough times hit, there was no glue holding the team together. The Allstar leaders couldn't appeal to common values and a shared direction, because they had built their organization on two faulty premises (see the myths in Chapter 1):

1. Brains are everything.
2. Money is everything.

The values assessment will help you answer questions like:

- What are the commonalities among our staff's personal values, those of the firm currently, and what people desire for the future?
- What are the four or five key words people use to describe our culture and our truths about who we are?
- What are the key differences between how our staff describes the current culture and the desired culture? What changes do these differences suggest?
- What incremental improvements or changes might we consider to foster an environment in which everyone can do their best work?

The values assessment was given to the entire staff at Ariel, and the results are shown in Figure 13.3.

Several facts jump out from these results.

1. First, as predicted, there are no limiting values/behaviors, in either the current or desired culture assessments. (Remember Allstar, which had all but two limiting factors in its current culture?) Limiting values/ behaviors are fear-based and generally cause the organization to operate at suboptimal levels. An example of a limiting value/behavior is blame. It is a very good sign of corporate health if no such words appear on the list.

2. Second, we see that both current and desired states reflect a full spectrum of values. In his research, Richard Barrett found that the best-performing companies were balanced between the survival needs at the bottom of the hourglass and the more selfless interests at the top. Firms that are lopsided, too much at the top or bottom, have cause for concern. Note that in Ariel's chart, no values are identified in the bottom level (the survival level). This is true of most highly successful investment firms (Brandes, Aronson+Johnson+Ortiz, William Blair, and others). Collins and Porras found that this is true of the truly great companies: They are not preoccupied with profit, but rather with providing great products or services. The absence of data in a level can also mean that there are simply no issues in this regard for the firm.

3. Third, we notice a strong match between the current values and the desired values. Fully seven of the current values are found in both lists:
   - Client satisfaction.
   - Community involvement.

Current Culture Values

1. *Client satisfaction*
2. *Community involvement*
3. *Diversity*
4. *Being the best*
5. *Accountability*
6. *Discipline*
7. Loyalty
8. Social responsibility
9. *Teamwork*
10. Long-term perspective

Desired Culture Values

1. *Client satisfaction*
2. *Diversity*
3. *Community involvement*
4. *Teamwork*
5. *Accountability*
6. *Being the best*
7. Clear performance goals
8. Balance (home/work)
9. Continuous improvement
10. *Discipline*
11. Ethics
12. Passion
13. Quality

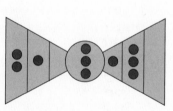

Legend

Bold and italics = Current Culture and Desired Culture match

L = Potentially Limiting (hollow dots)

FIGURE 13.3 Ariel Capital. (Reprinted with permission: Richard Barrett, Corporate Transformation Tools®, www.corptools.com.)

- Diversity.
- Being the best.
- Accountability.
- Discipline.
- Teamwork.

4. Finally, the real benefit of this values assessment is its capacity to indicate, even for the best of the best, where to focus continuous improvements. The staff of Ariel focused on two areas for further development: clear performance goals and balance. This gives the leadership information for planning and resourcing.

This tells us that Ariel is close to its optimal culture. They are truly walking their talk. Firms that have no limiting values and are nearly aligned with their desired culture are great places to work. They are also highly effective, as the values indicated in the desired state are specifically defined as those that "contribute to a high performing team." Ariel's employees are telling us that the values they are currently living out in the organization are one and the same as those that allow for optimal performance. This is tangible proof that Ariel is harnessing the full potential of its people assets.

Do these values square with what we learned about Ariel from Myers-Briggs and the trust survey? Absolutely. Rogers and his team expressed strong preferences for the Communal quadrant, which shows up in the values: client satisfaction, community involvement, diversity, and teamwork. The next strongest quadrant was Guardian, with its emphasis on Process. No surprise, then, that accountability and discipline appear as strong values in the Ariel culture. The third strongest quadrant was Rationalist, with an emphasis on Performance. We also see that "being the best" was chosen in both the current and desired value lists. Notice that the final quadrant, Adventurist, with its interest in innovation and pioneering, was not represented in Ariel's list of values. Again, no surprise, given that there are very few Adventurists in the firm and none in leadership. So, the Myers-Briggs and CAT Scan analyses fit tightly with the values assessment. This helps us feel secure that the leadership and culture at Ariel make sense. Just as we might examine a candidate's resumé to see that her experiences and education and hobbies are congruent, we get the same sense of congruency by looking at the various pieces of the picture for Ariel.

How does Ariel's value assessment square with its stated values? Are they like Enron, saying one thing and doing another? Or do they walk their talk? Here are Ariel's stated values:

We move forward knowing patience is the key to our long-term success.

Focus:
As we strive to be the premier small and mid-cap value investment firm, we will continue to grow our company with discipline and rigorous standards.

Contrarian:
Our tradition of independent thinking differentiates us from the crowd.

Teamwork:
Our diverse and experienced professionals work together toward a common goal of excellence in every aspect of our business. Through significant personal ownership in our firm, as well as in our mutual funds, our interests are squarely aligned with those of our clients.

Community:
We are committed to strengthening the neighborhoods and cities in which we live and work, practicing a unique model of corporate responsibility.

As one reads through this values statement, it is evident that the results of the values assessment reflect the congruence between these stated values and the day-to-day reality of working at Ariel. The stated goals of "patience" and "long-term success" are mirrored in the survey results of "discipline" and "long-term perspective." The value of "focus" reiterates the emphasis on discipline and rigorous standards, and the survey captures this spirit with the words "discipline" and "accountability."

The stated value of being "Contrarian," which correlates with the value assessment terms of "unique insights" or "innovation," is probably the weakest link between the stated values and the survey results. Because of the Myers-Briggs and CAT Scan analyses, we are not surprised that words like *innovation* do not appear as top values. Leadership at Ariel may want to examine this value further and ask questions like:

■ What exactly do we mean by "independent thinking"?
■ Do we mean that unique insights/innovation are key to our success?
■ If so, then how does the leadership team encourage more innovative, independent thinking?

The benefit of this rigorous examination is that it helps leaders to spot any inconsistencies and address them. We know from talking to senior leaders at Ariel, such as Merrillyn Kosier, that she manages an extremely creative group. When they design advertisements, for example, one of the criteria for success is that the ad must be completely distinctive, so that no other mutual fund could simply slap its name on the top. Kosier also insists that her team be made up of atypical members. None of them is an MBA and all have experience in different fields. In this sense, they are living out the value of diversity.

The stated value of "teamwork" is completely in sync with the results of the values assessment. Furthermore, the way in which Ariel states the teamwork goal reinforces its strong value of providing great service to its clients.

The final stated value, "community," also squares completely with the survey results. Two values of "community involvement" and "social responsibility" are clearly spelled out in Ariel's guiding-principles statement.

The values assessment, then, helps us see that Ariel has carefully thought out its guiding principles, and that it has woven them into the fabric of everyday life at the firm.

CONTINUOUS IMPROVEMENT

The additional benefit of the values assessment is that it provides a road map for continuous success. If we heard one mantra being chanted repeatedly by the best firms, it was, "good enough never is." Brennan at Vanguard said it most convincingly: "This had better be the worst you ever are." In other words, every day henceforth, you'll be better than you were today. Some employees find this attitude exhausting and torturous and leave Vanguard. Brennan told us, "I make no apologies for it. That's our attitude here." Collins and Porras found the same ethic in the *Built to Last* companies.

The values assessment points out areas for further improvement. In a case like Ariel's, these areas represent more tweaks than major overhauls. Nevertheless, it is precisely these tweaks—when performed year after year—that contribute to outstanding performance. An examination of the desired-culture values shows that "clear performance goals" is a newcomer to the list. Employees at Ariel are saying in the survey that clear performance goals are not highly valued in the current environment, but that they *should* be in an optimal environment. Leaders need to address this concern. The first step is to open a discussion of the topic and find out exactly what employees meant by "clear performance goals." (The Visual Explorer exercise discussed in Chapter 10 could be very useful for this.) When the opportunity has been identified and agreed upon, then they can outline steps for improvement. Similar steps can be taken around the other two values of "balance (home/work)" and "continuous improvement." Again, we are talking about tweaks in this instance. But in a finely tuned organization like Ariel, that's where you look for improvements.

The values assessment also identifies "independent thinking" as an area of possible improvement. Leaders identified Contrarian thinking/independent thinking as a core value, but employees did not identify these values in either the current or desired states. (They could have chosen synonyms like "innovation," "creativity," "thought leadership," or "unique insights," but they didn't.) The results of the cultural innovation survey may help in this regard.

INNOVATIVE CULTURE SURVEY

Precisely because innovation and thought leadership are so crucial to investment success, we have separate surveys that answer these questions:

- What are the individual creative styles of the leadership team?
- How does your current culture encourage or discourage innovation?
- What further actions can you take to foster creativity?

The results of the creative styles survey were in line with our expectations (see Table 13.4). Given that the leadership team has four Guardian temperaments, they were most likely to be Adaptors. Their style of creativity tends to be more in the box. They can be marvelous at continuous improvement, but tend to be skeptical of brand-new, break-the-mold approaches. The other four leaders, all Intuitives on the MBTI, are more comfortable with paradigm shifts and big ideas. They are split between Balancers and Innovators. It is not surprising at all that a culture led by mostly Adaptors and Balancers would value innovation less highly than other values such as "client satisfaction," "teamwork," and the like.

The question for Ariel—and many other firms—becomes, "What kind of creativity is important to your success?" In other words, do you need continuous improvements in already excellent systems? Or do you need periodic breakthroughs, including brand-new paradigms? Do active managers in the mutual fund industry need the former or the latter type of thinking? Gary Brinson succeeded nicely with the former, whereas Ralph Wanger has performed brilliantly with the latter. There is no right answer, but there should be clarity as to the approach and its fit with your firm and people.

The second question about innovative culture is also important to Ariel. Regardless of which type of creativity they are going for—incremental steps or breakthrough—the culture has to be supportive. Ariel's results from the

TABLE 13.4   Creative Styles Survey Results

Scores:

8–21	22–26	27–40
4 people	2 people	2 people
Adaptors	**Balancers**	**Innovators**
Analytical	Reliable	Innovative ideas are also practical
Solutions fit current structure	Find solutions quickly	Will work day and night on stimulating problem
Good in emergencies	Goal-oriented	High energy, generate ideas quickly
Stable and practical	Versatile	Welcome complex problems
Good team players	Calculated risk takers	Improvise readily
Task-oriented	Tolerant of extremes	
Conscientious	Fingers in many pies	
Very efficient		
Maximize available resources		
Possible Weakness		
Too detailed	Not strong at either extreme: detail work or	Hates being managed
Too risk-averse	big, new ideas	Bored easily

creative culture assessment indicate that employees largely feel supported in their efforts to be creative. Nearly all the responses in this survey were "4" (i.e., Agree) or better (i.e., 5 = Strongly agree). All questions are phrased in such a way that the higher the answer, the better for a creative environment. Only one factor was clearly identified as a negative in the environment:

I do NOT feel that there is too much work and too little time to do it.

On a 5-point scale, the answer to this question averaged 2.6, markedly below any other. There is good news and bad news here. The good news is that this is far and away the biggest negative factor in investment firms concerning creativity. (In a survey by Moss Adams LLP, "time management" was identified as the top challenge facing investment firms, even ahead of "capacity to serve clients.") People cannot be creative when they are overloaded with deadlines and assignments. Ariel is not alone in having this problem. The bad news is that they still have to deal with it. Other firms that have identified creativity as being absolutely essential to their success have devoted entire retreats to tackling this problem head-on. They ask, "How do we manage the workloads so that our people can still be highly creative?" Answers have included everything from enhancing time management skills to beefing up creativity skills, so that in the shorter amount of time staff can still be more creative by being more efficient. We reiterate that the purpose of this discussion is not necessarily to provide an answer to Ariel's creativity problem. Rather, the assessment and discussion are intended to point out areas that are ripe for continuous improvement.

ARIEL CAPITAL: IS IT BUILT TO LAST?

Now that we've discussed all these diagnostics, and shown applications for Ariel, we can address the basic question posed by this book. Is Ariel built to last? Has this company created a strong culture that will endure hard times and flourish over the long run?

Built to Last Scoresheet

For the answer, we turn our attention to the *Built to Last* scoresheet, which embodies the research of Collins and Porras. Using the information from the diagnostics discussed earlier, and our knowledge of Ariel from many interviews with leaders and staff, we've assigned the following scores for each of the 21 factors (see Table 13.5). The scoresheet uses the following ranking system:

+1 = Yes, the company definitely follows this *Built to Last* principle.
 0 = The company somewhat follows this principle.
−1 = The company does not appear to follow this principle.

Built to Last Analysis

Values and Vision

Having read Ariel's mission and values statement and seen the results of the values assessment, we had no hesitation in assigning 1s for all the categories A–D. The rating for the C category, "Purpose beyond profits," is supported both by the values assessment (no values relating to financial goals) and by remarks from Rogers himself: "Our purpose goes well beyond money. It's not just about dollars and cents. Community service is a huge concern of ours." Mellody Hobson, president, echoed these sentiments and told us that

TABLE 13.5 *Built to Last* Scoresheet for Ariel

Category	Built to Last Companies	Comparison Companies	Ariel Capital
I. Values and Vision	**2.56**	**−1.55**	**4**
A. Clarity of values and vision	.78	−.11	1
B. Historical alignment around values and vision	.67	−.89	1
C. Purpose beyond profits	.39	−.33	1
D. Alignment of words and actions	.72	−.22	1
II. Ambitious Goals	**1.50**	**−.73**	**2**
E. Use of ambitious goals to stimulate progress	.72	−.17	1
F. Choice of truly outrageous goals	.72	.00	0
G. Consistent use of ambitious goals to stimulate progress	.06	−.56	1
III. Strong Culture	**1.88**	**−.66**	**3**
H. Cultural indoctrination: Molding the new hires	.61	−.39	1
I. Strong, active culture	.44	−.33	1
J. Elitist attitude: "We're special"	.83	.06	1
IV. Creativity and Adaptability	**1.66**	**−1.28**	**3**
K. Consciously using an evolutionary process	.44	−.17	1
L. Employee autonomy	.39	−.39	1
M. Rewards for stimulating autonomy and evolution	.83	−.72	1
V. Leadership Continuity	**2.22**	**−.89**	**4**
N. Leadership continuity: Promote from within	.83	−.06	1
O. Absence of charismatic leaders	.67	−.11	1
P. Leadership training: "Homegrown"	.39	−.33	1
Q. Succession planning	.33	−.39	1
VI. Continuous Improvement	**1.72**	**−1.49**	**4**
R. Long-term focus	.33	−.28	1
S. Investment in people: Training and development	.56	−.44	1
T. Early adoption	.44	−.33	1
U. Improvement incentives from within	.39	−.44	1
Grand Total:	**11.54**	**−6.60**	**20**

one of her personal goals is to see that investment becomes a topic of conversation at the dinner table of every African American family. Furthermore, Rogers and Hobson spoke of their efforts to adopt a school—providing incentives like free college tuition to students who graduate from "their" high school—and the wish that every money manager would follow their example and also adopt a school to help.

Ambitious Goals

This was the only category in which Ariel did not receive a perfect score. The firm definitely has set its sights high: They want nothing less than to transform the community for the better. Part of that plan involves adoption of educational institutions, which the company supports both financially and through volunteer work. Ariel would like to see every financial institution follow their example and help kids get educated by adopting and supporting schools.

For investment performance, they have set a goal that goes well beyond top-quartile results. They aspire to be the number one small and mid-cap mutual fund in the country. Hobson uses an excellent phrase to capture the spirit of big, ambitious goals: "dreaming while wide awake." We gave Ariel positive scores for using ambitious goals and for doing so consistently. The only point we did not award was for category F, "truly outrageous goals," and this was purely a judgment call. The examples given by Collins and Porras for *Built to Last* companies were things like Boeing deciding to bet the company on building a jumbo commercial jet, which it had never done before. Are Ariel's goals in a league like that? Maybe, but we chose to give them only a medium, not top, rating for this category.

With regard to normal business goals, Ariel has excellent processes in place for setting them, monitoring them publicly, and achieving them. Merrillyn Kosier, executive vice president, told us that the public aspect of goals helps because no one at a high-performance shop like Ariel wants to look bad in front of their colleagues. So goals get achieved.

Strong Culture

No question here. Ariel's strong culture starts with its "ambassador program," which is designed to fully educate and submerge new recruits in the Ariel culture. By the time the first 100 days are finished, the new hires are fully qualified to be "ambassadors" for the company. They know its history, purpose, values, products, and all other relevant information. Kosier designed this program and runs it. Mellody Hobson chairs the culture committee at Ariel, which is specifically charged with making sure that Ariel maintains its strong culture. Each year at an offsite retreat, they discuss cultural issues and plans for improvement. As for category J ("we're special"), the attitude takes a little different form at Ariel. Under the direction of Rogers, a very modest man, "we're special" doesn't manifest as arrogance, but rather as incredible gratitude that the employees of Ariel get to participate in such a wonderful experience.

Creativity and Adaptability

As seen in the creative culture survey results, Ariel's culture is very supportive of creativity. The senior leaders do not micromanage, and Rogers himself strongly supports trying new things. Hobson says, "We throw a lot of new ideas against the wall to see what sticks." Hobson encourages employees to take small risks, see what works, and move on. She humorously sums up her attitude with the phrase "kill and drive on." This phrase also conveys some of the fun in Ariel's culture. Members of a creative culture don't take themselves too seriously. We gave Ariel perfect scores for its ability to create an innovative and adaptive culture.

Leadership Continuity

Ariel definitely promotes from within and plans for succession well in advance. Six years before she became president of the firm, Rogers told Hobson that she was slotted for the job and gave her assignments that would prepare her for the role. In his desk drawer at work, Rogers keeps an envelope containing detailed, exact instructions for succession should anything untoward happen to him. By now, it should be evident that Rogers is the antithesis of the charismatic leader. The simple act of naming the firm "Ariel," rather than "Rogers Capital," says a great deal about his ego.

Though quietly charismatic (in our opinion), Rogers has done much to prepare the firm for the day he steps down. He has not held the reins of power so tightly that no one else can step in. Hobson commented, "If you were writing this piece 10 years ago, it would have been fair to say that it was Rogers's company. But now it feels like it is our company." Again, on the *Built to Last* scoresheet, Ariel gets perfect scores for training, development, and succession of leadership.

Continuous Improvement

Clearly, the firm that has more than 1,000 turtle artifacts in its offices is concerned with the long term. It is written into Ariel's mission statement and embodied in its motto: "Slow and steady wins the race." Training averages more than 40 hours per employee per year. At this rate, Ariel exceeds the average number of training hours for the "100 Best Places to Work" investment firms. The statement from Hobson that best sums up Ariel's approach to continuous improvement is: "We've got so much to do to get better." This

TABLE 13.6   Metrics Summary for Ariel

Diagnostic Measure	Criteria for Excellence	Ariel Capital: Results/Comments
Built to Last principles	11.54 = average for *BTL* companies	20
Myers-Briggs	Good diversity, no overweighting of leader's type.	Good balance in three of four scales. Absence of Perceiving type (common to investment firms) means decision makers must work hard to explore all options. Their preference will be to decide quickly and move on.
CAT Scan	Coherent and aligned with Myers-Briggs.	Balanced across four quadrants. Absence of Adventurists is in keeping with Ariel's core business.
Values assessment	No limiting values. Full spectrum of values. High number of matches.	No limiting values. Good spectrum. Seven matches between current and desired cultures. Work on performance goals is indicated. Results also indicate desire for specific "next steps" with stated desire for continuous improvement.
Trust survey	Scores for top investment firms: Congruence: 5.6 Competence: 5.95 Caring: 5.8	Congruence: 5.88 Competence: 6.13 Caring: 6.02 Ariel's excellent scores tie in with clear performance goals from the values assessment. Desire for more clarity in roles/responsibilities is indicated.
Innovative culture	No major negative factors inhibiting creativity.	Culture is supportive of creativity.

firm is not resting on its considerable success. Rather, it's always gearing up for a better tomorrow.

For all these reasons, Ariel scored an astonishing 20 out of 21 on the *Built to Last* scoresheet.

SUMMARY

The combination of all the *Built to Last* factors allowed Ariel to get through some extremely difficult times. As a value shop, it woefully underperformed in the late 1990s when the tech bubble was fully inflated. Rogers and Hobson told us stories about losing clients on Christmas and New Year's Eve. Rogers told us that even his supportive and much-revered father suggested that Ariel was on the wrong track! Despite all the pressures, the team hung together. They were able to do so because of the excellent leadership and culture described in this chapter.

To summarize, we provide Table 13.6, which includes all the metrics we've discussed, as well as the relevant benchmark for each.

TEST YOURSELF

Go back to the beginning and retake the quiz at the end of Chapter 1.

CHAPTER 14

Continuous Improvement

We'd better be the worst we ever are today.
　　　　　—Jack Brennan, CEO at Vanguard, referring to
　　　　　　　　　the need for continuous improvement

Continuous improvement, or *renewal*, is the antidote to complacency. In this chapter, you will learn:

- The areas of your firm that are the best candidates for improvements.
- The best times for reevaluating your work.
- The most effective way to build on your experiences.
- Why client service in particular should demand your attention.
- Some foundational communication strategies.
- The guiding questions and principles for leading through renewal.

A possible definition for insanity is doing the same things repeatedly and expecting to get different results. At Allstar, leadership was unwittingly living out this definition. The more clients and top talent that left them, the harder they worked on the same old issues. They even hired a blue-ribbon consultant to help them improve their governance and reporting structures. When we asked one of Allstar's analysts to comment on the effectiveness of this work, he called it "money down the rathole." To him, it was an expensive and time-consuming way to end up just where they had begun, while still not addressing the leadership and culture issues we've described throughout this book. They had never established who they were and what they were trying to achieve together in the firm. What we know from our experience is that if people are not united on the founding principles, all the technical advice in the world won't resolve the debilitating tension. They won't be able to move forward.

This chapter addresses renewal. Having lived through the saga of poor Allstar, we are happy to include this optimistic ending note. After the final collapse of Allstar, I spoke with the director of research, who said:

> *Yes, we've been acquired. So the old firm and its name are gone. But our team is still intact and wants to make a go of it. We're bloodied and bowed but somehow there's an excitement about starting over. It will be very tough, but we've learned a few things over the past three years. We spent a morning recently discussing our investment philosophy and guiding principles that you helped us with. You would have been proud of us. We won't make the same mistakes again. And with a more solid foundation, I think we can really improve on the strengths that we already had. We'll be continually improving as we move forward.*

CONTINUOUS IMPROVEMENT AS A LIFESTYLE

One of the key findings in *Built to Last* is that visionary companies attain their extraordinary success not because of their spectacularly unique insights or their unusually sharp brainpower, but "largely because of the simple fact [that] they are so terribly demanding of themselves."[1] They do not adopt continuous improvement as a strategy of the month. Leaders understand that they must stimulate change *before* external forces demand it. Their annual planning commitments examine the status quo to see what's next, in at least the areas of:

- Process improvement.
- Staff development.
- Research and development.
- Implementation of new technologies and ideas.
- Evaluation and reevaluation of systems.

In these ways, *Built to Last* firms avoid the dangers of arrogance and complacency. During our research, we were constantly impressed with the attitude of the top firms concerning continuous improvement. Jack Brennan's quotation at the beginning of this chapter expresses the reality at Vanguard. Every day you have to challenge yourself to do better. The bar is always being raised. Brennan told us that he's seen this demanding attitude bring grown people to tears, shouting, "You don't know what it's like to be under this pressure. It's never good enough, we always have to do better." Brennan told us flat out that he does not apologize for this attitude. Continuous improvement is part of Vanguard's culture and you should think carefully if it's right for you before you join the firm.

Similarly, the Ontario Teachers Pension Plan in Toronto is known for its innovative approaches to investing. Leaders like Robert Bertram and Leo De Bever are frequently asked to present cutting-edge material at industry conferences. At first, then, it surprised me when they called and asked if I would make a presentation at their firm's annual meeting, on the topic of "Enhancing Creativity and Embracing Change." Here was a firm that, in my mind, was already doing just that. Why, I thought, does one of the most innovative organizations need a talk on being more innovative? Well, for precisely the reasons discussed in this chapter: *good enough never is*. The best firms are always looking for some way to tweak their already excellent processes.

Where to Start

Top firms are always improving. Other teams may decide to address problems when the pain is bad enough or results are poor enough. Team-building exercises or training in conflict resolution are often chosen as activities. The problem is that though nonwork-related activities often feel great at the moment, they don't have much residual value. Without a shared purpose that relates to work, the tensions quickly resume back in the office.

The operating rule is to deal with firm issues in this order:

1. Goals.
2. Roles and responsibilities.
3. Procedures.
4. Relationships.[2]

With this progression, you can avoid vicious circles and successfully tackle the real issues facing your firm.

The Right People First

In *Good to Great*, Collins stresses the importance of beginning with the right people.[3] Your attention to the cultural aspects of your firm will go a long way in helping distinguish who does and doesn't fit with your firm. Additionally, we found a strong correlation between the *Built to Last* firms' elaborate, extended hiring and orientation practices and those of the top investment firms.

Questioning Everything

All your processes should be reviewed regularly, being subjected to questions such as:

- What's going really well and what can we do more of?
- What would we like to improve?
- What can we stop doing?

The frequency of your reviews will make a big difference. If you wait too long, people forget the details of what happened. Generally speaking, the newer the project or the team, the more frequent the reviews should be. Other guidelines to remember:

- Review after all significant milestones.
- Review, at a minimum, every three months, if milestones are further apart than that.
- Review after anything really significant happens (the Army calls this an After Action Review).
- Review in an hour or less, to keep people focused and succinct.[4]

As a result of regular debriefing, your firm will continue to build its knowledge base, as people continue to learn from their experiences.

The trap to avoid is merely talking about the improvements you're going to make—when nothing happens thereafter. A few rounds of this, and at first you'll see a lot of eye-rolling; eventually, people will stop coming to the meetings altogether. People are already intensely busy with their regular workloads. If they're going to take on process improvement work as well, they'll have to see tangible results.

Collaborative Power

Chapter 10 covers innovation in considerable detail, but a comment about innovation is warranted here because innovative thinking is a key reason to conduct regular project and process reviews. Lewis reported on a study conducted at AT&T Bell Labs (and described by Kelley and Caplan in a 1993

Harvard Business Review article), in which the study authors attempted to discover why one set of engineers was considered so much more effective than another. The most remarkable difference was that the most effective engineers knew how to tap the information that already existed within their organizations. They not only reached out more, they also got timely responses from those they contacted. The researchers found that those who spent time building relationships with other members of the organization received timely callbacks, whereas the less effective group just left a bunch of unreturned messages.[5]

Much of the success of Templeton—the organization created by the famed Sir John—is credited to the relationships in the firm. Jeff Everett, president and CIO of Templeton Global Advisors, told us story after story about the emphasis they place on continuously strengthening the connection between analysts and portfolio managers. In one case, Everett had recruited a top analyst from Boston to join Templeton's South Florida team. Unfortunately, the analyst's son had a learning disability that required the expertise of a school in Boston. Everett valued this analyst so highly that he considered setting this person up as a one-man office in Boston. Eventually, though, they parted company, with the analyst joining a well-known Boston firm. His comments afterward were: "It's just not the same as Templeton. Templeton is tough, but collegial, you really work with each other and there is constant attention to improving the feedback."

At Templeton, analysts work with each other on a global basis to share information that is critical to one another's work. For example, the insurance analyst gets information on premium levels from analysts in many other sectors. The same is true of technology analysts and capital spending for products in various sectors. Everett pushes the team to continually improve its communication: "If there is no communication, there is no teamwork, then there is no degree of success."

We found that Russell Reynolds has based a practice strategy on these research findings about communication: People there employ the "Five-Call Rule." When kicking off a new assignment, they place five internal calls to let colleagues know of the assignment before they make any calls to the outside. They have found that by contacting each other whenever a new search gets underway, they can exchange valuable current information.

CONTINUOUS IMPROVEMENT IN CLIENT SERVICE

All of the top investment firms indicated that client service is a core value. Therefore, we'll address continuous improvement in this important area directly. Research shows that for a professional service firm, attention to client service will most likely bring more and better results than the creation of a new technology or brilliant model. The rub is that this is not a statistical exercise for your prized analysts to figure out on a spreadsheet. Creativity is called for here, to find new ways of doing things to leverage your strengths and highlight your advantages. Here are some ideas for continuous improvement in the client service area:[6]

- Can we hire in a different way to create a higher-caliber staff?
- Can we train in a different way on technical or consulting skills?
- Can we manage our accounts or transactions so that our service delivery is more effective and/or efficient?
- Can we systematize ways of ensuring that our people are skilled at client counseling, in addition to top technical skills?
- Can we become better than our competition at learning from our experiences, disseminating and building on our firm-wide expertise to broaden and deepen each person's knowledge base?
- Can we organize and specialize our people in innovative ways so that their focus on a particular market segment's needs is very well aimed?
- Can we become more valuable to our clients by being more systematic about collecting and responding to information about our clients' businesses?
- Can we become more valuable to our clients by investing in research and development on issues of particular interest to them?

Which two or three of these questions might be relevant to your firm at this time? As the leader, what do you need to do to create an opportunity for productive discussion on those questions?

Making the Difference

Service capability and *service passion* (that is, your staff's willingness to give the best service) are two well-researched factors that increase the value of a firm in the eyes of clients. In a study of three financial services organizations, the University of Maryland looked at which management practices correlated with service passion. Besides the obvious link with delivering to and interacting with clients, the next most important practices identified were:

- Hiring procedures.
- Performance feedback.

■ Internal equity of pay.
■ Training.

A different study, by professors at Harvard Business School, surveyed more than 9,000 employees and managers working in three divisions of two U.S. insurance companies. These researchers found six components of internal service quality that related statistically to service capability:

1. The right tools to do the job.
2. The right policies to get the job done.
3. Teamwork.
4. Management support.
5. Goal alignment.
6. Training.

Goal alignment also had the strongest connection with job satisfaction. This is one of the foundational elements of firm leadership and the basis of an effective performance evaluation system.[7]

GETTING THROUGH

We've given you some ideas about potential areas for continuous improvement, but how can you know exactly where to focus your efforts? This crucial area is still just a small percentage of where your firm will be spending its time. You all have full plates. Where will you devote your time? Where do you get the biggest bang for the buck?

In addition to all your financial measures, we have provided cultural metrics to help you understand the needs of your staff. You also have to listen carefully each day. I remember a senior leader stopping by my office, years ago, and asking if I had input for a current problem in the firm. Flattered that he had asked me, I perked up and spouted five or six ideas. He waited patiently as I spoke and when I was finished he said (this is absolutely true), "Well, if you get any ideas, stop by my office and let me know." Did he want me to come by his office and repeat what I had just told him?!

David Glass, Wal-Mart's ex-CEO, once told me that Wal-Mart's process of continuous improvement was remarkably simple. The leaders grabbed a pencil and a legal pad and set off to talk to employees on the floor about little things the firm could do better. In this very practical way, Wal-Mart has reduced its cost-of-goods-sold percentage every quarter since inception. Good listening and sincere interest are key.

Do you have good listening skills? Are you approachable in the first place? Do you create a safe environment for open and honest communication? Top investment firms, like American Century, Ariel, and Investec (South Africa), use trained facilitators to work with them on communication skills. Lyons at American Century said that he and his team learned, from their facilitated sessions, that "leadership isn't about being big and bold and decisive; it's about authenticity, communication, honesty, trust, and being connected." Lyons, at first a skeptic about the benefits of such retreats, now says, "Trust and cooperation levels are so high that we are much more efficient." Rogers at Ariel told us that a whole retreat was dedicated to improving listening skills for the leadership team. Hendrik du Toit, CEO of Investec, said simply, "You can never do enough retreats." Their facilitator is a trained psychotherapist who helps them "become aware of what is below the surface." Du Toit believes that communication is hugely difficult but critical to success.

When you and your team are ready to communicate with the rest of your firm, the first rule of thumb is that you can never communicate enough. You are never done. It doesn't matter how rousing your delivery or how enthusiastically your message was received. David Minella, while at LGT Asset Management, used to say, "Solutions must start and end with strong communication at all levels inside the organization."

Contrast Minella's attitude with that of a CIO in a large buy-side firm. He used to take perverse pleasure, during town-hall-style meetings, in disguising his message so cleverly that only the brightest people would get it. It was like a game to him: Can you read between the lines? Which of you is smart enough to see what I'm really saying? No surprise that half the department would end up in his office by mid-week, trying to tease out of him the gist of his message. (There's a whole *Seinfeld* episode along these lines, in which George misses hearing an assignment from his boss and spends the rest of the episode faking comprehension while trying to discover the real assignment.) This particular boss, who has distinguished himself as one of the world's truly bad communicators, would also get angry at subordinates who weren't smart enough to figure out his cryptic messages. You can learn much in life just by watching such people carefully and doing the opposite!

Leadership's responsibility is to implement a thorough communications plan. Here are some helpful guidelines:

- *Decide the outcome you seek.* Do you want to inform or get feedback? Do you want advice or clarification?

■ *Decide on your audience.* Is this a message for everyone, a few, or really just for one person?

■ *Decide the best mode for your message.* Meetings are the most expensive way to go, particularly if your intent is strictly informational. E-mails can cause a lot of trouble, because people can't discern your tone. Think about what's best for your desired outcome.

■ *Decide how you'll tell if the message was received successfully.* Silence doesn't necessarily mean either acceptance or understanding. How will you know if you have communicated well?

■ *Decide on alternative means.* If you find that the first pass didn't work, try something different.[8]

At Ariel, continuous renewal is built in through the cycle of annual planning and tied to the budget and performance evaluations. Once goals, objectives, and the budget are set, Ariel's leaders adhere to a regular course of communication, reporting in front of the board at least twice annually, with more regular postings internally. Everyone knows who's accountable for what by when. Everyone knows when he or she will hear next about what's happening. They don't have to guess; rumors get addressed. They are always reaching for the next level, with a shared understanding and common purpose. People come to work proud to be associated with a firm that is dedicated to improving and sustaining systems and processes that are designed to help them do their best work.

Collins and Porras offer questions like the following to keep the wheels of discontent moving at your firm. Everyone should get used to the idea that comfort is not the objective and that complacency will not be permitted to settle in:

■ What systems and processes can we put into place so that we reset the bar after each significant event or project?

■ What are we doing to invest in the future while doing well today?

■ Do we continue to build for the long term even during difficult times? What should we do in this regard?

■ What do we have to do to communicate that no matter how well we're doing, we're always going to target the next step and follow through on our decisions?[9]

Plan the big parties, but remember to celebrate the little victories along the way. Patrick O'Donnell understood the importance of encouragement:

We have a weekly meeting in which part of the time is devoted to reviewing everything that the analysts did right the previous week. For example, we recently had some great success with a stock because our analyst gave us an earnings estimate higher than consensus. She stuck her neck out on this, and we never let that go by unnoticed. We praise it and keep revisiting it. I might mention it three weeks in a row. We try to elevate all successes, even subtle ones, to a level of visibility that puts the "mistake" in a larger, more constructive context.[10]

Celebrating small wins will boost people's morale and keep them focused on the goal: the ongoing completions of all the ways you keep improving what you're doing for your staff and your clients.

IN CONCLUSION

Here are some grounding principles to consider as you embark on this work:[11]

- Who you are and what you stand for are just as important as what you sell.
- As so aptly demonstrated by Enron and Andersen, the rules you live by will play a huge role in what you create. Your capacity to live by the values, vision, and culture work you've done (see Chapters 2, 3, and 4) will be increasingly important in the public's perception of your firm's true worth and in its long-term success.
- Investment in personal fulfillment is essential for high performance. The metrics covered in Chapters 5 through 8 are excellent means by which to learn the needs and interests of your staff. Employee participation, meaningful work, and goal alignment, along with a climate of trust and openness, will foster an environment in which your staff can thrive.
- Relationships are the engines of success. Strong emotional intelligence means that you understand all of your stakeholder groups. You also understand yourself, how you communicate, and how your communication affects people. The leader-types chapter (Chapter 5) is intended to address these issues and give suggestions for ongoing improvement.
- Vision, evolution, and transformation drive long-term growth. Staying ahead of the markets, client expectations, and staff needs are central to goal setting and continuous improvement, as discussed in Chapters 9 and 14. Constant change demands that leadership stay open and question the status quo in meaningful and constructive ways.
- Organizational transformation begins at the top. Every leadership book worth its salt emphasizes personal development for leaders. One firm we know of brought in an excellent leadership development program

for its managers, but its leaders refused to take the training themselves. The director of the training company learned of this decision and said prophetically, "This is never going to work." Within a year, the top leadership had dropped the training and was promoting something new. Contrast that example with Bill Lyons at American Century, who wrote out his personal and professional mission statement, circulated it for feedback, learned that he needed to make some personal changes (we all do), and then undertook the transformation. Change, like charity, begins at home.

■ Connectivity builds strength. Teamwork and excellent communication across your stakeholder groups are the themes of successful leadership. Fierce competition must be met with fierce commitment to collaboration and learning from experience. As knowledge workers, investment professionals must remove any obstacles from the sharing of information.

Business structures are less bureaucratic today, with fewer levels, fewer rules, and fewer people. Smaller staffs are handling more and more data points, as sophisticated information systems deliver hourly. Firm cultures are more dynamic, as decision making is pushed downward and open, honest communication is expected.[12] The changes in business and people's expectations about their workplaces, which inevitably occur over time, mean that firm managers must be leaders who know how to unify people behind what's important and why. In this time of shaken confidences and uncertain markets, the principles of leadership and culture can solidify a foundation on which your firm can thrive. By establishing and reinforcing your firm's values, vision, culture, and cycle of improvement through goal setting, you will cultivate sustainable success.

TEST YOURSELF

1. Do you have a regular cycle of evaluation for your systems and processes?
2. Can you point to improvements you have made recently based on your learning from experience?
3. What can you do next to upgrade your ability to improve yourselves?
4. How would you do now on the first set of questions at the end of Chapter 1?

Other Audiences

CHAPTER 15

Consultant's View

If I had a nickel for every investment manager hired purely on past performance, I'd be a rich man.
—Harry Marmer, CFA, ex-Mercer and Frank Russell consultant[1]

Consultants can make or break an asset manager's chances to win more assets. In this chapter, you will see:

- How consultants weigh intangibles such as leadership and culture.
- Examples of qualitative data points that are important to consultants.

When I learned that the team at Allstar was going to get a second chance, with new ownership and a new name, I asked the director of research how he felt about their odds.

"Well, I won't lie to you," he said. "This is a long shot. You know how much we've lost and how bad our performance has been. So, we've got to stop the bleeding and get some decent numbers going. If we do that, we may be able to keep the clients we've got."

I had to ask the obvious question: "How have you kept your current clients?"

"One reason and one reason only," he said. Then he named one of the biggest consulting firms, the intermediaries who conduct searches for the plan sponsors. "They've stuck with us. They've continued to recommend that clients retain us."

"What is their rationale?" I asked, trying not to sound rude.

"They believe that three of the Ps are still in place. We still have smart people, our philosophy always made sense and is still operant today, and our process is intact. We just haven't delivered the big P, Performance."

"So," I said, "it all hinges on maintaining their blessing while you turn things around?"

"Yup."

INFLUENCE OF CONSULTANTS

Such is the power of consultants in the institutional investment market. The big consulting firms—Frank Russell, Callan, Mercer—do hundreds of management searches per year, influencing the placement of billions of dollars.

Big money managers must court these consulting firms if they want to win sizeable new accounts. This is especially true now, with all the defections, firings, and mergers of asset management firms. "There has been a lot of downsizing" at pension funds, reports Frank Russell's Paul Greenwood, and "increasing reliance on our manager research."[2] Evaluation Associates' Maisano agrees:

> Plan sponsors have dealt with constriction of their own staffs. The decision maker is more reliant on consultants. The burden is on us to do more, get further in making a recommendation. We now are being asked to pinpoint the person to have the assignment. Even if they don't trust the consultant, they have to trust the consultant.[3]

International Paper's Hunkeler also concurs. "Years ago, I might have been much more involved," he says. "Now I rely more on consultants."[4]

EXPERT SYSTEMS APPROACH

So, how do leadership and culture relate to the triangle in Figure 15.1? Harry Marmer's quip at the beginning of this chapter shows the key challenge that sponsors and consultants face in the manager search process: overreliance on past performance as a key selection criterion.

Ennis Knupp, based in Chicago, believes that expert systems will help plan sponsors select the best managers. An *expert system* helps one gauge a person or organization's performance potential. Medical examinations in connection with life insurance underwriting are an example of an expert system. They are designed to anticipate the longevity of the applicant. These

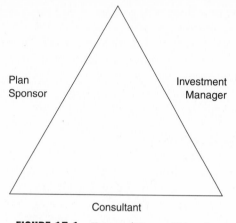

FIGURE 15.1   External Forces Triangle

examinations comprise several scientifically measurable factors (e.g., weight, height, blood pressure, chemical composition of body fluids, and EKG results). The examination also involves, at a minimum, a doctor's evaluation of the subject's heartbeat, which requires a trained (expert) judgment on the spot. Readings for the various factors are then correlated, or weighted, in such a way as to form the most reliable predictor of longevity. The method chosen for drawing together and evaluating the multiple factors—usually developed by a panel of experts who have had no direct involvement in a particular examination—invariably involves expert judgment, as does any conclusion rendered.

Other examples of expert systems abound. In professional sports, scouts employ an expert system in evaluating athletes for possible recruitment. Although each scout typically perfects his or her own system, the various systems have much in common for a particular position or role. For example, a major league baseball prospect who is a highly rated hitter invariably exhibits what is known as good *bat speed*, among other qualities. Without good bat speed, the prospect will not fare well against major league pitching. Credit ratings, driver's license examinations, and odds makers' point spreads for an upcoming game are all examples of the application of expert systems. All employ readings or evaluations of multiple factors that bear on performance potential.

Expert systems play an important role in business. They frequently represent the most efficient way to manage risk, allocate resources, and make choices, given the finite resources available to the decision maker. Thus, the function of an expert system is to allow the user to make the *best* decisions possible with the resources available.

So, how do expert systems help in the selection of asset managers? An investor selects an investment manager—an active investment manager, that is—in the belief that the market is inefficient and the manager will enable the investor to exploit security mispricing. Investors often seek the help of experts in selecting managers. The experts know a great deal about investing and conduct research to identify superior managers. They give investors the benefit of their expert knowledge, for a fee.

Extensive research has been done to identify factors that have some bearing on the future performance of a particular investment strategy, or of a manager who employs that strategy. Experts are familiar with this research, and thus know which factors are important to consider. They supplement this knowledge with what they learn from direct experience in evaluating managers. They also develop informed opinions on how to correlate the various factors they believe have a bearing on performance. The experts then research the universe of investment managers to identify those that offer the greatest promise of superior performance.

Devising an expert system enables an organization to make the best use of limited resources: primarily, professional time and travel costs. In this respect, an expert system is not intended to be the cheapest approach; rather, it's the one that uses finite resources optimally, and is therefore the best approach.

An expert system does not replace expert judgment, but leverages and channels it. In the absence of such a system, it takes many years to train experts. Unless they are exceptionally well trained, they will not be useful in identifying superior-performing managers, given the relative efficiency of markets and the costs of investing.

Ennis Knupp's expert system involves the eight factors shown in Table 15.1, plus a "gut-level adjustment."[5] From the scores in this table, a manager receives a total, which includes the gut-level adjustment. Interpretation of the score is shown in Table 15.2.

When we look at Ennis Knupp's expert system and the factors used in it, we note that the qualitative characteristics show up in several places. First, under #1—Perceived Skill—is the subcategory "Unusual insight." The description of *unusual insight* includes "teamwork and synergy." Much of our book is dedicated to the question of how great leaders create a culture where this happens. We also believe that great leaders will create strong cultures that attract and retain top talent. Ennis Knupp acknowledges that *talent* and *unusual insight* are nearly synonymous. Hence, we return to our original

organization. The *quality of service* (apart from rate of return) provided to clients is a determinant of client satisfaction.

Gut-Level Assessment

Note that a gut-level adjustment is allowed, to be used at the rater's discretion. This reflects the reality that any expert system is imperfect, by permitting the rater to increase or decrease the raw score by 2 points in arriving at the overall assessment.

The gut-level assessment is clearly the fudge factor in such an analysis. We have not seen it clearly explained by any of the major consultants, so part of the rationale for this book is to further that discussion. What exactly is the fudge factor, and how can we measure it more precisely?

FRANK RUSSELL: EMPHASIZING THE QUALITATIVE

Ted Aronson, head of his own investment firm and chair of AIMR's board of governors, says of Russell that they are "head and shoulders above most other consulting firms."[6] They are a force in the industry, to be sure. Marmer's experience at both Mercer and Frank Russell gave him good insight into the qualitative assessment factors that they considered in their evaluations:[7]

- Leadership strength and experience.
- Suitability of compensation program.
- Capability of attracting intellectual capital.
- Innovativeness and adaptability.
- Continuity of professionals.
- Succession program.
- Integrity and objectivity.
- Team vs. star approach.
- Intangibles: character, attitude, and desire to excel.
- Strategic direction of the company.
- Strengths and weaknesses of the organizational structure.
- Servicing capabilities and suitability to client's needs.[8]

I first saw this list of factors in Calgary, Alberta, where Harry was giving a presentation called "Managing Successfully within the Institutional Troika." It was one of 20 slides. I was struck by the similarity between the factors that Harry had listed and the ones I was about to present in my speech. In fact, I opened my talk by saying, "If Harry had elaborated on the qualitative factors he listed, there would be no need for me to say anything, and you could all eat in peace." In my subsequent discussions with Harry, he stated unequivocally that despite awareness of these factors, "the big challenge for sponsors, consultants, and money managers is to understand the qualitative criteria and how to apply them."

Consultants recognize this shortfall and are working to correct it.

In an effort to overcome the slippery nature of such qualitative information as whether or not a key staff member will stay with the firm or whether a product you might want to add to your asset mix will remain one of the manager's priority offerings or whether a merger is in the works, some consultants are designing quantitative models to tease out and analyze the numerous criteria that go into assessing a manager.[9]

Frank Russell claims that its approach to manager selection is much more heavily weighted toward People and Process than the typical search firm's approach, which is why Aronson likes the Russell company. Its analysts use a proprietary database of qualitative and quantitative characteristics, based on the factors listed earlier, to identify the managers that are most likely to outperform Russell's benchmark. Russell summarizes the quantitative and qualitative factors as shown in Table 15.3.

Russell has built models to evaluate the relationship between managers' beliefs about how they will perform and their subsequent performance. Among those beliefs are philosophies of research and portfolio construction. Russell has found that managers with similar philosophical tenets tend to show similar performance. Changes in investment behavior will set off alarm bells in this "Theory Directed Research" model. For example, is the firm selling stocks as aggressively as it once did? Does it continue to find stocks as early as before?

TABLE 15.3 Quantitative/Qualitative Comparison

Quantitative Factors	Qualitative Factors
Performance against peer groups	Personnel/administration
Performance against benchmarks	Investment philosophy
Transactions	Decision-making procedures
Portfolio characteristics	Economic and securities research

FS ASSOCIATES: ASSESSING THE QUALITATIVE

In researching the evaluation systems of consultants, we found that 30 percent was standard for the weight given to qualitative factors. One consultant, Fernand Schoppig of FS Associates, who shares our belief that leadership and culture are deciding factors in long-term performance, weights the qualitative factors at 33 percent and spells them out quite specifically. Some of the leadership and culture questions he considers are:

- Do they have a genuine corporate culture with a mission statement and a clear vision of where they want to go?
- Do they have a COO who is responsible for running the firm, rather than having the firm run by the same people who are running the portfolios?
- How long have the senior people been working together at their current firm, or as a team at another firm?
- Is management hierarchical or participatory?
- What is the ownership structure?
- How has the company planned for succession?
- What is the firm's compensation structure?
- How is performance defined and calculated for figuring out bonuses?
- Is there equity participation?
- If yes, is it throughout all levels, or limited to very senior professionals?
- How important is client servicing?
- Can the firm demonstrate that it is willing to accommodate the client as much as possible?
- Is overall client satisfaction measured regularly, and is this aspect made part of the bonus considerations and remunerated accordingly?

Schoppig's rigor in the area of leadership and culture stems from his 25 years of experience in the industry, which taught him that

> *The asset management industry has less to do with assets and much more with people. This is an industry which is human-resource intensive, where brainpower, creativity, vision, and quality of leadership matter. Consequently, it is also an industry where a lack of people skills, accentuated by huge egos and overshadowed by temporary investment success, can take its toll and destroy an otherwise great money management firm.*

Schoppig believes this so strongly that he will not award a top rating to a money manager that is performing well unless the cultural and organizational aspects of the organization can be considered outstanding as well. He says:

While investment performance is, without any doubt, a very important factor in recommending a money manager, it is the starting point; the other 3 Ps—philosophy, process and people—followed by the organizational aspects like culture, commitment to human resources, from the pecuniary side but also offering them a stake in the firm, via equity or phantom equity, matter very much as well!

Having seen many market cycles, Schoppig agrees with our position when he says that

Every money manager, even the best ones, will have periods where they have to deal with below average investment performance. The firms with a strong culture and an understanding of what it takes to make a great organization will be able to handle the stress resulting from such periods of underperformance clearly better than those firms which do not put a lot of weight on the organizational and cultural aspects mentioned.

Leadership and culture are the only defenses against the inevitable tough times.

QUANTITATIVE VERSUS QUALITATIVE

The quotation from Harry Marmer that opened this chapter pokes fun at the fact that past performance still plays a key role in manager selection. Evidence shows clearly that lay people—and even experts—are strongly influenced by the latest hot fund. Knowing this, some investment firms still tout their latest quarter or year, despite the SEC-mandated advertising disclaimer that "Past performance is no guarantee of future results." We asked many consultants why past performance is still such a big part of the manager search, even when it is known to be a notoriously poor predictor of future performance. The best answer we have heard, which sums up all the others, is from Steve Cummings at Ennis Knupp: "In a word, *convention.* Everyone does, always has, and almost certainly will continue doing so for the foreseeable future." Company founder, Richard Ennis, agrees: "The decision to retain managers often turns on relatively recent performance. I refer to this as the 'performance syndrome.'"[10] Cummings went on to say:

Performance, after all, is what we are seeking from the manager, and past performance has the allure of being just about the only "hard evidence" concerning the manager's ability to perform well in the future.

> *And inasmuch as past performance is a standard consideration in manager evaluation, including it helps ensure that the manager evaluation system contributes to discharging one's fiduciary duty.*

This last statement carries a lot of weight. The people who select managers want hard data to fall back on if the choice turns out to have been a poor one. Past performance has that appeal.

Nevertheless, we see clear evidence of a trend away from reliance on quantitative toward consideration of the qualitative. Seasoned experts like Charles Ellis, founder of Greenwich Associates, are making statements about investment firms such as, "[O]ver the very long term, culture dominates"[11]; when that happens, you know it's only a matter of time before the reality of the situation overtakes the convenience of simpler measuring systems.

The case for the qualitative side really came home to me when I read a remark from Lou Gerstner, retired CEO at IBM, who said that the culture of a firm is not just important but "the whole game."[12] Gerstner's friend, Andrew Tobias, heard this remark and commented, "Gerstner's not a warm, fuzzy individual."[13] Our point exactly! Factoring in culture as an important attribute is not a call for a kinder, gentler workforce. (Many would argue that the Marines have an admirable culture, but certainly not a soft one.) The mistake lies in abandoning the search for the right metrics to measure qualitative factors. Wilshire Associates is very much aware of this shift from past performance to qualitative factors, and commented:

> *Wilshire places great emphasis on the assessment of qualitative variables when evaluating investment managers and their respective products. Our manager selection process is forward-looking, with predominant weighting given to qualitative factors we believe are supportive of manager out-performance.*

In addition to Wilshire's Odyssey Group, which is responsible for collecting data from managers, the Manager Research Group at Wilshire includes investment professionals who are exclusively dedicated to qualitative manager due diligence.[14]

CALLAN ASSOCIATES: DEFINING THEIR OWN CORE VALUES

Callan Associates provides even more evidence that the consulting world is taking the qualitative side more seriously. When consultants resort to "eating their own cooking," you know they are serious indeed. In the summer of 2001, Ronald Peyton, Callan's CEO, put this question to his firm: "What are our core values?" His interest in this question stemmed from his years of experience in working with clients and seeing that culture was a main determinant of success. He says,

> *What does [a healthy culture] have to do with values? Everything! To generate the kind of effort and results that are needed in today's world, associates must feel ownership of the business. And this shared responsibility will germinate and grow only in a values-oriented culture that encourages commitment, loyalty, and true dialogue.*[15]

In his quest to identify and define the core values at Callan, Peyton revealed one of the most common misconceptions that we find in working with clients:

> *I felt I knew precisely what our firm's values were. But one day it hit me that perhaps I was taking too much for granted in assuming that all associates of the firm understood those values. For, although we regularly go through a regimented process to clearly articulate our vision and the core strategies for realizing that vision, we had never discussed our values in an open forum.*[16]

Peyton initiated a process that involved all 18 members of Callan's management committee and a good cross-section of the associates.

> *The ensuing dialogue was both revealing and rewarding. What we all learned, sitting around that table and reviewing the listed values, was that we truly do share the same high standards of professional behavior and client service. If we make a promise to a client or prospect we make sure we deliver. Equally important, we place great importance on building and maintaining a corporate culture that encourages individual creativity, teamwork with both clients and co-workers, and taking action. And last, but hardly least, we want, and work to have, a corporate environment that recognizes the pressure our clients are under, yet also supports our associates' needs. Whether it is by promoting and participating in their continuing education, providing flexible hours that allow them to meet family obligations, or assisting them during an illness, we strive to help our associates flourish personally, as well as professionally.*[17]

Once the Callan group had identified the company's core values, they set about developing concise definitions of those values. The resulting statement was as follows:

> *In serving our clients and their beneficiaries, Callan values:*
>
> - *Quality and integrity—in everything we do.*
> - *Honoring every commitment we make.*
> - *Encouraging creativity, collaboration, and action.*
> - *Respecting the needs of each client and associate.*

Exactly tracking the steps that we've found effective with clients, Callan then communicated these results to all associates and planned a firm-wide conference to discuss them and weave them deeper into the fabric of the firm. The values will become an ongoing theme in all of Callan's discussions and meetings.

Did Peyton feel that he had changed his view of the words that describe the firm's values? "Yes. Were they better? You bet! A real example of a creative and collaborative process."[18]

Peyton added a comment that we strongly agree with, based on our scuttlebutt research of talking to as many employees as possible. He said,

> *It is, of course, valuable to discuss these value statements with associates and use them to base decisions and conduct business. But, in the end, the only way to know if your values are really being embraced is by watching and listening to the ways in which your associates treat clients, beneficiaries, vendors, and each other.*[19]

As a result of this exercise, Callan is even more committed to evaluating the qualitative side of asset managers. They see the benefits of strong culture and clear values firsthand in their own firm and realize that superior managers also promote this clarity in their organizations.

PREMIUM ON STABILITY

One of the signs of a strong culture is stability. We see this in the top organizations that we've studied. Until consultants figure out a more precise metric for measuring culture, they can at least focus on its outcome: stability. David Holmes, senior consultant at Mercer Manager Advisory Services in Louisville, Kentucky, says that it used to all be about product, but "people now recognize the effects of reorganization after reorganization and mergers and acquisitions, and want to see stable organizations and stability in personnel."[20] Holmes's colleague in Boston, Ravi Venkataraman, says, "We want to feel good about the team and their approach."[21] Jim Carmack, president of the Carmack Group in Alhambra, California, agrees that "qualitative data is at least as important as portfolio data. Even if the manager is going to have a turn in the tank, you want consistency of style and team."[22] His advice to consultants, when the time comes to explain poor performance to a plan sponsor, is "make sure you have a qualitative story to go with it."[23]

Plan sponsors and consultants have the same goal: to select managers that will produce superior performance and provide excellent service over the *long term*. Investment managers want to be the company selected to provide the long-term performance and service. Cliff Kelly, who heads up the global manager research group at Callan Associates in San Francisco, agrees, noting that they "are looking for a long-term-oriented culture."[24] In this sense, all three entities—the consultant, the plan sponsor, and the asset managers—have an interest in the characteristics and factors that contribute to the long-term success of asset managers.

For our part, we believe that the tools and metrics in this book are a step in the right direction. Their possible superiority lies in the fact that they attempt to measure leadership and culture directly, rather than looking at outcomes like stability and performance.

TEST YOURSELF

Imagine that your firm is being evaluated by a consultant. How would your senior team respond to the following yes/no statements? What are your next steps in regard to any of these points?

1. We can clearly define our culture.
2. Our leadership priorities can be clearly articulated.
3. Our leadership is consistently recognized as a contributing factor to our firm's success.
4. We have distinct systems and processes in place that result in a high retention of talent.
5. We have a distinct reputation as a great place to work.
6. We have a shared ownership plan in place.
7. Our shared ownership plan is clearly understood by the relevant parties.
8. We have a succession plan that is clearly understood by the relevant parties.

CHAPTER 16

Stock Picker's Corner: Rounding Up the Un-Usual Suspects

Analysts in most places are doing what they have always done: reading a lot, traveling a lot, massaging familiar data, making heroic efforts to explain why the latest quarter differed from their forecasts . . . . Yet, we are becoming increasingly aware that much of this work may be a waste of time.

—Peter Bernstein[1]

Applying the principles of leadership and culture, as discussed in this book, to stock analysis can yield superior investment returns. In this chapter you will learn:

- Criteria for analyzing the qualitative side of a company.
- Strategies for using the "Analyst Scoresheet" when performing fundamental research.
- How to spot the Enrons, Tycos, and Vivendis *before* a meltdown.

Stock picking and corporate culture may be more related than we think. Allstar's weak culture—described throughout this book—certainly affected its ability to retain top investment professionals. But did it also affect the actual stock picking? From discussions with Allstar's analysts, we know that they paid very little attention to the qualitative side of a business. One of the biggest losers in Allstar's portfolio was Tyco. Many of Allstar's most heated arguments were over the valuation of this one stock. In the end, they stuck with the stock and rode it all the way down.

To be fair, lots of smart people got taken in by Tyco. In a November 2001 article, when Tyco's stock was trading at $58 per share, Robert Hunter compared Tyco to Enron:

> *CEO Kenneth Lay of Enron holds a Ph.D. in economics—and everyone knows that Ph.D.s make bad traders. (Most of the principals at Long Term Capital Management boasted doctorates—including two Nobel laureates—and look what happened there.) Far more troubling, Lay acknowledged during an August conference call with analysts that one question was above his head. That suggests that Dr. Lay didn't fully grasp Enron's vast array of dealings. Ugh.*
>
> *Kozlowski, by contrast, is an accountant by training, and had spent most of his career working in M&A. He personally pores over potential acquirees' books, and understands the accounting implications of all the deals he makes. In fact, there's probably no one in America with a more intimate knowledge of M&A accounting than Kozlowski. I bet he could have recited Financial Accounting Standards Board rules verbatim to SEC investigators. That's the guy I want at the helm when regulators start sniffing around.*[2]

From our perspective—fans of leadership and strong culture—we always view numbers as being only half the story. The qualitative side of the story is your safeguard against the Tycos and the Enrons. Using the 21-item scoresheets (Tables 16.1–16.6) at the end of this chapter, you can nearly guarantee that the next Tyco or Enron won't appear in your portfolio. If you are only looking at the numbers, though, as Hunter did, watch out. You could end up with the likes of these guys running the company you just invested in:

> *"The defendants are charged with running a criminal enterprise," prosecutor John Moscow told the judge. The numbers were staggering: a 94-page indictment alleging enterprise corruption and 38 counts of grand larceny, conspiracy, and falsifying business records. The prosecutor accused the two of "simply stealing" $170 million from Tyco. Including stock sales, he alleged, their ill-gotten gains totaled a jaw-dropping $600 million. Kozlowski and Swartz pleaded not guilty and prepared to post astronomical bails: $100 million and $50 million, respectively.*[3]

Examining the qualitative side of the company is your best defense.

This chapter is intended as a stand-alone piece for analysts and portfolio managers. The underlying principles are identical to those presented in the remainder of the book, but the perspective is different. Rather than addressing the concerns of leaders who want to create long-term success, this chapter addresses the needs of stock pickers who want to buy superior stocks. All the evidence suggests that companies that follow the *Built to Last* principles will outperform their peer companies and the general market.

In contrast to Allstar, a company like William Blair, which is very attentive to its own culture, focuses on company culture as part of its fundamental analysis. In fact, William Blair himself was known to base investment decisions largely on the qualitative side of a business: How do we rate the company's leadership? Would we want to do business with these people? Under the direction of Bob Newman, the Blair sell-side research team places heavy emphasis on the qualitative factors, and even has a product called *Current Better Values (CBV)*. An article in *Shareholder Value* magazine underscored Blair's emphasis on the qualitative side, noting that "William Blair managers don't invest until they really get to know you."[4] A *CBV* list has been published every 2 months for more than 25 years. The lists have outperformed their benchmarks (including the most widely used benchmark, the S&P 500) 77 percent of the time. The most recent 9 lists (established since Newman has been director of research) had outperformed their benchmarks 85 percent of the time as of December 2002.

The weight that Blair gives to qualitative factors may explain why it performed so well, and avoided the trap described by Peter Bernstein in the opening quotation: "Analysts in most places are doing what they have always done . . . [y]et, we are becoming increasingly aware that much of this work may be a waste of time."[5]

Analysts concentrate on well-illuminated (and much-used) stock facts such as price, earnings per share, dividends, sales, return on equity, and so on. If you pick up any random issue of *Financial Analysts Journal* and skim the table of contents, you'll find that virtually every article examines one of these usual suspects. The latest publication from AIMR, *CFA Magazine,* has an article about stock picking that lists "Tools of the Trade":[6]

- Dividend discount models.
- Free cash flow models.
- Residual income models.
- Price-to-earnings ratio.
- Price-to-book ratio.
- Price-to-sales ratio.
- Price-to-cash flow ratio.

- Enterprise value to EBITDA.
- Dividend yield.
- Return on equity.
- Operating and profit margins.
- Asset turnover ratios.
- Earnings growth rates.
- Free cash flow growth rates.
- Growth rates of dividends, cash flow, and earnings.
- Risk-free rate and risk premium.

See anything even vaguely approaching a measurement of leadership or culture? No. Every one of these tools is based on the collection and analysis of hard data.

In contrast, Blair's analysts are not simply massaging familiar data or tinkering with quarterly estimates. They are instead challenging the status quo by assessing the leadership and cultural aspects of companies. Lisa Shalett, chairman and CEO of Sanford Bernstein, agrees that "[t]he real way to make money is to figure out what else is going on that the numbers don't tell you."[7] The remainder of this chapter provides ideas and guidelines for making this qualitative evaluation.

Skeptics might challenge this qualitative approach. How do we know leadership and culture are important? Remember the earlier study that we cited, by Kotter and Heskett.[8] They surveyed 75 Wall Street analysts and asked them to separate their industries into the attractive and unattractive companies (buys and sells, basically). When they then asked the analysts what factors differentiated the two groups, 74 of the analysts said that a firm's culture explained the difference. Despite all the work by Michael Porter at Harvard, showing that competitive strategy and competitive advantage determine winners and losers,[9] analysts realize that culture is a major factor. Look at some of the success stories in the past three decades—Circuit City, Southwest Airlines, Tyson Foods, Wal-Mart—and you'll realize that their success had nothing to do with being in a cushy industry. Charles Ellis's comment about the investment industry holds for companies in general: Over the very long term, culture dominates.[10]

The idea that the qualitative side of the business is important is not new. Phil Fisher, a legend in the field and author of *Common Stocks and Uncommon Profits*, wrote in 1958 that the quality of management was critical to a company's success. He also encouraged analysts to use his "scuttlebutt" technique of gathering data: Question the company's vendors, competitors, and even ex-employees. Peter Lynch said in jest, "I want to buy a company that any fool can run, because eventually one will,"[11] but the truth is that leaders are the caretakers of a corporate culture. And culture dominates.

So, why stick with the hard data—the usual suspects—when we know that the soft data is valuable?

One possible explanation is our love of computers. Computing power has grown so enormous that it's nearly impossible to resist its attraction. Consider: One of those musical birthday cards that sings "Happy Birthday" has more computing power in it than existed in the entire world before 1950. A digital watch has more computing power than existed before 1960. Your camcorder has more computing power than an IBM 360 mainframe. Your kid's video game base has more power than the original Cray supercomputer. We analysts love our toys. Give us the numbers and we delight in crunching them . . . "garbage in, garbage out" be damned! The alchemist analysts will turn the compost heap into filet mignon: just give them a few more algorithms and a lot more gigabytes!

Phil Fisher's tips on analyzing the soft side of a business are anecdotal and from his gut. Jim Collins and Jerry Porras, in *Built to Last,* took a huge step forward in providing hard evidence for the importance of culture. Equally important, they showed how to quantify it. In their 5-year study, Collins and Porras examined the records of 18 exemplary companies and 18 "comparison" companies (ones that were in the same industry but without the distinguished record). The research method they used was empirical: Start with no hypothesis and just let the data speak. Five years and 100,000 pages of information later, the two summarized their findings in 21 factors that differentiated the built-to-last companies from the also-rans.[12] Why these factors are not standard course material for stock pickers and CFA candidates eludes me. After all, the *Built to Last* stocks outperformed the index of stocks from 1926 to 1990 by a factor of 10. They outperformed the also-ran comparison stocks by a factor of six. If money talks, then analysts need to turn up their hearing aids. The results are screamingly obvious, and yet the soft side is still ignored in favor of the large crunching sounds emanating from the computers interrogating the usual suspects.

For those analysts who are interested in finding some new suspects, I have chosen 8 of the 21 *Built to Last* factors and described how they can be used to determine the potential of a stock. These 8 factors follow the Pareto principle (80/20 rule). They are both powerful differentiators and readily understandable. Using Fisher's scuttlebutt technique, a good analyst should be able to imitate the Collins and Porras approach of rating a company as high, medium, or low on each factor. To allow one to work

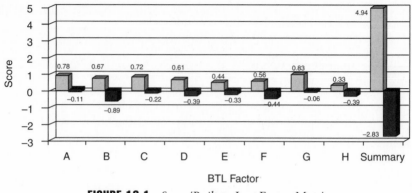

FIGURE 16.1   Score/*Built to Last* Factor Matrix

with these factors quantitatively, I simply translated the ratings into +1, 0, and −1. The eight factors, which are discussed later, scored as follows for the exemplary (light) and mediocre (dark) companies (see Figure 16.1).

THE UN-USUAL SUSPECTS

Here, then, are the eight unusual suspects that can help you pick top stocks.

1. Clarity of Values and Vision

Look for evidence that the company has identified and articulated its core values and vision and uses them as a source of guidance. Collins and Porras call values and vision the "core ideology" of a company, and the major finding of their research is that ideologically driven firms outperform and outsustain purely profit-driven companies.[13] Core ideology answers these questions:

- ■ Who are we?
- ■ What do we stand for?
- ■ What is our purpose (beyond profit)?
- ■ Where are we going?

Core ideology gives direction and purpose. There's an old joke about the airline pilot who says over the intercom, "I've got good and bad news. The good news is that we're making excellent time. The bad news is we're lost." Surely there were a number of buggy-whip companies that were efficiently and skillfully producing whips right up until they closed their doors. The role of leaders is to identify a purpose that is broad enough and compelling enough to guide the company for decades. Examples of such purposes for the *Built to Last* companies are:

- 3M: innovative solutions for problems.
- Johnson & Johnson: alleviate pain and disease.
- Merck: preserving and improving life.

> *STRATEGY*: Ask five employees at the firm (separately) to articulate the firm's vision and core values. Compare their answers for common understandings and differences. You are looking for:
>
> +1 Significant evidence that the company has identified and articulated its core values and purpose and uses them as a source of guidance. Key leaders speak of the values and vision and have communicated them to the employees.
>
> 0 Some evidence of the above.
>
> −1 No evidence that the company has made serious attempts to identify and articulate core values and purpose.

2. Historical Alignment around Values and Vision

Look for evidence that the values and vision have undergone little change since inception. The top companies not only have clearly stated their ideologies, but also have remained true to them over time. In the cases just mentioned, each of the three companies (3M, Johnson & Johnson, and Merck) has left its vision and values unchanged for more than 100 years.

> *STRATEGY*: Review old annual reports and talk to longtime employees. Determine how consistent the firm's purpose and core values have remained over time. You are looking for:
>
> +1 Evidence that the values and vision (described in factor 1) have changed very little since inception and are continually reinforced by the leaders.
>
> 0 Evidence that the values and vision have changed over the years and that the company has been inconsistent in reinforcing them.
>
> −1 Little evidence that there has been a consistent set of values or central purpose for the company.

3. Alignment of Words and Action: Walking the Talk

Okay, so the company has a clear ideology, and that ideology has been in place for a long time—but does it really "live" in the organization? For example, one client we worked with had printed its four core values on lovely wall plaques and placed them in all the hallways and reception areas. When we asked employees to name the firm's core values, we found only one person out of 300 who could, and that person was in charge of human resources! The point is that people have to *know* the values if they are to live them. This firm would get a –1 score on "walking the talk."

For another example, consider the following values and descriptions. Ask yourself, "How would I feel about having my son or daughter work at this firm?"

Communication
We have an obligation to communicate. Here, we take the time to talk with one another . . . and to listen. We believe that information is meant to move and that information moves people.
Respect
We treat others as we would like to be treated ourselves. We do not tolerate abusive or disrespectful treatment.
Integrity
We work with customers and prospects openly, honestly and sincerely. When we say we will do something, we will do it; when we say we cannot or will not do something, then we won't do it.
Excellence
We are satisfied with nothing less than the very best in everything we do. We will continue to raise the bar for everyone. The great fun here will be for all of us to discover just how good we can really be.

Pretty good set of values, wouldn't you say? You'd feel good about your child working there, right? Well, these were Enron's values—before its collapse. Again, the point is that any firm can go offsite and craft a beautiful set of guiding principles, but the important thing is what really happens at the firm day-to-day. What values and behaviors are really endorsed? An ex-Enron employee reported that the culture there was so cutthroat that he didn't worry about being stabbed in the back, he worried about being stabbed in the front!

STRATEGY: Ask employees if management's actions are consistent with the vision and core values of the firm. When interviewing leaders, ask them behavioral questions like, "When was the last time you spoke to employees about the core values? What did you say? Give an example of how the core values are incorporated in strategic planning. How are core values incorporated into compensation?" You are looking for:

+1 Significant evidence that vision and values are lived out in practice in the company. Major strategic initiatives and organizational policies are guided by the vision and values.

 0 Some evidence of the above, but less pronounced and inconsistent.

−1 Little evidence that vision and values tie into or guide the actions and behaviors in the company.

4. Cultural Indoctrination: Molding the New Hires

Teaching the values and vision to new hires is an important part of building a strong culture, where *culture* is defined as the "collective programming of the mind (values, beliefs and behaviors) which distinguishes the members of one organization from another."[14] Gary Brinson understood this concept well. He compared organizational cultures to different religions. One isn't necessarily better or worse than any other, but each should be carefully defined. Brinson repeatedly emphasized that "knowing and understanding the firm's culture is important for the people to yield maximum results." As you can imagine, the culture at Brinson Partners (now part of UBS Global Asset Management) was clearly defined.

In defining culture, leaders need to ask the deeper questions, such as:

- What do we really believe?
- Can analysts add value?
- Can the market be timed?
- How do we manage egos?
- How do we set up compensation to align with our values? (Many firms talk of team efforts and then continue to compensate on individual performance.)

The answers to these questions are enormously important in shaping the culture of an organization. David Fisher at Capital Guardian is very aware of the importance of culture and therefore won't start a hedge fund, simply because it might give the wrong impression, both internally and externally.

STRATEGY: Ask employees about their orientations. You are looking for:

+1 Significant evidence of a formal indoctrination process, which may include:

- Orientation program that teaches values, traditions, guidelines.
- Ongoing training that reinforces those values, traditions, and guidelines.
- Internal publications emphasizing company values and traditions.
- Leaders discussing and promoting the values and traditions.
- Use of special language or terminology that reinforces a unique culture (such as Disney calling employees "cast members" or Vanguard calling them "crew members").
- Hiring young, promoting from within, shaping the employee's thinking from the start.

  0 Some evidence of the above, but to a lesser extreme.

−1 Little or no evidence that the company has a formal indoctrination process.

5. Strong, Active Culture: "Our Way or the Highway"

Strong, active cultures tend to draw binary reactions: Employees either love them or hate them. For example, in visiting with Jack Brennan and his senior team, we learned about the advantage of strong culture in recruiting. Mike Miller was working at another financial firm when a colleague said, "Mike, I know you and I know the Vanguard culture; trust me, you'd love it." Mike went to Vanguard and does, in fact, love it. Conversely, I met a woman several weeks later who commented that she had worked at Vanguard and "hated it." Rather than making me second-guess my judgment that Vanguard really was a strong culture, this woman's view confirmed it. Yes, Vanguard has a strong culture that some people will love and others will run from like the plague. The key is to listen for words that convey pride when employees speak of their firm. Strong cultures, like that of the Marine Corps, typically have rabid support.

Leaders of strong cultures also understand the importance of hiring for both skills and fit. Typically, firms hire for skills: "Get me the smartest person available!" The leading-edge firms understand that they need a cultural fit as well. That's why firms like MFS in Boston and William Blair in Chicago have candidates interview with as many as 30 employees before a decision is made. Barrow Hanley, a $30 billion manager in Dallas, learned this the hard way in 1999 when it hired a smart young guy to pick stocks in this value-oriented firm. No sooner had the young man started than he bought subscriptions to six high-tech magazines; his first recommendations were dot-com companies that had no earnings and no sales! Needless to say, this was a bad fit at a value shop, and they soon parted ways.

> *STRATEGY:* Talk to an ex-employee who did not fit with the culture and therefore left. What were the values or behaviors that caused the split? What did this person find praiseworthy about the culture? Do current employees use words like "proud" to describe their feelings about working there?

+1 Strong evidence that culture is well-defined and binary (that is, some people love it and others hate it). Indications of strong culture are:

- Rewards and recognition for those who fit in with the culture, and negative reinforcement for those who do not.
- Severe penalties for those who violate core values.
- Hiring for fit and careful monitoring of employees based on vision and values.
- Heavy emphasis on loyalty.
- Employees are proud to work there.
- Employees are expected to join fully in the company and espouse its values.

  0 Some evidence of a strong culture, but not to the extent indicated above.

−1 Little or no evidence of a strong culture.

Tip: To find out what the buzz is on hiring, firing, and orientation at various firms, try www.thevault.com. This web site is a rich source of information for evaluating the qualitative side of a business.

6. Investment in People: Training and Development

A strong culture invests in its people even in downturns. The exemplary cultures realize that people are their key asset and actively recruit and develop the best people, even in bad times. An example from the investment industry is MFS in Boston. Despite having to lay off several hundred of its 2,700 employees in 2002, it still added to its professional investment staff at a time when other firms were laying off investment professionals. MFS employs the classic Warren Buffett "buy it when no one else wants it" philosophy. The number of full-time investment professionals at MFS went from 200 to 210 during 2002.

> *STRATEGY:* Ask leaders, employees, and ex-employees about the company's training programs. Does the firm cut back during tough

times? Are employees encouraged to stretch and learn? Is it clear that leaders take the investment in people seriously? You are looking for:

+1 Significant evidence that the company invests in recruiting, training, and development, even in downturns.

 0 Some evidence of the above.

−1 Little or no evidence of the above, especially in downturns.

7. Leadership Continuity: Promote from Within

The numbers speak for themselves on this one. Over the collective life of the *Built to Last* companies, there were 121 CEOs, only 4 of whom came from outside the company. Contrast that statistic with the record of the mediocre companies. They had 158 CEOs collectively, and 31 of them were from outside the ranks of the organization. Tenure was a similar story. Average tenure for the exemplary companies was 17 years, versus 12 for the mediocre companies. The exemplary companies value their culture and want to preserve it with someone who truly understands it. They don't look outside for a savior.

> *STRATEGY:* Examine the company's track record for CEOs. Are they homegrown from within, or are they brought in from the outside? You are looking for:
>
> +1 Significant evidence that the CEO is selected from within the company.
>
> 0 Evidence that the CEO is primarily selected from within the company, with one or two exceptions.
>
> −1 Evidence that the company has deviated from the "promote from within" strategy for choosing CEOs more than twice.

8. Succession Planning

As with the concepts in items 6 and 7, exemplary companies carefully groom successors by giving them plenty of mentoring and leadership development opportunities. The low-key, nonegocentric leaders of the exemplary companies realize that the culture is much bigger—and more important—than they themselves are, and they look for capable leaders who can preserve and protect the culture. Charismatic leaders like Lee Iacocca at Chrysler or Stan Gault at Rubbermaid were credited with great successes while they were in charge, but the stock charts in each case show what happened when they left: collapse. Sustainable success depends on leaders who understand the culture and strengthen it. That's why MFS has selected its CEO, CIO, and CFO all from the ranks of the company. Each of them started as an analyst in the 1980s, became a portfolio manager, and then ascended to the current leadership position.

> *STRATEGY:* Ask the leadership team about the succession process. Does the CEO have his or her successor picked out already? How was the decision made? How many were in the running? What is the training process for developing new leaders? You are looking for:
> +1 Significant evidence that the company has a history of careful succession planning and formal CEO grooming.
> 0 Less evidence of the above.
> +1 Little or no evidence that the company has a history of careful CEO succession planning.

SUMMARY

Peter Lynch may joke that he likes to buy companies that "any fool can run, because eventually one will,"[15] and Sandy Weill may quip, "What is culture but something that is found in yogurt?"[16] Despite the jokes, analysts who ignore these factors in their research do so at their peril.

Using the eight factors listed in the preceding section, and the scuttlebutt method suggested by Phil Fisher, an analyst can round up the *un*usual suspects and add value to the analysis of a stock. Watch a few reruns of *Columbo* and start asking questions of ex-employees and vendors.

All 21 factors for evaluating leadership and culture are included in the scorecard that constitutes the rest of this last section.

Analyst Scoresheet for Identifying Companies with Outstanding Leadership and Culture

The following scoring system allows you to measure the leadership and culture of a company. There are 21 items, each considered a "timeless principle" of outstanding companies.[17] Each item should be scored with a +1, 0, or −1 depending on how closely the company in question matches the description of the timeless principle. In our experience, the best research is done apart from senior management, which is obviously vested in a positive outcome. We recommend talking with ex-employees, suppliers, customers, and others who meet these four criteria:

- ■ Objective (no vested interest in the outcome).
- ■ Knowledgeable (familiar enough with the company to provide accurate information).

- Revealing (willing to talk openly about the question).
- Accessible (can be reached for an interview).

The concept behind each broad category is described briefly, with specific statements that you are to assess based on your knowledge of the company.

At the end is a tally sheet (Table 16.7) on which you can summarize the score and see how the company you are analyzing compares with outstanding companies and average companies.

Good luck and good hunting.

TABLE 16.1 Values and Vision Scorecard

Category for scoring:	Score
I. Values and Vision	

Concept: Does the company have a well-thought-out ideology? Have its leaders taken the time to determine clearly who they are and where they are going? Have they articulated the answers to the preceding questions to the employees? Finally, do the leaders reinforce the values and vision so that they "live" within the company?

A. Clarity of Values and Vision	
+1 Significant evidence that the company has identified and articulated core values and purpose and uses them as a source of guidance. Key leaders speak of the values and vision and have communicated them to the employees.	
0 Some evidence of the above.	
−1 No evidence that the company has made serious attempts to identify and articulate core values and purpose.	
B. Historical Alignment around Values and Vision	
+1 Evidence that the values and vision described in part A have undergone little change since inception and are continually reinforced by the leaders.	
0 Evidence that the value and vision have changed over the years and that the company has been inconsistent in reinforcing them.	
−1 Little evidence that there has been a consistent set of values or central purpose for the company.	
C. Purpose Beyond Profits	
+1 Evidence that the role of profitability or shareholder wealth is only part of the company's objectives, not the primary objective. Use of phrases like "fair" return rather than "maximal" return.	
0 Evidence that profits are highly important, equal to or greater than any other goals or values.	
−1 Evidence that profit is the main driving force, and all else comes second.	

TABLE 16.1   *(continued)*

Category for scoring:	Score
D. Alignment of Words and Actions: "Walking the Talk"	
+1 Significant evidence that vision and values are "alive" in the company. Major strategic initiatives and company policies are guided by the vision and values.	
0 Some evidence of the above, but less pronounced and inconsistent.	
−1 Little evidence that vision and values tie in to the actions and behaviors in the company.	
Score: Values and Vision	

TABLE 16.2   Ambitious Goals Scorecard

Category for scoring:	Score
II. Ambitious Goals	

Concept: Outstanding companies stimulate progress by setting ambitious goals. The core ideology described in part I provides stability for the company, whereas the ambitious goals stimulate change and motivate employees.

	Score
E. Use of Ambitious Goals to Stimulate Progress	
+1 Significant evidence that the company repeatedly uses ambitious goals to stimulate progress.	
0 Some evidence that ambitious goals are used, but inconsistently and less prominently.	
−1 Little or no evidence that ambitious goals are used. Conservative strategies and certainty of results is emphasized.	
F. Choice of Truly "Outrageous" Goals	
+1 Significant evidence that the ambitious goals were truly outrageously difficult and highly risky.	
0 Some evidence that the goals were outrageous, but not as pronounced.	
−1 Little or no evidence that the goals were outrageous.	
G. Consistent Use of Ambitious Goals to Stimulate Progress	
+1 Evidence that the company has used ambitious goals over time and through multiple generations of leadership.	
0 Some evidence of the above.	
−1 Little evidence that the company uses ambitious goals.	
Score: Ambitious Goals	

TABLE 16.3   Strong Culture Scorecard

Category for scoring:	Score
III. Strong Culture	

Concept: Top companies hire for fit and then mold their employees to the same set of values, beliefs, and behaviors. There is a strong sense of employees being on the same page. Employees express pride in belonging to such a company. The culture is binary: either you hate it or you love it. Rarely do people have a lukewarm or neutral feeling.

H. Cultural Indoctrination: Molding the New Hires	

+1   Significant evidence of a formal indoctrination process, which may include:

- Orientation program that teaches values, traditions, and guidelines.

- Ongoing training that reinforces those values, traditions, and guidelines

- Internal publications emphasizing company values and traditions.

- Leaders discussing and promoting the values and traditions.

- Use of unique language or terminology that reinforces a frame of reference.

- Hiring young, promoting from within, shaping the employee's thinking from the start.

 0   Some evidence of the above, but to a lesser extreme.

−1   Little or no evidence that the company has a formal indoctrination process.

I. Strong, Active Culture: "Our Way or the Highway"	

+1   Strong evidence that the culture is well defined and binary (that is, some people love it and others hate it). Indications of strong culture are:

- Rewards and recognition for those who fit in with the culture, and negative reinforcement for those who do not.

- Severe penalties for those who violate core values.

- Hiring for fit and careful monitoring of employees based on vision and values.

- Heavy emphasis on loyalty.

- Expectation that employees will join fully into the company and espouse its values.

TABLE 16.3 *(continued)*

Category for scoring:	Score
0 Some evidence of a strong culture, but not to the extent indicated above.	
−1 Little or no evidence of a strong culture.	
J. **Elitist Attitude: "We're Special"**	
+1 Significant evidence that the company reinforces a sense of belonging to something superior or special. Some indications of this are: <ul><li>Verbal and written emphasis on belonging to something special.</li><li>Secrecy as it relates to internal information or processes.</li><li>Celebration to reinforces successes, belonging, and elitism.</li><li>Nicknames or special terminology for employees (such as "crew members" at Vanguard, "cast member" at Disney).</li><li>Emphasis on "family" feeling.</li><li>Physical isolation (company has its own campus and minimizes the need for employees to deal with outsiders).</li></ul>	
0 Less evidence that the company has reinforced a sense of belonging to something special.	
−1 Little or no evidence that the company emphasizes a sense of belonging to something special.	
Score: Strong Culture	

TABLE 16.4   Creativity and Adaptability Scorecard

Category for scoring:	Score
IV. Creativity and Adaptability	

Concept: Top companies are careful not to stagnate. They create an environment in which employees try many things to see what works. This requires management to trust the employees and not micromanage them. Management uses different rewards and techniques for stimulating creativity and initiative.

K. Consciously Using an Evolutionary Process	
+1 Evidence of consciously using an evolutionary process of variation and selection (à la Darwinian evolution). Strategic shifts resulted from it.	
0 Some evidence of conscious evolution.	
−1 Little or no evidence of using an evolutionary process.	
L. Employee Autonomy: Empowering "Hands off" Management	
+1 Evidence of high employee autonomy. Employees have wide personal discretion in how to fulfill their responsibilities.	
0 Some evidence that the company historically has encouraged and practiced employee autonomy.	
−1 Little or no evidence that the company empowers its employees.	
M. Rewards for Stimulating Autonomy and Evolution	
+1 Significant evidence that the company uses a variety of ways (other than the above) to stimulate autonomy: rewards for creativity, safety to make mistakes, incentives for discovering new opportunities.	
0 Some evidence that employee autonomy is stimulated in the above ways.	
−1 Little or no evidence that the company has a history of using different methods to stimulate autonomy.	
Score: Creativity and Adaptability	

TABLE 16.5 Leadership Continuity Scorecard

Category for scoring:	Score
V. Leadership Continuity	

Concept: Top companies spend a great deal of time developing and strengthening their culture, so they want to preserve it over time. Hence, they carefully train and develop future leaders so that the new CEO can be homegrown. Evidence shows that internal succession (skillfully done) provides far better results than looking for an outside CEO to come in and rescue the firm (the *savior syndrome*).

N. Leadership Continuity: Promote from Within	
+1 Significant evidence that the CEO is selected from within the company.	
0 Evidence that the CEO is primarily selected from within the company, with one or two exceptions.	
−1 Evidence that the company has deviated from the "promote from within" strategy for CEOs more than twice.	
O. Absence of Charismatic Leaders: No Savior Syndrome	
+1 No evidence that the company cannot find a highly qualified successor or is looking outside to find a savior to help in troubled times.	
0 Evidence that the company has experienced the above at least once in its history.	
−1 Evidence that the company has experienced the above at least twice in its history.	
P. Leadership Training: "Homegrown"	
+1 Significant evidence that the company develops leaders through training, rotation of jobs, mentoring, and careful grooming of future leaders.	
0 Some evidence that the company develops leaders as described above.	
−1 Little or no evidence that the company develops future leaders.	
Q. Succession Planning	
+1 Significant evidence that the company has a history of careful succession planning and formal CEO grooming.	
0 Less evidence of the above.	
−1 Little or no evidence that the company has a history of careful CEO succession planning.	
Score: Leadership Continuity	

TABLE 16.6   Continuous Improvement Scorecard

Category for scoring:	Score
VI. Continuous Improvement	

Concept: Top firms promote a "never satisfied" view of their efforts. Employees continually strive to improve their skills. Management is willing to get on board with new technology. (*Note:* Technology does not drive progress, but is supportive of it.)

R.	**Long-Term Focus**	
+1	Significant evidence that the company has a history of reinvesting earnings for long-term growth (PP&E, R&D, payout ratio).	
0	Some evidence of investing for the long term.	
−1	Evidence that the company is short-term oriented.	
S.	**Investment in People: Training and Development**	
+1	Significant evidence that the company invests in recruiting, training, and development, even in downturns.	
0	Some evidence of the above.	
−1	Little or no evidence of the above, especially in downturns.	
T.	**Early Adoption**	
+1	Significant evidence that the company has a history of being an early adopter of new technologies, processes, management methods, and the like.	
0	Some evidence that the company has been an early adopter.	
−1	Evidence that the company is a late adopter.	
U.	**Improvement Incentives from Within**	
+1	Significant evidence that the company has a history of "mechanisms of discomfort" that impel change from within before the market demands it.	
0	Some evidence of the above.	
−1	Little or no evidence that mechanisms of discomfort exist.	
	Score: Continuous Improvement	

TABLE 16.7 Total Scorecard Tally Sheet

	Scores		
Category	*Built to Last* Companies	Comparison Companies	Company under Analysis
I. Values and Vision	2.56	−1.55	
A. Clarity of Values and Vision	.78	−.11	
B. Historical Alignment around Values and Vision	.67	−.89	
C. Purpose Beyond Profits	.39	−.33	
D. Alignment of Words and Actions	.72	−.22	
II. Ambitious Goals	1.5	−.73	
E. Use of Ambitious Goals to Stimulate Progress	.72	.17	
F. Choice of Truly "Outrageous" Goals	.72	0	
G. Consistent Use of Ambitious Goals to Stimulate Progress	.06	−.56	
III. Strong Culture	1.88	−.66	
H. Cultural Indoctrination	.61	−.39	
I. Strong, Active Culture	.44	−.33	
J. Elitist Attitude	.83	.06	
IV. Creativity and Adaptability	1.66	−1.28	
K. Consciously Using an Evolutionary Process	44	−.17	
L. Employee Autonomy	.39	−.39	
M. Rewards for Stimulating Autonomy and Evolution	.83	−.72	
V. Leadership Continuity	2.22	−.89	
N. Leadership Continuity: Promote from Within	.83	−.06	
		Scores	

TABLE 16.7   *(continued)*

	Scores		
Category	*Built to Last* Companies	Comparison Companies	Company under Analysis
O. Absence of Charismatic Leaders	.67	−.11	
P. Leadership Training: "Homegrown"	.39	−.33	
Q. Succession Planning	.33	−.39	
VI. **Continuous Improvement**	1.72	−1.49	
R. Long-Term Focus	.33	−.28	
S. Investment in People: Training and Development	.56	−.44	
T. Early Adoption	.44	−.33	
U. Improvement Incentives from Within	.39	−.44	
Grand Total:	11.54	−6.60	

TEST YOURSELF

1. How much do you consider the qualitative side of a company in your analysis?
2. Can you think of examples where the qualitative side definitely was a factor?
3. What creative strategies can you use to quantify the "soft" side of a business and give yourself a competitive edge?

Notes

PREFACE

1. Aaron Lucchetti, "Janus Debates How Much to Change," *Wall Street Journal*, 22 April 2002, C1.
2. References to "I" in this book indicate Jim Ware as the lead author. "We" refers to Jim, Beth, and Dale.
3. Comments after speeches in Lugano, Milan, and Rome, Italy, in April 2003.
4. "The Hot Topic in EMBA Programs," *Fortune*, 31 March 2003, 157.
5. William J. Nutt, "Aligning the Interests of Clients, Management, and Owners," in *Organizational Challenges for Investment Firms* (Charlottesville, Va.: AIMR Proceedings, 2002), 25.
6. Thomas J. Dillman, "Attracting, Motivating, and Retaining Professionals," in *Ethical Issues for Today's Firm* (Charlottesville, Va.: AIMR Proceedings, 2000), 43.
7. Alison A. Winter, "Managing Investment Professionals Who Deal with Individual Client Accounts," in *Managing Investment Firms: People and Culture* (Charlottesville, Va.: AIMR Proceedings, 1996), 60.
8. James C. Collins and Jerry I. Porras, *Built to Last* (New York: HarperBusiness, 1994).
9. Jim Collins, *Good to Great* (New York: HarperBusiness, 2001).

CHAPTER 1 LEADERSHIP AND CULTURE IN THE INVESTMENT INDUSTRY

1. David I. Fisher, "Words of Wisdom on Managing a Global Investment Firm," in *Managing Investment Firms: People and Culture* (Charlottesville, Va.: AIMR Proceedings, 1996), 9.
2. Patrick O'Donnell, "Managing Investment Research Professionals," in *Managing Investment Firms: People and Culture* (Charlottesville, Va.: AIMR Proceedings, 1996), 31.

3. Warren Buffett (as company chairman), Annual Report of Berkshire Hathaway (1992), 12.
4. Paul David Schaeffer, "Competitive Challenges: Managing Profitability and Productivity," in *Organizational Challenges for Investment Firms* (Charlottesville, Va.: AIMR Proceedings, 2002), 19.
5. Gary P. Brinson, "Organizational Culture," in *Managing Investment Firms: People and Culture* (Charlottesville, Va.: AIMR Proceedings, 1996), 7.
6. Denis Bryay, *Einstein: A Life* (New York: John Wiley & Sons, 1997), 45.
7. David H. Maister, *Managing the Professional Service Firm* (New York: Simon & Schuster, 1993), 291.
8. Charles B. Burkhardt Jr., "Evaluating Business Models," in *Organizational Challenges for Investment Firms* (Charlottesville, Va.: AIMR Proceedings, 2002), 31.
9. Schaeffer, "Competitive Challenges," 19.
10. Jeffrey S. Molitor, "A Client's View of Business Models in Investment Management," in *Organizational Challenges for Investment Firms* (Charlottesville, Va.: AIMR Proceedings, 2002), 33.
11. Details from Frank Russell Company, www.russell.com; last accessed April 2, 2003.
12. James C. Collins and Jerry I. Porras, *Built to Last* (New York: Harper-Business, 1994), 233.
13. "Best Places to Work" companies: Goldman Sachs, Principal Group, SEI Corporation, A. G. Edwards, Schwab. Comparison companies: Citigroup, Morgan Stanley, Bear Stearns, Merrill Lynch, Lehman, Franklin Resources, Janus, T. Rowe Price.
14. Peter Lynch, speech given 13 April 1999.
15. Sandy Weill, quoted in an interview with Jeff Everett on 15 November 2002.
16. John P. Kotter, *Leading Change* (Boston: Harvard Business School Press, 1996), 26.
17. Ibid., 73.
18. Quoted in Richard Barrett, *Liberating the Corporate Soul: Building a Visionary Organization* (Woburn, Mass.: Butterworth-Heinemann, 1998), 159.
19. Russell Reynolds presentation at AIMR conference, Boca Raton, Florida, 8 December 2000.
20. You can purchase instruments based on Hersey and Blanchard's model from Pfeiffer, to measure your practices against this model.

Call 800-274-4434 for a catalog, or visit Pfeiffer on line at http://www.pfeiffer.com.

21. James P. Lewis, *Team-Based Project Management* (New York: AMACOM, 1998), 91.
22. Edward L. Gubman, *The Talent Solution: Aligning Strategy and People to Achieve Extraordinary Results* (New York: McGraw-Hill, 1998), 58.
23. John P. Kotter and James L. Heskett, *Corporate Culture and Performance* (New York: Free Press, 1992), 114.
24. Collins and Porras, *Built to Last*, 234.
25. Gubman, *The Talent Solution*, 297.
26. James F. Rothenberg, "Star versus Team Approaches: Missing the Point," in *Managing Investment Firms: People and Culture* (Charlottesville, Va.: AIMR Proceedings, 1996), 13.
27. Thomas M. Luddy, "Building a Global Investment Network," in *Managing Investment Firms: People and Culture* (Charlottesville, Va.: AIMR Proceedings, 1996), 49.

CHAPTER 2   CORE VALUES

1. William Lyons, "My Vision," letter to authors, 15 June 2002.
2. David I. Fisher, "Words of Wisdom on Managing a Global Investment Firm," in *Managing Investment Firms: People and Culture* (Charlottesville, Va.: AIMR Proceedings, 1996), 12.
3. Fisher, "Words of Wisdom," 12.
4. Lyons, "My Vision" letter.
5. Fisher, "Words of Wisdom," 10.
6. Gary P. Brinson, "Organizational Culture," in *Managing Investment Firms: People and Culture* (Charlottesville, Va.: AIMR Proceedings, 1996), 8.
7. James C. Collins and Jerry I. Porras, *Built to Last* (New York: Harper-Business, 1994), 16.
8. Roger Siboni, "Culture and Performance," *Fast Company*, 10 January 2002, 62.
9. Collins and Porras, *Built to Last*, 4.
10. Brinson, "Organizational Culture," 8.
11. Collins and Porras, *Built to Last*, 85.
12. Paul David Schaeffer, "Competitive Challenges: Managing Profitability and Productivity," in *Organizational Challenges for Investment Firms* (Charlottesville, Va.: AIMR Proceedings, 2002), 19.

13. Jeffrey S. Molitor, "A Client's View of Business Models in Investment Management," in *Organizational Challenges for Investment Firms* (Charlottesville, Va.: AIMR Proceedings, 2002), 33.
14. Brinson, "Organizational Culture," 4.
15. "Andersen Story," *Chicago Tribune*, 1 September 2002, 1.
16. Peter Drucker, *The Leader of the Future* (San Francisco: Jossey-Bass, 1996), xiii.
17. Jim Collins, *Good to Great* (New York: HarperBusiness, 2001), 45.

CHAPTER 3   VISION: WHERE ARE WE GOING?

1. Alison A. Winter, "Managing Investment Professionals Who Deal with Individual Client Accounts," in *Managing Investment Firms: People and Culture* (Charlottesville, Va.: AIMR Proceedings, 1996), 56.
2. James C. Collins and Jerry I. Porras, *Built to Last* (New York: Harper-Business, 1994).
3. Edward M. Hallowell, *Connect* (New York: Random House, 1999).
4. David I. Fisher, "Words of Wisdom on Managing a Global Investment Firm," in *Managing Investment Firms: People and Culture* (Charlottesville, Va.: AIMR Proceedings, 1996), 12.
5. Jim Collins, *Good to Great* (New York: HarperBusiness, 2001), 42.
6. Richard Barrett, *Liberating the Corporate Soul: Building a Visionary Organization* (Woburn, Mass.: Butterworth-Heinemann, 1998), 106.
7. John P. Kotter, *Leading Change* (Boston: Harvard Business School Press, 1996), 68–72.
8. Ibid., 84–85.
9. See their web site: www.interactionassociates.com.
10. Collins and Porras, *Built to Last*, 54.
11. Quoted in Mihaly Csikszentmihalyi, *Creativity* (New York: Harper-Collins, 1996), 54.
12. Collins, *Good to Great*, 98.
13. Collins and Porras, *Built to Last*, 237.
14. Warren Buffett (as company chairman), Annual Report of Berkshire Hathaway (1992).
15. Ed Oakley, *Enlightened Leadership* (New York: Fireside, 1994), 180.
16. Warren Bennis, *On Becoming a Leader* (New York: Perseus Publishing, 1994), 183.
17. William Lyons, "My Vision," letter to authors, 15 June 2002.

18. Quoted in Peter Drucker, *The Leader of the Future* (San Francisco: Jossey-Bass, 1996), 103.
19. Kotter, *Leading Change*, 82.

CHAPTER 4   STRONG CULTURES

1. Pat Ward, Goldman web site: www.goldmansachs.com. Last accessed 25 February 2003.
2. Thomas J. Dillman, "Attracting, Motivating, and Retaining Professionals," in *Ethical Issues for Today's Firm* (Charlottesville, Va.: AIMR Proceedings, 2000), 43.
3. Stuart M. Robbins, "Managing Institutional Brokerage Professionals," in *Managing Investment Firms: People and Culture* (Charlottesville, Va.: AIMR Proceedings, 1996), 52.
4. James C. Collins and Jerry I. Porras, *Built to Last* (New York: Harper-Business, 1994), 25.
5. Ibid., 143.
6. David H. Maister, *Managing the Professional Service Firm* (New York: Simon & Schuster, 1993), 308.
7. Dillman, "Attracting, Motivating, and Retaining Professionals," 44.
8. Edward L. Gubman, *The Talent Solution: Aligning Strategy and People to Achieve Extraordinary Results* (New York: McGraw-Hill, 1998), 304.
9. Patrick O'Donnell, "Managing Investment Research Professionals," in *Managing Investment Firms: People and Culture* (Charlottesville, Va.: AIMR Proceedings, 1996), 30.
10. Collins and Porras, *Built to Last*, 224.
11. John P. Kotter, *Leading Change* (Boston: Harvard Business School Press, 1996), 157.
12. Gubman, *The Talent Solution*, 306.
13. Collins and Porras, *Built to Last*, 138.

CHAPTER 5   LEADER TYPES

1. Clayton Christensen, *The Innovator's Dilemma* (Boston: Harvard Business School Press, 1997).
2. Ted Bililies, "Does Your Fund Manager Play Piano?" *Fortune*, February 1992, 45.

3. The Economist Intelligence Unit (in cooperation with Pricewaterhouse-Coopers), "Tomorrow's Leading Investment Managers," February 1996.
4. Katrina Sherrerd, *The Future of the Investment Industry* (Charlottesville, Va.: AIMR Proceedings, 2000), 5.
5. Damon Darlin, "Picking a Loser," *Wall Street Journal*, 8 April 1982, C1.
6. Herb Greenberg, "Does Tyco Play Accounting Games?" *Fortune*, 17 March 2002 (Sunday), 73.
7. Peter Lynch, speech given on 13 April 1999.
8. Jeffrey Krug, "The People Toll of Mergers," *Harvard Business Review*, February 2003, 15.
9. Ibid.
10. Michael Goldstein, *The Future of the Money Management Industry in America* (New York: Sanford Bernstein, 1998), 34.
11. Daniel Goleman, *Emotional Intelligence* (New York: Bantam, 1995).
12. Jonathan P. Niednagel, "Head Games," *American Way*, 15 December 1998, 78.

CHAPTER 6 MEASURING CULTURE

1. Peter Drucker, *The Essential Drucker* (New York: HarperBusiness, 2001), 124.
2. Edward L. Gubman, *The Talent Solution: Aligning Strategy and People to Achieve Extraordinary Results* (New York: McGraw-Hill, 1998), 60.
3. Charles Ellis, *Winning the Loser's Game* (New York: McGraw-Hill, 1998), 125.
4. Kim Cameron and Robert Quinn, *Diagnosing and Changing Organizational Culture* (Reading, Mass.: Addison Wesley, 1999), 5.
5. Robert S. Kaplan and David P. Norton, *The Balanced Scorecard* (Cambridge, Mass.: Harvard Business School Press, 1996).
6. www.cradv.com; last accessed 29 June 2003.
7. Frederick Herzberg, "One More Time: How Do You Motivate Employees?" in *HBR Classics* (Boston: Harvard Business Review Business Classics, 1998), 42.
8. James C. Collins and Jerry I. Porras, *Built to Last* (New York: HarperBusiness, 1994), 114.

9. A.G. Edwards web site, www.agedwards.com; last accessed 29 June 2003.
10. John P. Kotter and James L. Heskett, *Corporate Culture and Performance* (New York: Free Press, 1992).
11. Robert Levering, available on http://www.greatplacetowork.com/education/articles.php; last accessed 29 June 2003.

CHAPTER 7 DIAGNOSING CULTURE BY MEASURING VALUES

1. David I. Fisher, "Words of Wisdom on Managing a Global Investment Firm," in *Managing Investment Firms: People and Culture* (Charlottesville, Va.: AIMR Proceedings, 1996), 12.
2. Richard Barrett, *Liberating the Corporate Soul: Building a Visionary Organization* (Woburn, Mass.: Butterworth-Heinemann, 1998), 55–101.
3. Abraham Maslow, *The Farther Reaches of Human Nature* (New York: Penguin, 1965), 35.

CHAPTER 8 LEADERSHIP AND TRUST

1. Quoted in Frederick F. Reichheld, *Loyalty Rules* (Boston: Harvard Business School Press, 2001), 29.
2. Paul David Schaeffer, "Competitive Challenges: Managing Profitability and Productivity," in *Organizational Challenges for Investment Firms* (Charlottesville, Va.: AIMR Proceedings, 2002), 19.
3. John Emshwiller and Rebecca Smith, "Corporate Veil: Behind Enron's Fall, A Culture of Operating Outside Public's View," *Wall Street Journal*, 5 December 2001, 1.
4. Quoted in Del Jones, "Do You Trust Your CEO?" *USA Today*, 25 February 2003, 7B.
5. Ibid.
6. Brian Billick, James A. Peterson, and Andrea Kremer, *Competitive Leadership: Twelve Principles for Success* (New York: Triumph Books, 2001), 10.
7. Quoted in Peter Drucker, *The Leader of the Future* (San Francisco: Jossey-Bass, 1996), 251.

8. Details of this study, "The Human Capital Edge: 21 People Management Practices Your Company Must Implement (or Avoid) to Maximize Shareholder Value," are provided on Watson Wyatt Worldwide's web site: www.watsonwyatt.com/research/. Last accessed 23 April 2003.

9. Ibid.

10. James C. Collins and Jerry I. Porras, *Built to Last* (New York: Harper-Business, 1994), 154.

11. As reported in Dan Richards, *Getting Clients, Keeping Clients* (New York: John Wiley & Sons, 2000), 35.

12. Robert Bruce Shaw, *Trust in the Balance* (San Francisco: Jossey-Bass, 1997), 57.

13. John C. Bogle, speech for United Way, Rochester, New York, 2 October 2001.

14. Claude N. Rosenberg Jr., "Leading Investment Professionals: Start with Fundamentals," in *Managing Investment Firms: People and Culture* (Charlottesville, Va.: AIMR Proceedings, 1996), 23.

15. Reported in Roy C. Smith and Ingo Walter, *Street Smarts* (Boston: Harvard Business School Press, 1997), 65.

16. Ibid., 66.

17. Ibid., 20.

18. Edward L. Gubman, *The Talent Solution: Aligning Strategy and People to Achieve Extraordinary Results* (New York: McGraw-Hill, 1998), 124.

19. Shaw, *Trust in the Balance*, ch. 9.

CHAPTER 9   AMBITIOUS GOALS AND IMPLEMENTATION

1. Rich Blake, "Massachusetts Miracle: MFS Defied the Odds and Its Own Consultants to Become a Force in Institutional Asset Management in Less Than a Decade," *Institutional Investor*, 1 December 2001, 37.

2. James C. Collins and Jerry I. Porras, *Built to Last* (New York: Harper-Business, 1994).

3. Ibid., 94.

4. Ibid., 112.

5. Ibid.

6. Jon Birger, "Leader of the Pack," *Money* (June 2002): 126.

7. Ibid., 126.

8. Ibid., 129.

9. David Rynecki, "Can Sally Save Citi?" *Fortune* (June 2003): 68.
10. Blake, "Massachusetts Miracle," 38.

CHAPTER 10   THE INNOVATIVE CULTURE

1. Guy Moszkowski, speech given at AIMR conference, Boca Raton, Florida, 7 December 2000.
2. Art Zeikel, "Organizing for Creativity," *Financial Analyst Journal* (November/December 1983): 54.
3. Gary Hamel, *Leading the Revolution: How to Thrive in Turbulent Times by Making Innovation a Way of Life* (Cambridge, Mass.: Harvard Business School, 2002).
4. Robert Arnott, e-mail to authors, 1 February 2003.
5. Thomas Edison, quoted in *The Forbes Book of Business Quotations* (New York: Forbes, 1997), 269.
6. Center for Creative Leadership, www.ccl.org. Last accessed June 30, 2003.
7. Ibid.
8. Clayton Christensen, *The Innovator's Dilemma* (Boston: Harvard Business School Press, 1997).
9. James C. Collins and Jerry I. Porras, *Built to Last* (New York: HarperBusiness, 1994), 89.
10. See http://www.ccl.org/products/keys/ for more information on KEYS. Last accessed June 30, 2003.
11. See www.ccl.org for more on Visual Explorer. Last accessed June 30, 2003.
12. Alison A. Winter, "Managing Investment Professionals Who Deal with Individual Client Accounts," in *Managing Investment Firms: People and Culture* (Charlottesville, Va.: AIMR Proceedings, 1996), 55.
13. Ibid.
14. Denis Bryay, *Einstein: A Life* (New York: John Wiley & Sons, 1997), 47.
15. For example there are seven chapters on individual creativity in Jim Ware, *The Psychology of Money: An Investment Manager's Guide to Beating the Market* (New York: John Wiley & Sons, 2000).
16. Claude N. Rosenberg Jr., "Leading Investment Professionals: Start with Fundamentals," in *Managing Investment Firms: People and Culture* (Charlottesville, Va.: AIMR Proceedings, 1996), 24.
17. Winter, "Managing Investment Professionals," 55.

CHAPTER 11   COMPENSATION AND OWNERSHIP

1. Luke D. Knecht and Richard S. Lannamann, "Special Report: Job Satisfaction among Investment Professionals," in *Managing Investment Firms: People and Culture* (Charlottesville, Va.: AIMR Proceedings, 1996), 41.
2. Ibid., 37.
3. Capital Resource Advisors web site: www.cra.com. Last accessed 28 June 2003.
4. Mark Tibergien, presentation at AIMR conference, Amelia Island, 8 December 2001.
5. Lawrence E. Lifson and Richard A. Geist, *The Psychology of Investing* (New York: John Wiley & Sons, 1999), 154.
6. Ibid.
7. Thomas M. Luddy, "Building a Global Investment Network," in *Managing Investment Firms: People and Culture* (Charlottesville, Va.: AIMR Proceedings, 1996), 49.
8. AIMR compensation study, 2001; available at www.aimr.org. Last accessed 7 July 2003.
9. David H. Maister, *Managing the Professional Service Firm* (New York: Simon & Schuster, 1993), 255.
10. James F. Rothenberg, "Star versus Team Approaches: Missing the Point," in *Managing Investment Firms: People and Culture* (Charlottesville, Va.: AIMR Proceedings, 1996), 14.
11. Survey (2002) available on www.greatplacestowork.com. Last accessed 7 July 2003.
12. Maister, *Managing the Professional Service Firm*, 261.
13. Alison A. Winter, "Managing Investment Professionals Who Deal with Individual Client Accounts," in *Managing Investment Firms: People and Culture* (Charlottesville, Va.: AIMR Proceedings, 1996), 60.
14. Patrick O'Donnell, "Managing Investment Research Professionals," in *Managing Investment Firms: People and Culture* (Charlottesville, Va.: AIMR Proceedings, 1996), 33.
15. Maister, *Managing the Professional Service Firm*, 259.
16. Ibid., 261.
17. Ibid.
18. O'Donnell, "Managing Investment Research Professionals," 33.
19. Winter, "Managing Investment Professionals," 60.
20. Margaret Eisen, letter to authors 21 March 2003.
21. Dean LeBaron, e-mail to authors 28 March 2003.
22. David A. Minella, "Managing the Virtual Global Organization," in

Managing Investment Firms: People and Culture (Charlottesville, Va.: AIMR Proceedings, 1996), 48.

23. Charles B. Burkhardt Jr., "Evaluating Business Models," in *Organizational Challenges for Investment Firms* (Charlottesville, Va.: AIMR Proceedings, 2002), 30.

CHAPTER 12   HOMEGROWN LEADERSHIP

1. James C. Collins and Jerry I. Porras, *Built to Last* (New York: Harper-Business, 1994), 172.
2. Ibid., 176.
3. Ibid., 220.
4. MFS statement available on www.mfs.com. Last accessed 7 July 2003.
5. Rich Blake, "Framed by Tradition," *Forbes*, 11 November 2002, 35.
6. Ibid., 35.
7. James M. Kouzes and Barry Posner, *The Leadership Challenge* (San Francisco: Jossey-Bass, 1987), 283.

CHAPTER 13   THE BEST OF THE BEST: ARIEL CAPITAL

1. John Rogers, in company literature, "Ariel Capital Management, Inc., Historical Timeline" (January 2003).
2. For a more detailed description of strengths and weaknesses, see James Ware, *The Psychology of Money: An Investment Manager's Guide to Beating the Market* (New York: John Wiley & Sons, 2000).
3. Lu Hong and Scott Page, "Diversity and Optimality," working paper February 2003).
4. Michael Mauboussin, "Consilient Observer" [in-house publication of Credit Suisse First Boston], 19 November 2002, 4.
5. Marty Zweig, *Winning on Wall Street* (New York: Warner Books, 1997), 57.
6. Richard Barrett and Associates, "Corporate Transformation Tools," available on www.corptools.com. Last accessed 7 July 2003.

CHAPTER 14   CONTINUOUS IMPROVEMENT

1. James C. Collins and Jerry I. Porras, *Built to Last* (New York: Harper-Business, 1994), 186.

2. James P. Lewis, *Team-Based Project Management* (New York: AMA-COM, 1998), 154.
3. Jim Collins, *Good to Great* (New York: HarperBusiness, 2001), 56.
4. Lewis, *Team-Based Project Management*, 150.
5. Ibid., 126.
6. David H. Maister, *Managing the Professional Service Firm* (New York: Simon & Schuster, 1993), 224.
7. Edward L. Gubman, *The Talent Solution: Aligning Strategy and People to Achieve Extraordinary Results* (New York: McGraw-Hill, 1998), 311.
8. Lewis, *Team-Based Project Management*, 166.
9. Collins and Porras, *Built to Last*, 199.
10. Patrick O'Donnell, "Managing Investment Research Professionals," in *Managing Investment Firms: People and Culture* (Charlottesville, Va.: AIMR Proceedings, 1996), 32.
11. Richard Barrett, *Liberating the Corporate Soul: Building a Visionary Organization* (Woburn, Mass.: Butterworth-Heinemann, 1998), 212–214.
12. John P. Kotter, *Leading Change* (Boston: Harvard Business School Press, 1996), 172.

CHAPTER 15   CONSULTANT'S VIEW

1. Harry S. Marmer, *Perspectives on Institutional Investment Management* (Toronto: Rogers Publishing, 2002), 71.
2. Paul Greenwood, in "Beyond Performance Measurement," *PlanSponsor*, February 2002, available at www.plansponsor.com. Last accessed 2 July 2003.
3. Ibid.
4. Ibid.
5. Taken from the Ennis Knupp web site, www.ennisknupp.com, which includes a description of the full model and factors. Last accessed 1 July 2003.
6. Ted Aronson, e-mail to authors, 3 March 2003.
7. Marmer, *Perspectives on Institutional Investment Management*, 71.
8. Harry S. Marmer, "Managing Successfully within the Institutional Troika," speech in Calgary, Alberta, 12 February 2003.
9. Greenwood, in "Beyond Performance Measurement."
10. Richard Ennis, in "Beyond Performance Measurement."
11. Charles Ellis, *Winning the Loser's Game* (New York: McGraw-Hill, 1998), 47.

12. Quoted in Del Jones, "Do You Trust Your CEO?" *USA Today*, 25 February 2003, 7B.
13. Ibid.
14. From the Wilshire Associates web site, www.wilshire.com. Last accessed 7 July 2003.
15. Ronald Peyton, *Callan Letter*, Summer 2001, at 1; available at www.callan.com. Last accessed 28 June 2003.
16. Ibid., 1
17. Ibid., 2.
18. Ibid., 2.
19. Ibid., 8.
20. Quoted in "Beyond Performance Measurement," 3.
21. Ibid.
22. Ibid.
23. Ibid.
24. Cliff Kelly, quoted in "Beyond Performance Measurement."

CHAPTER 16   STOCK PICKER'S CORNER: ROUNDING UP THE UN-USUAL SUSPECTS

1. Peter Bernstein, "The Expected Return of the Security Analyst," *Financial Analysts Journal* 54, no. 2 (March/April 1998): 4.
2. Robert Hunter, "The Numbers Game," www.Smartmoney.com, 1 November 2001. Last accessed 23 June 2003.
3. Nicholas Varchaver, "Criminal Charges at Tyco," *Fortune*, 13 October 2002, 45.
4. Bill Mahoney, "Serious Research," *Shareholder Value* 2, no. 2 (March/April 2002): 24.
5. Bernstein, "The Expected Return of the Security Analyst," 4.
6. Cynthia Harrington, "Fundamental vs. Technical Analysis," *CFA Magazine* 14, no. 1 (January/February 2003): 37.
7. Lisa Shalett, "Unconflicted Research," *Shareholder Value* 3, no. 2 (March/April 2003): 35.
8. John P. Kotter and James L. Heskett, *Corporate Culture and Performance* (New York: Free Press, 1992).
9. Michael Porter, *Competitive Strategy* (New York: Free Press, 1998).
10. Charles Ellis, *Winning the Loser's Game* (New York: McGraw-Hill, 1998), 47.
11. Peter Lynch, speech given 13 April 1999.

12. James C. Collins and Jerry I. Porras, *Built to Last* (New York: Harper-Business, 1994).
13. Ibid., 187.
14. Geert Hofstede, *Cultures and Organizations* (New York: McGraw-Hill 1996), 76.
15. Lynch, speech given 13 April 1999.
16. Sandy Weill, quoted in an interview with Jeff Everett on 15 November 2002.
17. Collins and Porras, *Built to Last*, 258–288.

Index